Stories from the Land
A NAVAJO READER ABOUT MONUMENT VALLEY

Robert S. McPherson

Robert S. McPherson is Professor of History Emeritus at Utah State University–Blanding Campus and author of numerous books about the history and cultures of the Four Corners Region.

Other books of related interest by the author:
Navajo Women of Monument Valley: Preservers of the Past
        (distributed by University Press of Colorado)
Traditional Navajo Teachings, A Trilogy
        Volume I: Sacred Narratives and Ceremonies
        Volume II: The Natural World
        Volume III: The Earth Surface People
        (distributed by University Press of Colorado)
Traders, Agents, and Weavers: Developing the Northern Navajo Region
        (University of Oklahoma Press)
Both Sides of the Bullpen: Navajo Trade and Posts of the Upper Four Corners
        (University of Oklahoma Press)
Viewing the Ancestors: Perceptions of the Anaasází, Mokwič, and Hisatsinom
        (University of Oklahoma Press)
Under the Eagle: Samuel Holiday, Navajo Code Talker
        (University of Oklahoma Press)
Dinéjí Na'nitin: Navajo Traditional Teachings and History
        (University Press of Colorado)
Navajo Tradition, Mormon Life: The Autobiography and Teachings of Jim Dandy
        (University of Utah Press)
Along Navajo Trails: Recollections of a Trader, 1898–1948
        (Utah State University Press)
A Navajo Legacy: The Life and Teachings of John Holiday
        (University of Oklahoma Press)
Navajo Land, Navajo Culture: The Utah Experience in the Twentieth Century
        (University of Oklahoma Press)
The Journey of Navajo Oshley: An Autobiography and Life History
        (Utah State University Press)
Sacred Land, Sacred View: Navajo Perceptions of the Four Corners Region
        (University Press of Colorado)
The Northern Navajo Frontier, 1860–1900: Expansion through Adversity
        (University of New Mexico Press)

CONTENTS

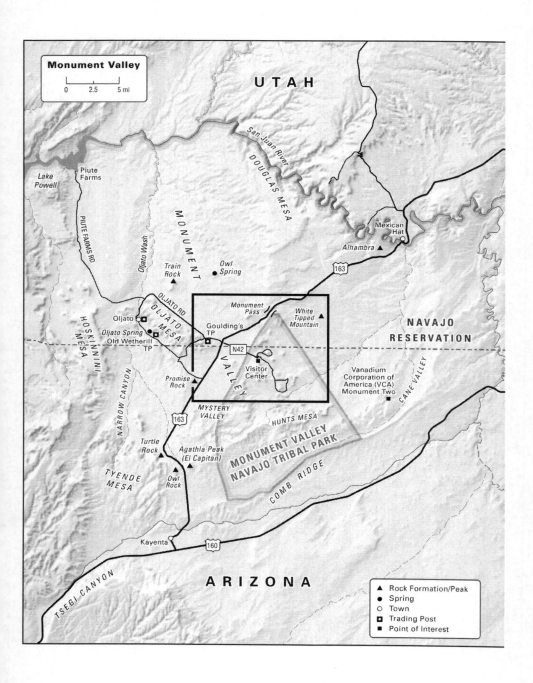

Monument Valley

0   2.5   5 mi

UTAH

Lake Powell

Piute Farms

PIUTE FARMS RD

San Juan River

DOUGLAS MESA

Mexican Hat

Alhambra ▲

163

NAVAJO RESERVATION

HOSKININI MESA

Oljato Wash

MONUMENT

Train Rock ▲

Owl Spring ●

OLJATO RD

Oljato

OLJATO MESA

Oljato Spring ●
Old Wetherill TP

Goulding's TP

Monument Pass

White Tipped Mountain ▲

N42

VALLEY

Visitor Center

Vanadium Corporation of America (VCA) Monument Two ■

CANE VALLEY

Promise Rock ▲

MYSTERY VALLEY

HUNTS MESA

NARROW CANYON

163

Turtle Rock ▲

Agathla Peak (El Capitan) ▲

MONUMENT VALLEY NAVAJO TRIBAL PARK

COMB RIDGE

TYENDE MESA

Owl Rock ▲

Kayenta

160

TSEGI CANYON

ARIZONA

▲ Rock Formation/Peak
● Spring
○ Town
◻ Trading Post
■ Point of Interest

vi

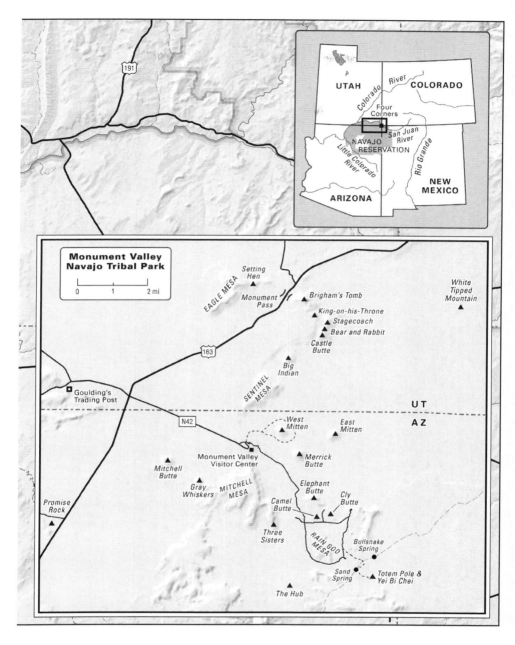

Map by Erin Greb Cartography

Embracing Monumental Memories

T ime is the greatest eraser of memories, both individually and collectively. When one considers that Native Americans have inhabited Monument Valley for 13,000 years (documented) and may have been there as early as 15,000 years ago, it is interesting to think about what all of those many generations experienced and how much of it has been forgotten. Until science creates a time machine that allows us to revisit those days, we have to be content with what archaeology can unearth and what a paper-thin historical record may say. Change is certain and inexorable, and for many people in today's society, not only welcomed but highly sought after. But for those looking to history for understanding, each day the older generation loses a member, the record of individual thoughts and events becomes impoverished. Memory shared through oral history is perhaps the most fragile and fleeting of all. In the grand scheme of millennia, the Navajo (Diné) are among the newcomers, arriving in the Southwest perhaps as early as 1200 AD, but even their experience is folded into the mists of history with only a small amount of information existing about who they are and what they encountered.[1]

This book is about preserving a small but rich body of oral history shared by Navajo elders of Monument Valley in the late 1980s and early 1990s, when most of them were in their seventies and eighties. These men and women had been raised during the first quarter of the twentieth century, a time when traditional teachings and practices were still very much in vogue and religiously (no pun intended) pursued. They came from a long line of practitioners, who kept their beliefs and lifeways alive through an oral tradition steeped in spiritual understanding. Their worldview was markedly different from that of the dominant culture that first rubbed up

1

against, then later invaded, their land and changed their way of life. The account presented here is at the tail end of that experience, but the thoughts and framework belong to a previous age explained through the presence of holy people and a traditional understanding.

Perhaps it is best to start by clarifying some terms and defining what this book is and is not. I am already in trouble. The slippery term of "traditional," of course, depends on the era of history being referred to and the age of those using the term. A person living in the mid-1800s might be considered radically new in their approach to life by a person born in the 1700s, while for someone alive in the 1900s the earlier person might be either old-fashioned or someone to emulate from the "good old days." Here the term is used to identify those Navajo men and women who were born in the first quarter of the twentieth century when the livestock and agricultural economy was in full sway, the ceremonial belief system was at its height, and Navajo culture had not been seriously changed by events from the dominant culture. When I interviewed most of the people cited in this volume, many were born during this time period, and so have become the reference point for using the term traditional.

The subtitle raises another question associated with the term "reader," which goes to the heart of this book's objective. A reader is defined as "a book of collected or assorted writings, especially when related in theme, authorship, or instructive purpose."[2] In this volume "collected," "theme," and "instructive in purpose" are central to what is discussed. Most of what is presented here is never-heard-before oral history that reaches into the depth of Navajo thought and experience. The interviews were often impromptu and held in many different settings. Those elders sharing their thoughts were anxious to pass this information along to the following generations since they understood that dramatic change moving toward the twenty-first century was sweeping across the Navajo Nation and irreparably shifting their way of life. They were right. Looking back from today and listening to young Navajos talk about their history, it is evident that much of the traditional view is now gone. This is not a criticism but only recognition of reality as even their parents and grandparents show concern about what is being lost—language, traditional teachings, historical perspective, and other areas that bring stability to cultural identification. Hopefully, in some small way, this book will stem a part of that loss by preserving the thoughts of the elders.

An anthology or reader usually comprises an author's or group's previously published works. Much of what is presented here is put in writing for the very first time. However, having spent over thirty years writing about

Navajo topics, primarily focusing on the People in southeastern Utah including Monument Valley, it should not come as a surprise that in this reader, I have drawn upon some of that material. For instance, in 2005 John Holiday, a medicine man from Monument Valley, and I worked together to publish his autobiography, *A Navajo Legacy, The Life and Teachings of John Holiday*; in 2021, I published *Navajo Women of Monument Valley: Preservers of the Past*, in many ways a companion volume to what is presented here.[3] I used excerpts from both books, since to leave these important sources out would cause the reader to go find them. In each of these books there is so much more information, but on some topics, those people provided important perspective, and so were included here. While Anglo commentary and experience is kept to a minimum, in the chapters about traders and Harry Goulding, I used interview materials to capture their perspective and provide thoughts with which to compare what Navajo informants were saying.[4]

I have studiously avoided taking away the "voice" of the elders. This is their book. I have kept academic paraphernalia to a minimum, using endnotes primarily to identify sources—who was saying it—and an occasional explanation, but skirting heavy documentation in order to maintain their tone. For those who wish to have a more contextualized approach with dates, explanations, and a more complete overview of a topic, let me suggest two possibilities. In *Navajo Land, Navajo Culture: The Utah Experience in the Twentieth Century*, the reader will find a more academic approach in chapters concerning trading posts, introduction of the automobile, livestock reduction, the film industry, and uranium mining—all of which have sections dealing with the Monument Valley area. Here, far more dependence on oral history comprises the text, whereas in *Navajo Land*, different sources, many of them Anglo, tell the story from a more documentary perspective. Each has its place and approach.

Much of what the elders share has been translated by expert interpreters and is straightforward for the reader. However, a person unfamiliar with Navajo culture may have questions about how something works—divination, relationships with the unseen, cultural practices, kinship responsibilities, and so forth. There may also be those who just want to get into greater depth on a particular topic. To that end, let me recommend a trilogy on Navajo beliefs entitled *Traditional Navajo Teachings: A Trilogy*, containing volume 1, *Sacred Narratives and Ceremonies*, volume 2, *The Natural World*, and volume 3, *The Earth Surface People*.[5] A companion text that looks at specific aspects of Navajo beliefs of yesteryear as well as those of today is *Dinéjí Na'nitin, Navajo Traditional Teachings and History*.[6] There are, of course, hundreds and hundreds of books written about the Navajo, some of which are by top scholars like Gladys Reichard, Father Berard Haile, Clyde Kluckhohn, Charlotte J. Frisbie, J. Lee Correll, Leland C. Wyman, and a host of others. Their works, for the most part, are for those who want a deep anthropological approach and scholarly treatment in defining and categorizing Navajo culture and history.

My approach here has been different. Any terminology, classification, and explanation come from the Navajo. In working with the translation of what they talked about, I have strong confidence in what my interpreters said. In the field, I worked with Baxter Benally and Marilyn Holiday. Baxter, recently deceased, was a jovial interviewer who seemed to know every Navajo person in southeastern Utah and what they had done. His fluency in the language was excellent and he was always on target with follow-up and clarification questions. He also enjoyed putting me in a "fix" to see how I would react, but he was also good at getting me out of it. There is nothing like being introduced for the first time as a person from the IRS who might be interested in marrying the informant's daughter. I also found time for payback. Marilyn was my primary interpreter for Monument Valley both in the field and in transcribing the information. It is hard to overstate the respect I hold for her in this role. She knew everybody in the community, having been raised there herself. Highly respected by all, wonderful at keeping informed about what took place with families and individuals, aware of how to approach a sensitive topic, and just as wise in not asking particular questions—she is the star in preserving much of her community's history. As with many of the elders, Marilyn understood kin and family relationships—who was the grandfather, father, son, uncle, nephew, and other ties on both the male and female side of the families. This can at times be bewildering for an outsider, but she kept it straight. I still occasionally call her about a person, place, or thing and she continues to have the ability to go back in time and provide an answer.

My role as recorder, questioner, and writer has been to take what Baxter and Marilyn provided and make it accessible to the public—a goal that all of the interviewees understood and wanted to have happen. People who have worked with oral history, either from within or outside of their own culture, realize that there are trade-offs that are made to get a translated, transcribed oral text into a readable format. Speaking expectations and reading expectations are two different things. In order to hold a reader's attention, there needs to be sentence variety, a flow in words, avoidance of repetition, the pairing of topics, maintaining clear references, and an underlying sense of context. None of this is demanded in oral history where assumptions of what is understood, the jumping around in conversations, repetition for emphasis, the interview environment, and an active system of cultural kinesics are all present during the interview but absent on the written page. The writer's job is to work with these shortcomings and issues and provide an interesting, clear, and accurate text. To that end, I have taken some liberties in editing the spoken word, moving around paragraphs, adding words for flow and connectivity, and inserting a phrase or two when necessary for clarity based on other parts of the text. For some purists, who demand that everything in an interview—including chuckles, poor grammar, repetition—be faithfully reproduced, what I have done may be unacceptable. My goal, on the other hand, is to provide a text that accurately portrays the feelings and information provided by these individuals but at the same time is something that a wide variety of people—from relatives of the deceased to a curious tourist who wants to learn about Monument Valley and its inhabitants—will pick up to learn and also enjoy. I often ask a person who knew the elder providing information if they can "hear his or her voice." When they say they can, then I know I have succeeded. Please note that the "correct" spelling of some names and terms can be difficult to determine, even with the help of Navajo linguist Clayton Long, because spellings and pronunciations vary among Navajos. In those cases we've spelled them to the best of our ability and made them consistent within this book, sometimes with a [?] following if we resorted to a phonetic spelling.

Each community or area on Navajo land has its own history, heroes, and issues. The people of Monument Valley want their story told. Recently, I was in an Oljato Chapter meeting, working to get the old Oljato Trading Post preserved. Following my presentation, an elder spoke, saying that it seemed like no one ever wrote about that area. She listed a few contemporary events that had taken place in Monument Valley, then said she was tired of everybody writing about Kayenta to the south, but nothing about the valley's history. Others agreed. In another instance, I was talking to a Navajo tour guide, who was one of the best in the area. As we discussed what he shared about the land and its people, it became apparent that he was not familiar with a lot of the specifics of the region—place names, stories, history—that would enliven his presentations. He was highly educated, knew a huge amount about traditional teachings, practiced hand trembling, participated as an assistant in ceremonies, and had come from a line of medicine people. Much of what he was saying was accurate, but generic and not focused on the specific views of the elders of the land he lives and works on. The same is true of the Navajo Tribal Park that is inundated all year long with tourists who want to come and learn. The museum displays are brief and accurate but generic, for the most part. Very little is said specifically about the valley. This is not to criticize any of the above, but only to point out that now there is a rich history and interpretation of the land that comes from the elders who lived in it and understood its teachings from a Navajo perspective.

There are twelve chapters in this book that focus on specific topics of interest to the people of Monument Valley. Each is told in their words. I am sure that outsiders have written books about its geology and topography, produced beautiful coffee-table photo albums of sunsets and rock formations, and have dabbled, in a general sense, in telling about the land and its people. This book is from the Navajo elders to subsequent generations. Some readers might not agree with things that are said, others may not understand, still others may find fault with how the informant may contradict others. Welcome to oral history. While Anglos often seek the ultimate "final word" or defensible truth or attempt to find mistakes or inconsistencies, Navajo people accept what they have been taught as it has come through traditional prayers, songs, and ceremonial knowledge. How a person is taught, not what is the latest theory or ever-changing "proof," becomes the standard of measure. Still, it is interesting to see how close sometimes the traditional teachings are in concordance with explanations from the scientific Anglo community.

Taking a chronological view in organizing this rich heritage, the first chapter discusses the land, its creation, and how Navajos think about it. The material is presented so that the reader, after understanding the naming process and thinking about the land, could actually drive on the roads from Monument Pass (north) to El Capitan (south) and from Oljato (west) to the eastern end of the tribal park and see many of the places John Holiday identified with traditional teachings. The Anasazi were an important people who illustrate some very specific lessons about behavior for the Navajo. The second chapter reveals who these people were, the reason for their abandonment of southeastern Utah by 1300 AD, and how their experience teaches people today what to do and not to do. The Long Walk period comes next, showing how this time of aggression changed the Navajos forever. Wolfkiller and Hashkéneiniihii Biye' give their accounts of what life was like during the "Fearing Time." These two men lived through it. I felt that many of the chapters dealt with big events, movements, or specific individuals without giving a sense of the daily life of families. Chapter 4 looks at what it was like to be a child during the early twentieth century and what one's responsibilities and tasks were. Life was difficult, at times teetering on the edge of survival, so the reader will not be surprised that the elders recounting their lifestyle compare it to the ease of today and why they want children and parents alike to remember that life was not always easy and that hard work and sacrifice built devotion and character.

Chapter 5 gives a brief glimpse into sickness and ceremonies. Navajo religion is complex. When one considers that there are two types of illness—physical such as a broken bone that is treated with splinting or ailments like a stomachache that might require specific herbs—it is not difficult to see how cures parallel those of Anglo medicine. But when that same stomachache or other malady manifests itself in certain ways, the cause may be spiritual and require a ceremony. Different forms of divination can reveal the cause, particular ceremonies may provide the cure, and the holy people can be called upon to help in most instances. The 1918 influenza epidemic is used as an example of how much of this comes together. Trading posts, a welcomed addition to the Navajo economy, form the next chapter with a special emphasis on the Oljato posts built by John and Louisa Wetherill (1906–10) and a second store started in 1921. The role they played in the community by introducing desirable goods and other elements from the dominant culture speak to the adaptability of the Navajo. But all was not peace and harmony, as chapter 7 discusses the livestock reduction of the 1930s and the trauma it introduced to almost every Navajo family. Second only to the Long Walk in the tribal memory, this episode became a major change agent of the traditional culture, which is also the theme of chapter 9 with the introduction of the car, expanding road networks, boarding schools, and the Civilian Conservation Corps programs that brought increasing Americanization to the Navajo. The movie industry in chapter 8 was a time during the John Ford–John Wayne years, when the people of the outside world caught a glimpse of the land and were indirectly introduced to the Navajo, who served as actors in many of the movies. Harry Goulding and his wife, Mike, not only played an important role in luring Hollywood to film in the West, but also by operating a trading post, encouraged tourism and helped promote the burgeoning uranium mining industry in the post–World War II Cold War. An entire chapter is devoted to the Navajo experience in mining and how they felt at the time as well as later, using twenty-twenty hindsight. The last chapter examines how these elders viewed the changes that had played out in their lives and on their lands—the price of living in an iconic landscape, how loss of control of the land to the tribal park has affected them, and what they hoped for in the future. The last segment looks at what has since evolved—playing a part

in promoting the 2002 Winter Olympics, being the staging area for a Red
Bull flying contest and balloon festivals, and their contemporary response
to the COVID-19 pandemic when compared to that of influenza in the
past. Ultimately, where are the Navajo people now in their response compared to what the elders would say?

Recognizing the ways and contributions of the past provides a basis
to think about the present and prepare for an uncertain future. If a single
motivation can be ascribed as to why these elderly men and women were
willing to share their thoughts and experiences, it was to guide future generations and to explain what it meant to be Navajo at a time when there
was no self-doubt and the world was framed by the holy people. The elders'
words are a gift to their posterity, at a time when cultural loss is great, the
world is confusing having lost its central rudder, and the younger generation is crying for stability and a firm understanding of who they are. It is
to them that the elders have dedicated this book.

CHAPTER ONE

Teachings of the Land

Living in Sacred Space

T he approximately thirty square miles that compose the rugged terrain of Monument Valley is some of the most photographed, dramatic landscape in the United States. From its towering mesas, buttes, and spires to its arches, dunes, and volcanic necks, the countryside is a kaleidoscope of form that testifies of the power of wind, water, and temperatures carving through differential erosion. Occasional vistas tease the traveler with the promise of shady pine-clad mountains and the possibility of water, a highly sought-after commodity in this high desert environment. To the east are the San Juan Mountains, south the Carrizo and Lukachukai, west Navajo Mountain, and north the Blue or Abajo—all of which are the first to receive any moisture coming into the region. The valley's 5,000-foot elevation cannot compete with the 4,000-to-9,000-foot difference of its tall, dark, and handsome neighbors in each of the cardinal directions. Still, the desert has its own appeal, one that has become increasingly popular over the years. Once considered by Anglo visitors a wasteland, home of the rattlesnake and scorpion, the valley has since blossomed into an iconic crown jewel and destination for tourism. To the Navajo or Diné, it has always been an important place to make one's home and to wrest a living from the land. Holy people are there and make it possible.

The Navajo see Mother Earth, Father Sky, and everything that exists in between as sentient beings powered by an Inner Form That Stands Within (Bii'yistiin), comparable to a spirit. Each rock, tree, spring, cloud, and animal has one inside, holding its own inherent powers received at the time of creation. This spiritual essence can be appealed to for different types of assistance—healing, protection, increase, information—if approached respectfully and with offerings. Specific songs, prayers, and guidance provided at the beginning of time call forth these powers as outlined by the holy people (diné diyinii). Thus, a relationship (k'é) is formed between man and everything that exists in the universe. Ultimately, what may seem to be a barren landscape devoid of life and meaning, is actually one filled with power, energy, and potential if shown respect. Put another way, the homeland of the Navajo is truly a home, inhabited by familiar beings who participate and provide when called upon.

Luke Yazzie from Cane Valley, east of Monument Valley proper, explains the breadth of this relationship:

> The ground is our Mother Earth. Corn pollen was carried for her. This all branched out in the growth of plants and water. Men in the past carried corn pollen to where the water seeped out of the earth at the base of a butte and where their livestock came to get a drink. They prayed to the rock that talks (echoes), Mother Earth, and the dark heavenly body, saying, "We walk upon you this way. We sit on you, lie upon you, and grow in numbers on you." This is how a song is sung, a prayer is offered to them, but we were also told not to do this if it would endanger ourselves or kin. It was through these teachings that harmony was set in place.[1]

Betty Canyon noted the effect of this kind of activity and what it meant. "It is sacred in most places. My father used to put his sacred offerings at Organ Rock and the Gray Ridge just west of here and also around Train Rock. John Holiday and several other medicine men have done so for many years. It has kept our community at peace and in good health."[2] Fred Yazzie personalized this type of relationship even more when he noted, "These buttes around here are my fences and inside is where I live. This is what I think. I look at them every morning. The rocks remain the same. The sun coming up is the same. The sunrise is beautiful. I am happy about this beauty. With this my mind is strong, which makes me strong. With this my plans are strong. This is how I think when I am sitting here. I am a desert rich man." His father, Hastiin Adakai Yázhí (Little Gambler—a.k.a. Frank Adakai), identified these same monuments as if they were family. "He would ask, 'Is it raining on the Father Mesa?' or 'Is it snowing on the Uncle Mesa or the Mother Mesa?' He named them this way for his own geographical familiarity with the land. It was his way of knowing what was happening in each area."[3]

Everywhere one looks, sacred powers are manifest. Not far from the northern end of Monument Valley runs the San Juan River, displaying its own personality. This meandering body of water with its sinuous, reptilian curves is said to be the home of Big Snake, a mythological guardian that demands respect. It is holy, so when a person approaches it, corn pollen is offered for a safe and prosperous journey. The people plead with this holy being that, after crossing, they will receive many goods if trading and be covered by its protection. A long time ago, the river was a physical and spiritual boundary that kept enemies away. It at times runs fast and dangerous as a male, powered by Big Snake that swims within, comes there to drink, and lives nearby. Holiness is in there; the hill that runs behind it (Navajo Blanket) holds the design of Big Snake's home as a warning. That is another reason why people make an offering to it. Other rivers that are considered female run more calmly. One cannot just walk around on its banks without calling upon spiritual protection because of the sacredness of the snake that is in the river. It has ba'at'e' or a power flowing within that can strike an individual, and it is dangerous if one is not prepared or respectful.[4]

The winds and air are also thought of as holy beings. Shone Holiday, former Oljato Chapter president and elder in his community, taught about the relationship of these elements to the Navajo.

One should not mock the lightning because it can hear and punish you. On the other hand, if you pray to it properly, it will reward you. Lightning travels by the holy wind (nítch'ih). Our elders used to advise us to leave wild animals like bears, cougars, and other powerful creatures alone and only talk to them reverently, for they also can hear. They are among the holy beings who are present right now and listening to everything we say. That is why we continuously praise them for all things. The same is true of the winds. We pray and talk to them—"nítch'ih dithił" (black air), "nítch'ih dootł'izh" (blue air), "nítch'ih łitso" (yellow air), "nítch'ih łigai" (white air), "nítch'ih noodǫ́ǫ́z" (striped air). The east is black, the south is blue, west is yellow, and north is white. The reasons for these colors are that sunsets are yellow, the south is blue because the sunshine reflects that color from the mountains and sky, the north is white because of the mountains covered with snow. These colored winds are named in our prayers in a certain order, just as they are in a ceremony or sing. They also have different strengths. Some are big while others are little winds, depending on where they are located in the four sacred directions. Medicine men name all of them in their songs and prayers, and although we cannot see them, they are there. When there is a tornado or big wind, medicine men will blow it away with ashes and prayers. This is part of the teachings of the Windway Ceremony.

A man named Hastiin Tsé'naa'í (Mr. Across) used to sing these songs and prayers, but I think he was the last medicine man to know them. Even the little whirlwinds or "dust devils" that blow around in the sand can be either good if twirling clockwise or bad if going counter-clockwise because ghosts can travel in them. It is said that as long as one of these does not run over you, you will be alright, but if one passes over, it will affect one's breathing and you will become sick. Medicine men can perform a sing for this type of illness to cure the bad air.[5]

Creating the Earth's Surface

Anthropologists often refer to Navajo religion as being "land-based" in that the stories, names, and knowledge are tied intimately to specific points on the landscape. There is no guessing as to where events in a narrative occurred as it begins and ends at a certain place, with a number of sites mentioned in between. There is also no exaggeration in suggesting that almost every rock formation, pool of water, canyon system, riverbed, or other unique topographical feature will have a story or teaching and been named either on a local or a broader regional level. Whether it appears in the songs, prayers, or mind of a local inhabitant, there is something to be learned and respected. Often there is more than one explanation or teaching derived from the same site. This is not to suggest necessarily that one person's beliefs are more correct than another's, only that they have been taught differently through the narratives, accompanying ceremonies, or personal experience. The oral tradition, as means of transmission until fairly recently, accepts variation based upon how an individual has been taught.

Many of the landforms and creatures that inhabit the Monument Valley region are associated with the creation story, explaining how they came into existence. The most basic narrative tells how everything was made spiritually before it existed physically and how each being inhabited a different form, ranging from humans and animals to rocks and water. The Inner Form That Stands Within is encased in a particular shape, which if removed, would have human qualities capable of thinking, speaking, and acting as well as controlling its special powers assigned to it by the gods. These first existed in three or four different worlds (depending on the account of the creation story) beneath the level of the Glittering World, in which we exist today. There are many different versions of what took place during the emergence and shortly after the holy people arrived here.[6] These narratives explain how each of these worlds had its own color, starting at the lowest level with black, then blue, yellow, and white before reaching the one we now inhabit. Each also had its own set of creatures that grew in complexity as one ascended—beginning with ants, insects, and other small creatures in the Black World—and culminating with all elements of the animal kingdom and the physical creation of man in the Glittering World. Every level provided new prototypes for what would exist on this level, fostered experiences and teachings that emerged with each being as it moved to its next stage of existence, and opened doors to a growing sophistication. Many of these new experiences encouraged learning control and understanding what not to do. Indeed, the reason that these beings migrated from world to world was that they had done things incorrectly and so were forced out.

Susie Yazzie, a woman who lived her entire life in Monument Valley, tells how pristine water covered most of the earth, as the holy people abandoned the world beneath this one. They were leaving because Coyote the trickster had stolen a water baby. The water monster, angry at her loss, flooded the world beneath this one, forcing its inhabitants to crawl through a tall reed into the sky before reaching the bottom of today's land. Once these fleeing creatures worked their way through the earth's crust and entered upon this level, they found themselves on a small spit of land surrounded by water that needed to be drained. There are a number of different accounts telling how this was accomplished. One mentions how four holy beings, each setting off in one of the cardinal directions with a big knife, carved a channel through which the water could flow over the ground and into a river system, leading eventually to the ocean. Another tells of four colored rocks that whirred and buzzed like saws through the surrounding land formations, while Susie describes how a holy being, Badger, dug a hole that drained the water. Regardless of the version, the earth became exposed, leaving behind the rock formations of Monument Valley and the Four Corners region. Susie begins:

> Long ago, it was said, the earth was covered with water, like the ocean. The holy people wanted to drain it to expose the earth, but they were unsure, once the water was gone, if the land would remain dry. There were many types of fish and animals in these waters, just like in the ocean today. These creatures swam beneath, floated on the surface, and gathered in groups, searching for food and following underwater pathways. Take

for instance The One Who Grabs and Holds You to Him (Tééhóółtsódii), with many legs. These creatures were huge, some like giant lizards and fish, others like large cockroaches that ran on top of the water. There was a wide variety of different insects and animals, a number as big as boats. Other creatures looked like donkeys, but they lived under the water. Grandfather Atini mentioned another creature he called Yellow Coming Out (Bił Hajootsoii) that had a horn and might have been related to our cows or horses. In earlier times, these animals had different names from those used today.

The deep gorges and canyons that you see now were exposed and formed as the water drained. The mesas were on a higher ground level, where trees grew, but as the water dropped, much of the soil washed away, leaving some of the rocks standing upright. It was said there was also vegetation under the water where some dinosaurs and reptiles lived. These creatures came from the east and went through these passages toward Navajo Mountain on an underwater trail. This is what my grandfather told me. He cautioned that no one was to make their homes on these trails, but today, we see many dwellings at these sites. Oljato Mesa is called Rock Going Down (Tsé Yanii Áhá) because that land formation descends down to the west but rises up on the eastern end. Where the rock opens near the former Seventh Day Adventist Hospital and mission is Between the Rocks (Tségiizh). This is one of the trails of the huge reptile dinosaurs (tł'iish tsoh). The pathway is called "Tł'iish Tsoh Bitiin" (Big Dinosaur Trail). They left their tracks along the edges of the boulders close to where the hospital building now stands above the Seventh Day Adventist Church. These rocks were dynamited when construction workers widened the road through the canyon. Some say that people took these tracks with them. Now they are gone.

The large body of water remained until Badger (Nahashch'idí) dug a tunnel to let it out. Everything turned very muddy with animals falling into the slime, leaving tracks behind. The draining mud and water destroyed all of the plants and animals that had been under the water, then solidified into the rocks and mesas we see today. Once the swamp was gone, the land started drying and the sandstone became mesas shaped by the flowing liquid. The "Holy One" planned it that way. He made the land so that the people could live on it, although it took many, many years for this change to occur; it did not just happen overnight. Grandfather used to say, "You can still see the line of the water level as it went down. It probably stayed at these heights for years before descending to the next visible mark that is still there." Once the water drained, it left the

Silhouettes and shadows, colors and contrasts, rocks pointing to the heavens—Monument Valley is one of nature's classic creations, said by some to be the Eighth Wonder of the World. Home to the Navajo, this land's stories speak of its beginning and continue through today. (Courtesy Special Collections, J. Willard Marriott Library, University of Utah)

pillars of rock standing, creating the monuments that others come to see. Vegetation began to grow. Some animals that lived before the flood were buried in the mud and became the minerals of today like uranium. Some of these elements are dangerous to human beings.[7]

Gladys Bitsinnie, living on Douglas Mesa at the northern end of Monument Valley, offered additional details that confirm Susie's beliefs. Gladys said,

My father and grandfather told me about the different rock formations. There are holes in them, almost as if they had been made by man, but they are old and were formed when the rocks were mud. Past Kayenta, there is a place called Ndeelk'id (Long House Valley, literally "Side of the Hill"). We were traveling by there and my father talked about it. The rocks looked like they were stairs and he said that they were from the time of the mud. All different kinds of wildlife, like big lizards, were around this place.[8]

This is one way to think about the land. Another is to see specific sites, individual rock formations, and natural resources as an integrated framework tied together with stories about holy beings, historical incidents, and supernatural powers understood by the Navajo living in the area. Indeed, the rich tapestry of cultural knowledge that is unfolded here is, for the most part, specific to a limited area that is multiplied numerous times in different ways across the reservation. Some landmarks such as mountain ranges, rivers, a rock formation like Shiprock, and a historic site like Fort Sumner will have its own more generalized teachings understood by many, but much more of this knowledge is on a local level known only to those who live there. Understanding this information, both local and regional, is the role of medicine men and those who are intimately familiar with the songs, prayers, and ceremonies that have their beginnings in events that occurred during the creative period or "palm of time," when spiritual rules and teachings were put into place by the holy people. John Holiday (1919–2016), a highly respected elder and teacher, was such a person. In 2001, I had an opportunity to travel with him throughout the Monument Valley region as I recorded information for his autobiography. We started from his home north of Train Rock and spent the day visiting familiar sites including the Navajo Tribal Park and the Oljato area. What immediately became apparent was the intensity of his understanding and conviction of his beliefs about the land. "Our great men used to give offerings to all the mesas and mountains around here, which made these places holy and sacred. I noticed these things and wondered about them. Even right here where I live, I can sometimes hear the wind blowing, with sounds down underground, and then it rains or the wind blows. I sometimes 'think' let it rain and it does. It is strange, but this is the holiness of the place. This is what I know about the sacred places. They are holy."[9] Unless otherwise noted, much of what follows are his teachings.

Categorizing the Land

John saw the land as one inextricably entwined catalogue of names. It was a huge memory-jogger or mnemonic device that conveniently fell into the five categories that geographer Stephen C. Jett identified in his book *Navajo Placenames and Trails of the Canyon de Chelly System, Arizona.*[10] In it, he examined and classified 250 such identifiers and determined that there were five primary ways that Navajos thought about the land through its names. Although John, without prompting, would not think of them in this manner, it is a helpful way to evaluate the different meanings associated with specific sites. In ascending order of complexity, they are (1) description based on physical characteristics, (2) possession or who lived there, (3) travel and boundaries, (4) livelihood and resources, and (5) events (history) or stories (hané).

Listen to the descriptive terms that identify places based on physical characteristics, requiring little further explanation. As John and I traveled that day in November, a list of these place names rolled off his tongue. For example, there was The Road Coming Up, Mr. San Juan River's Water, Rocks Fallen Down, Pointed Rocks Coming Up, Creviced Rock, The Crooked Road, Between the Rocks, Beneath the Rock, Willow Springs, Swinging Around the Rock, Water that Boils Out, Pointed Rough Rock, Black Spot on the Rock, Jagged Rocks, and Hole in the Rock. These were all landmarks or geographical names of the places where we moved in and around the VCA (Vanadium Corporation of America—Cane Valley) area. Near Train Rock were places called Red Strip of Sand, Under the Cottonwood Spring, Red Hill, Salty Water Spring, and Sitting Red Object. On the northern side of this area is a catch basin with trees at a place called Stump Ears. It got its name from a spotted horse with short ears that used to go there to drink. Beyond that is Downward Sloped Red Meadow and across from it Among Young Juniper Trees. Rough Red Rock Bluff acts like a mountain. Sometimes at night one hears a roar inside, making the sound of gushing water. This noise occurs when the wind is going to blow or when it is going to rain. Sure enough it happens.

There is also Narrow Canyon (Tséyaa' Tsʼózí Chʼinílíní—Where the Narrow Canyon Runs), where a number of families live and large cornfields existed nearby. All of the watering holes have been given Navajo names. For instance, "Bullsnake Spring" (Diyóósh Bitóʼ) is located north of Totem Pole Rock in Monument Valley and farther down the wash is Dune or Sand Springs. Many of these descriptive names have since been forgotten, but to those tied to the land through the livestock industry of the past, they were well-known terms shared on a local level.

Another way of describing the land was by where people lived. This is a familiar process in today's dominant society when one refers to the location of a home or where a group of related families reside. Gray Whiskers Mesa near the tribal park's Visitor's Center is a good example, named after a prominent medicine man (Bidághaa Łibáí) who lived at that site. The mesa is also said to be one of the doorposts of a giant hogan formed by Monument Valley with a second post being Sentinel Mesa and the fireplace in the Goulding's area. Gray Whiskers used to move around this whole valley near White Tipped Mountain, where there used to be a lot of wild horses, with a number of stallions each having their own herd. Some were white, others red, and some black. There were other herds of horses with black manes, golden horses, yellow ones, pintos, and roan. Occasionally, the people rounded them up. Some horses were butchered for meat while others were tamed for riding.

Continuing on John's tour, we descended into the Monument Valley Park and drove past the remains of a male hogan that sat weathering under the desert sun. He pointed out,

> That big hogan is where two or three families lived even before there was a road near it. They shared space and food and did not fight but lived peacefully. It first belonged to Mister Lefty (Tł'aa'í—Left Handed), named after an old headman who died in 1934 and is buried at the foot of Cly Butte. That formation is named after him but the name changed because of a mispronunciation of his Navajo title. He was called that because he did things with his left hand. He had a lot of children whose last name is now Cly and they have many generations of both paternal and maternal grandchildren. After he left, his son-in-law, His Big Adopted Son (Hastiintso Biye' Íí'íní), took the hogan.
>
> In those days people did not claim ownership of the land or hogans. Whoever was moving to the area for the season and found the hogan empty got to live in it. People would say so-and-so is now living in the hogan. They were kind and considerate of each other. Back then they used to say, "Go ahead and bring your sheep and let them feed anywhere you can find a good grazing area. There is water for your sheep." They never turned anyone away. The people were afraid to claim any piece of land because they believed that when one died, the place where he or she was buried became his or her land. For this reason, the people did not claim ownership and one never said "my land." But now everybody says this and is stingy and protective. As soon as someone argues about owning the land it is for sure that not too many days will pass before they die. It happens every time, so I believe those old wise people and never say, "my land."[11]

On a slightly different note, between 1906 and 1910 John and Louisa Wetherill owned a trading post roughly a mile south of the now standing Oljato post started in 1921. Both of these stores' history will be discussed in a later chapter, but today there is nothing left at the Wetherill site beyond a pool of water used by livestock. At one point there remained three upright wooden posts protruding from the ground and so the place became known as Where the Wood Is Pointing Out (Tsindeez'áh) and was one of the sites where horses were kept during the era of livestock reduction. The names of the previous owners had been forgotten. Perhaps one of the best-known places associated with Monument Valley is named after two other traders, Harry and Leone ("Mike") Goulding, who arrived there in the fall of 1925. After moving their tent around to various locations including the base of Mitchell Butte because of the availability of melting snow water, and beside the trail going through Monument Pass (Atiin Nahoneeshtł'iizhí) because of the cooling summer breezes, the couple settled in the store's present location at what they called Rock Door Canyon. The Navajos referred to this site as Between the Rocks, in which there was a small spring important for its water.[12]

A third way of thinking about the land is as a mental map or itinerary filled with landmarks and boundaries encountered when traveling. This same pattern is prominent in the many narratives outlining the journeys of the holy people. Indeed, medicine men who are highly aware of the sacred landscape described in the stories, may recount verbally or reenact physically the retracing of the same steps described in the narrative behind the ceremony that they are using. This may include the gathering of materials employed in the healing process. The location of the plants, minerals, or object is identified, and the healer follows the ritual pattern established previously, while the travel and how it is conducted is as important as obtaining the physical item. It is all part of the healing process.

The annual life cycle of a family herding livestock may follow a seasonal round that is just as detailed. John spoke of the pattern his family pursued when he was a young man and moving about in search of resources available during certain times of the year. The route could mean the difference between economic success and hardship.

> During the summer, when I was a child, our home was a tent and a circle of sagebrush that served as a windbreak. Back in those days all families used to move around a lot. We lived alongside Comb Ridge (Tséí K'áán—Rocks Standing Up) at a place called Soft Ground Water. We also lived down by Much Rocky Ground and just below that at Red Sand Rocks, at Little Coyote, at The Cottonwood Tree, at Black Streak down the Rock, then at the base of Douglas Mesa at a place called Wind Blowing around the Rock, and at Water Streaming Off the Top. We lived in all these places. We searched for good grazing land and when we learned where there was an abundance of vegetation, we moved to that pasture for the sheep. This was the main purpose for traveling around so

much. "It rained over there and there's plenty of vegetation; let's move there!" Then in the winter, "The vegetation has not been touched over there; it is fresh; let's move there." We moved everywhere, never staying in one place.

The land was filled with Navajo names. One place was called Silhouette of Person beneath the Rock along Comb Ridge. This came from a crevice that runs down the mesa. When someone went up or down it, he would see his shadow or silhouette against the rock. As we moved from Where the Rocks Came Ashore (near Lake Powell) down by Piute Farms, we headed east through Water Under the Cottonwoods (the mesa south of Train Rock), Sitting Red Mesa, Owl Spring (which received its name from the owls hooting at night), then down into the valley on the northeast side of the rock formations of Monument Valley to Salty Springs, then White-Tipped Mountain, and on to Wind Blowing Downward Off the Rock, then to Wind Blowing Through the Rock and Canyon of Trees and Road Coming Up. When we got to Wind Blowing Through the Rock we had to shear the sheep because it was nearly summer.[13]

This leads to a fourth way that the Navajo identified and interacted with the land—the practical search and location of resources and means of survival. The basis of the Navajo economy in the early days depended on livestock—sheep, goats, horses, and cattle—and agriculture supplemented by hunting and gathering. Much of the hunting was done north of the San Juan River and so will not be discussed here, but gathering wild plants was well integrated into the search for grazing areas for the sheep. June Black Yazzie explained,

When you are herding sheep, you took a sack for things that came from the land and you filled that bag with wild onions that you dug out of the ground, then took home. They were then used in gravy, and bread was dunked into the gravy. Sumac berries were ground and eaten and seeds were gathered in cloths. Hashch'ééd££' was also used, ground and added to porridge, while cornmeal was eaten with a sweet clay (dleesh). Then there was tł'ohdei found growing outside of our home, but it was generally hard to come by. People would ride to where these plants grew in patches, pick, and then bake them in the ground in the same kind of process they did with corn bread.[14]

As a medicine woman, Ada Black was keenly aware of the location of healing herbs and the reason that they grew in certain areas. In the midst of Monument Valley there is a large volcanic neck named El Capitan (Spanish: The Captain; Navajo: Aghaałą́—Much Wool/Fur) that is prominent in many traditional stories, some of which will be discussed later. Ada, speaking of this formation, noted:

> On the east side of this rock is a hole where Big Snake, one of the holy beings who traveled with Changing Woman at the time of creation, used to have his home. It is said that he traveled only at night on the wind and a rainbow before returning by daylight. During the spring when there was a new growth of plants, it would come out and live on the mesa. El Capitan served as the doorway for this snake. That is why the lizard and snake people are so abundant and consider all of Monument Valley as their sacred land. Monument Pass, at the northern end of the valley, has a lot of them there as well as many medicine plants such as ts'iis tsoh bik'ą', and one for birthing called doo bich'į' achíí. If a person is injured, there is the Iináájí azee' (Lifeway medicine) that heals. All of these plants grow there. The medicine men who perform the Iináájí ceremony use herbs in water that grow in this place. The white man called this disease ajizeeh [?], which bothers a woman who does not take care of herself during her monthly. Her ankles, knees, back, or fingers will hurt unless she takes some of this herb that grows there. It can be found clustering in areas, because it is holy ground and should not be disturbed in any way. Navajo people have medicine growing all over this place with numerous sites to offer prayers to holy people like Talking God (Haashch'ééłti'í), whom we call our maternal grandfather, Mother Earth, and Tsé asdzą́ą́, all of whom can serve as a shield and a power.
>
> Near Much Fur/Wool [El Capitan] people used to tan antelope and deer hides.[15] There was a lot of fur around the area and so that is how it got its name. People were very scared of the fur because they did not want the sheep to wander into the area and they did not want people to urinate at that place because it would get them sick and they would not be able to relieve themselves.[16]

Other names associated with the livestock industry have their own story to tell. Dibé Bichaan Bito' (Sheep Manure Spring) and Dził Naakai Tł'ízí near El Capitan have obvious ties. Another site is called Where the Sheep Drowned, which is found in the farthest canyon of Mystery Valley southeast of Promise Rock. There were some deep and steep watering holes

The Three Sisters, said to be holy people frozen in stone, graphically depict the power of differential erosion that separated these rocks from their neighboring mesa. To the Navajo they are a place of power embedded in a sacred landscape. (Courtesy Photo Archives, Utah State Historical Society)

there. They say one winter when the water froze, some sheep got on top of the ice to drink. Since they were all standing on one side, the sheet of ice flipped over, spilling them into the water, then trapping and killing them. One spring was named Buffalo Skin in the Water because the moss growing on the ledges under the water looked curly and dark like buffalo hair. Near another source called Mourning Dove Spring was a place known as Hanging Paiute. This got its name because Paiutes used to pick berries off the trees there. One of them jumped off a branch, got his shirt caught on a limb, and he hung there for some time. A formation of black rocks near the VCA mine is called "Rocks [volcanic] of Hunger for Meat." They were named that because when people grazed their flocks in the area, the sheep would not get fat enough to butcher. The land is harsh in this place.

Some of the places found today in Monument Valley have received more recent names such as Clearing Amidst the Rocks (Tsé Bii' Ndzisgaii), now known as Mystery Valley. Randall Henderson, a writer for *Desert Magazine*, gave it this epithet in the 1950s when he was touring through the area with Harry Goulding. Henderson was impressed with how around each corner and rock formation a new arch appeared, a different sight unfolded, and another Anasazi ruin loomed ahead, with pleasing vistas everywhere.[17] To Guy Cly, the mouth of Mystery Valley, when added to Monument Valley and Dennehotso, were the three most prominent planting fields in the region.[18] This Clearing Amidst the Rocks had a more fundamental utility then, whereas now, there are far more greenbacks changing hands than green-leafed cornstalks.

During the 1930s, some of that corn as well as fruit, either grown locally or purchased in Kayenta at the southern end of the valley, made its way to alcoves and other hidden spots in Monument Valley, preferably with a seep or spring. There the manufacture of bootleg alcohol ignited a prosperous trade among locals, much in keeping with the spirit of the times. Some people mention that the trader in Oljato was in on the commerce, while the children of one of the notable Navajos in the valley became excited when Dad came back with a lot of luscious fruit that disappeared into a still before they had a chance to sample it. At this time there was not a lot of money on the reservation and so barter was the general practice. Those selling the moonshine (dah tsidígii) were more interested in cash but were also amenable to advancing credit once the spirits had been brewed. Local people say that Promise Rock, a site known as one of the places for these transactions, received its title as the place that the buyer would return to make good on his purchase.[19]

The fifth and final way of thinking about the land is based on its history and sacred teachings. Many of the historical events such as the Long Walk era, livestock reduction, and uranium mining will be developed more fully in later chapters. The more complex derivation of names connected to Navajo traditional narratives will be the primary focus here. The landscape is one large stage across which history has played. A few examples follow. When the Utes and Mexicans sought out Navajos in hiding during the Long Walk period, the land offered secluded places, one of the favored ones of retreat being the rocky canyons along the lower San Juan River and Oljato Creek. One of these, known as Adahch'íjííyáhí Canyon on the northern end of Tséyii'déé' Mesa, became an important place to flee. A prominent headman named Giving Out Anger (Hashkéneiniihii) lived at the southern end of Monument Valley and fled far beyond this site to Navajo Mountain. Still, a mesa to the west of Oljato is named after him (Hoskininni Mesa), the east side of which became known as Where the Mexicans Chased Them Upwards (Naakai Híhoniiłkaad). Susie Yazzie, a great-granddaughter of Giving Out Anger, will in chapter 3 explain some of the events surrounding this name. In the tribal park there are Mitchell

(Tsé Ntsaa—Big Rock) and Merrick (Tóshjeeh—water barrel) Buttes named after two prospectors, Hernan D. Mitchell and Charles S. Merrick (actually Myrick), who were killed near the formations bearing their names.

There are also more recent historical events—either personal or recognized by the community—that are tied to the land. For instance, it might be as simple as when June Yazzie was dumping ashes in the Oljato area called Náházhóóh one night. She and some of her family members spotted a skinwalker trotting by, seized a rifle, and shot, wounding it. They heard a woman's cry before it disappeared. The next morning, they looked for tracks in the direction it had fled and followed them until they went over some rocks and then turned into human footsteps. The creature only walked on the middle of its paws, but once on top of the rock, "its tracks were in the right way."[20]

Compare that simple experience to John Holiday's use of the land that brought much-needed water to the entire Monument Valley community.

> Approximately 30 years ago, Train Rock seemed to always have rain around it. A small cloud would gather just above the formation and it would rain all the time in a little area surrounding the mesa. I had noticed it was this way for about thirty years. Then one day it rained and a huge slab of rock slid down on the west side facing Oljato. A man named Gray Whiskers, my grandfather by clan from the southern end of Monument Valley, was asked to make a special prayer offering at this site. So he performed the offering, but there had been no rain ever since and we did not know why. Then about 20 years ago there was another rock slide. This time it was towards my home. I went up there and gave the sacred offerings. I took a jug of water which had a mixture of water from the ocean, sacred mountains, and local springs.[21] With this water I "cooled" the area of the rock slide, prayed that the rain cloud would reappear because it had been gone for so many years, and that it would rain again like it did long ago. The next day was the fair in Monticello held in mid-summer. My oldest son, Albert, and I went to the fair and played cards with the Utes. He said, "I think it's raining at home in Oljato."
>
> We left for Monument Valley after dark. There still was no rain in Monticello, however, as we got closer to home, we saw it had been raining there. We were just east of Train Rock when we noticed that the red sand was wet and muddy, and before we knew it, we were stuck in a large puddle. Gradually, we backed out of it by shoving brush under the tires then took another route on sandy soil to get back home. It had rained really hard and water was everywhere.

I recall seeing a little cloud above the Bears Ears while we were driving to Monticello that morning. I guess it moved to Train Rock that afternoon, but only a narrow strip of rain had fallen all the way from the Bears Ears to Train Rock. People said the cloud dissolved there. Now it remains there and each time the cloud forms, it rains. People often ask why it rains only on Train Rock. Teddy Holiday from Douglas Mesa asked me once, "Why are you getting all the rain? You're the only one who will survive for sure!"

"I don't know," I said, "It's the rock that's getting blessed from above, not me."

"But you're the only one to get all the rain! It's your fault."

"You should learn the rain ceremony," I said. He did not answer and just walked away. That is how mesas are; they are naturally blessed.[22]

Perhaps the most interesting and complex understanding about the land is found in the names and teachings derived from the stories associated with many of the rock formations. Much of this information has been forgotten and so these spires, monoliths, buttes, and mesas have been given contemporary titles based on someone's imagination dealing with a supposed shape. For example, a quick perusal of many of the names found in the tribal park have little connection to traditional Navajo beliefs or experience—Brigham's Tomb, King on His Throne, Castle and Camel Butte, or Totem Pole Rock—for example. Navajo elders that have now passed away had a very different story to tell. What follows is some of that information left behind before their passing. Tallis Holiday, a lifetime resident of this area, provides a starting point:

> The rocks standing in Monument Valley are part of a home for what lives there including the wind. There is a doorway formed by two rocks that stand apart at some distance on the east side of the valley. The formations that stand upright and point north toward Douglas Mesa encase part of a path used by the holy people. That is why these rocks are in a row. If people live too close to where the holy people dwell, they will get sick, so one should live away from these places.[23]

Some sites have more than one meaning or story associated with them, which is very much in keeping with past beliefs and various narratives tied to the same formation. John Holiday takes the lead in this discussion. Starting at the northern end of the valley after entering through Monument Pass, large rock configurations loom on each side of the road.

On the far right or west side sits Eagle Mesa, said to be a large "Water Basket Sits." Other names for Eagle Mesa include Wide Rock and Trees Hanging from Surrounding Belt because there used to be a lot of trees around the mesa. Standing beside the main mesa is a slender pinnacle that looks like a perched eagle, hence the name Eagle Mesa. Navajo names for this rock include Eagle Alongside Mesa, Standing Slim Rock Alongside, and Big Finger is Pointed. John noted:

> People say there is a male hogan on top of it. Awhile back when I used to live within view, we used to see moving lights on top. I do not know which direction the lights went down the mesa and I do not know who it was. The rock standing by itself beside Eagle Mesa is The Key and the one behind it that looks like a sitting bird is called Turkey [Setting Hen]. It was said to be a live turkey before it turned to rock. The red hill next to it is Porcupine, which also was alive but turned to stone. The three rocks [Big Indian] pointing up are people who came down from the top of the mesa [Sentinel] and were sitting together visiting when they also turned to rock. If a person looks at it from a different angle it appears to be a jackrabbit's head with three ears. That is why it is named Jack or Big Rabbit. Next to it is a formation [Castle Butte] named after a Feather Ceremony, Wide Wood, and next to that is another rock named after the Feather Ceremony.
>
> Other rocks around Eagle Mesa have sacred teachings as do Train Rock and Totem Pole down in the valley. The monument of "The Bear and the Rabbit" is also sacred. The bear is really a coyote, not a bear. Legend says that the coyote did not have ears at that time, and that he caught the rabbit for a meal. "I will eat you," said the coyote.
>
> "Wait. Let's talk first," pleaded the rabbit.
>
> "The Diné usually wrap their arrows around their bow before eating," said the rabbit as he pressed his hands and arms against the coyote's chest. Then they suddenly changed into rocks.
>
> The coyote's ears used to be shaped like a bear's ears long ago and were not pointed like they are today. There is a story that tells how this change came about. One day the coyote crept up on a sleeping bobcat. He pushed in the bobcat's nose and chopped off its tail to a length where it could not move anymore. Later, when the bobcat found the coyote asleep, he crept up to him and pulled his nose and ears very hard. The coyote awoke, but his ears were pointed. Stagecoach Mesa, next to the earless coyote and rabbit, was said to be the spectators watching what went on between these two, but they were also changed into rocks. All

The oral tradition is a powerful means of telling about the past in preparation for events in the future. Baxter Benally, a fun-loving and skilled interpreter, listens to John Holiday, a highly accomplished medicine man who knew well the history of Monument Valley, his lifetime home. (Photo by author)

are sacred. If there is a drought, one can place corn pollen at these mesas and they will bring rain.

Further down the road just above the Monument Valley High School is a formation named Rock Blocking the Way because it is in front of the two other rocks. It is a gate that protects Oljato Mesa and other formations to the west. Husky Standing Rock [Mitchell Butte] is said to be where Talking God lives. He comes out at dawn to pray and bless all the rocks and mesas. It is a sacred place. Continuing south but before reaching El Capitan there is a black jagged rock believed to be two horned toads lying crisscrossed. It is said that the Thunder, a holy being and ruler of all things, tied together these two creatures with curled blades of grass. Another god finished by tying them to a bush, where they remained bound for twelve days before their pleading led to their release. The other gray hills below that are two female toads lying face down. Further down the road sits Turtle Rock, said to be a turtle that had just left his home of piled rocks on the other side of the road. People placed their offerings there for rain. Nearby was a natural spring at Water under the Cottonwood but this has since been covered. The water used to bubble up from the ground, but now it is pumped from the well. This was also a sacred place for offerings.[24]

Some of the teachings about El Capitan have already been discussed. Stephen Jett (see endnote 15) also noted that this dramatic, pointed tuff-breccia volcanic neck has been said by some Navajos to be the center of the world, by others a pedestal serving as a Sky Supporter that holds up the heavens like an umbrella, or a wool twiner, or a means of communication like an antenna between the Sun, First Woman, and Changing Woman, who has her home in the ocean, tying in to her close association with the Western Water Clans that she created. Some of their number traveled by this location and camped there before moving on to settle in Oljato. To Kayo Holiday, El Capitan was placed there by the gods and assisted in the killing of four monsters roaming the earth. That is why sacred offerings are made here for those who have bad dreams, especially those involving teeth. "These you give as sacrifice so that it [the formation] may help you to stay in harmony as you go about. The rocks that are standing, these you give sacrifice to."[25] Directly across the road from El Capitan sits Owl Rock, said by John to be Changing Woman. If one observes closely, they will see her gray and red flared skirt with white sole moccasins sticking out from under her dress. A legend says that she was angry, sat down, and turned into a rock. According to Blessingway singer Billy Yellow the rock is a spindle left behind by the holy beings.[26]

Returning to the tribal park, Tallis Holiday explains that when the "coughing sickness" came in the past, the thin rock near the ranger station called Tsé Áłtsoozí Siláhí was used as a shield against sickness. It was like a banner against any illness because it was made of electricity in every part of it.

John continues his narration.

Merritt [Merrick] Butte is called Poking (Standing) Rock. The formation sticking up nearby is Desert Weasel and next to that is a snake that is also sticking its head up. The weasel put his hands together and that is how he was turned into a rock. There is a legend about this area that a long time ago everything was very small. This entire area was once underwater, but it went away little by little. These were the only rocks above the water. Then the gods blew on this region to make it really wide. That is when these rocks and everything became big. Even the people became big people, tall people. The water ran out and made big canyons. The Three Sisters formation is a lady walking toward us with her two children while the rock that is in front is a man with a cane leading them. Right by Wide Rock Butte or Holding Things Like a Bowl [Rain God Mesa—Dahazkání (?)][27] are three standing rocks that are gods to whom the people pray. Nearby is Tracks of Sheep Leading Down. The people used to water their sheep at a place called Bullsnake Spring in the Sand. Southwest of Rain God Mesa, there are rocks that form a rough circle. In the middle there was a fire [The Hub] whose remains have turned to stone and a pile of sand left behind from making sand paintings at a No Sleep ceremony (Doo Da'iigháashjí). The rocks that are sticking up in the middle of the flat were buffalo who turned to stone, some big and some small.

The rocks around Water in the Sand are said to be people standing near a hogan with a fire.[28] Nearby are the Yé'ii who dance at dawn and these people are watching them dance. They sing making the sound, "O hoo woo ho, I hii yee he." In the distance is Woman Carrying the Baby. The rock that is near her side is the Water Sprinkler (clown).[29] He has the hide of a coyote. The rock sticking out in front of them is a traditional whistle [Totem Pole Rock], and the other rocks are more people standing and watching the dance while the round ones on the side of the mesa are their heads. That is what I was told.[30]

To Tallis Holiday these formations are the home of the mirage (hadahoniye') people as well as the air people because there are usually holes going down the side of the formation.[31]

John concluded:

About five years ago, a medicine man from the valley came to visit me. He said, "We never have rain, we are experiencing drought, and the wind continues to blow for many days." We did not go directly to a water hole to give the offering, but took the sacred materials to Totem Pole Rock in the valley, where we asked for rain in all four directions. As we returned home in his pickup truck, the rain came and there were flash floods everywhere. It was pouring and the washes filled with water. The rain started coming again to this area after that. It was truly a sacred and holy blessing. If these holy places are destroyed, then I do not know what will happen. They are sacred so that when we lack rain, we can place our offerings there.[32]

I dropped him off at his home north of Train Rock and began my long journey across the sand and gravel road, out to the highway, and home.

The sun was setting over the rock formations I had spent the day learning about, bathing them in a yellow light that accentuated the red sandstone. The land took on a life of its own, one filled with stories and history, with teachings and promise. John and the other elders had opened the door that allowed recognition of its power and importance. Each of the land's features had taught of its own importance, something that speaks to the Inner Form That Stands Within.

CHAPTER TWO

Lessons from Deep History

The Anasazi Legacy

Monument Valley has been home for a number of prehistoric Indian groups long before the Navajo arrived. Primarily the domain of the archaeologist studying material remains, the earliest groups extend all the way back to the last ice age, ending around 10,000 BC. Starting with the Clovis culture, identified as the earliest, these people are viewed as operating in small, highly mobile hunting and gathering groups. Their material remains indicate they had a notable focus on big game hunting of megafauna such as mastodons, mammoths, camelids, and other now-extinct animals. Because they rarely utilized dry alcoves for shelter, all that exists of these cultures to help archaeologists understand them is primarily their stone tools, everything else having deteriorated beyond recognition. As the climate became warmer following the end of the Pleistocene (Ice Age) Epoch, the Archaic period began with a general shift in material culture that adapted to hunting smaller game and gathering plant materials of a drier environment. Because these Native Americans made much more use of alcoves, not only stone tools have survived, but also woven baskets, blankets, cordage, and rock art. For six thousand years, this way of life persisted, although despite its length of time, relatively little is known beyond their physical lifestyle with the exception of rock art, which hints at how they viewed the nonmaterial world. Neither of these groups is identified by the Navajo.

This is not the case, however, when it comes to the Anasazi (Anaasází), who left extensive remains, including their dwellings, tools, and rock art, all of which are of keen interest to the Navajo. Indeed, there are extensive stories about who these people were, how they lived, and why they abandoned a homeland that they had lived in for centuries. While Anglo culture wrestles with questions about physical evidence, the Navajo have their own answers that offer religious reasons about what happened and why, providing insight that archaeologists generally refuse to accept. This dichotomy could not be more pronounced—science versus religion, tangible versus intangible, spiritual versus physical causes. In this chapter, after presenting a highly abbreviated archaeological view of the ruins found in every nook and cranny of the northern part of the reservation, the remainder will outline the highly different perspective of Navajos living in Monument Valley. For additional information on their views along with those of the Ute and Hopis, see *Viewing the Ancestors, Perceptions of the Anaasází, Mokwič, and Hisatsinom.*[1]

There is a profuse literature written by archaeologists, rock art specialists, and a host of related science and social science scholars anxiously trying to understand and explain who the Anasazi were and what happened to them. Their efforts have greatly aided in categorizing this Indian group's physical experience living in the Four Corners area. Extensive surveys and excavations have unearthed information not otherwise available, but at the same time they were highly offensive and contrary to what the Navajo thought and wished. To understand why there was such a contrast to each group's approach as to what had happened so long ago, it is important to understand their perspectives.

For the Anglo, starting approximately 1000 BC, there was a gradual shift from the hunting and gathering lifestyle of those Indians classified as Archaic to a different cultural phenomenon that would be labeled as the Anasazi or Ancient Puebloan culture. Glimmers of maize horticulture provided the impetus. As the culture grew in sophistication and complexity, though never entirely leaving hunting and gathering while greatly expanding its dependence on domesticated plants, it evolved through various stages. Archaeologists still use the Pecos Classification system devised by Alfred Kidder and others at the Pecos Conference in 1927 to subdivide these people into two major categories—Basketmaker (early and late) and Pueblo (Periods I, II, III, IV, and V).

Because of the difficulty of distinguishing between the Archaic hunters and gatherers and the first phase of Anasazi development during the Basketmaker I period, the latter is considered transitional between the two cultural expressions and so only Basketmaker II or early Basketmaker is discussed. This cultural horizon began when these people developed shallow pit houses, circular storage pits, skillfully crafted baskets and sandals, feather and fur robes, and a greatly expanded tool kit, much of which was stored in the rock overhangs of the canyon floors or amid the juniper and piñon groves of the lands above. By 500 BC, Basketmaker II groups depended heavily on maize and squash, while continuing to seasonally move to various sites to harvest wild foods, returning at times to care for their crops and hunt game with atlatls.

The Late Basketmaker period started around 450 AD and is distinguished from the earlier phase by the introduction of pottery and the bow and arrow, as well as the creation of larger, more elaborate pit houses with internal storage facilities and antechambers found alone or in small clusters. Another significant addition was that of beans to the larder. While corn served as the primary food staple because of its ability to be stored, beans and squash added nutritional variety, composing a complete diet. Garden plots were maintained through dry farming techniques utilizing runoff, moistened floodplains of a river, or pot irrigation with water carried in jars to the crops. For over a thousand years this agricultural system supported a generally expanding population base.

By 750 AD the Anasazi had reached the next stage of development, that of Pueblo I. As the name suggests, there were some significant changes in their dwellings, though elements from earlier phases persisted. For instance, they now built their homes above ground in connected, rectangular blocks of rooms, using rocks and jacal (a framework of woven saplings and sticks packed with mud), and some stone and adobe masonry for construction materials. One or more deep pit houses have been found in each of the building clusters and may have served a ceremonial function. These communities were located along major drainages or on mesa uplands at elevations of 5,500 feet. Evidence of prolonged drought and a warming trend suggests that they moved to areas where the growing season and water were adequate. The Pueblo II period started during the 1000s AD and lasted for the next 150 years. A change in climate provided more dependable precipitation, higher water tables that affected springs and seeps, and temperatures conducive to agriculture. The people reacted by moving from a pattern of clustering population in strategic locations to a far-ranging decentralization. An apparent link that unified different areas is evidenced by a new phenomenon—clearly constructed roads with associated specialized building sites. The most dramatic examples of road activity are found in Chaco Canyon, New Mexico, but are also present in southeastern Utah. Several of these roads converge on "great houses" (multistory room blocks) and great kivas—large, semi-subterranean ceremonial chambers—whose roofs were supported by pillars and spanned by long-beam construction. Unlike the smaller kivas found with most habitation sites, great kivas had a specialized ritual function not totally understood by Native Americans and researchers today. These structures were located where significant concentrations of people lived and worshipped, with satellite communities on the periphery.

By the Pueblo III phase, the Chaco phenomenon had ended and Mesa Verde had become a bustling epicenter, spreading its construction and pottery characteristics over a large area of the northern Anasazi domain between 1150 and 1300 AD. The dramatic cliff dwellings of Mesa Verde offer a good picture of buildings and changing lifestyle during this era. The general pattern of events is characterized as a shrinking or gathering of dispersed communities into a series of larger villages in more defensible areas. Large communal plazas, tower clusters around springs or at the head of canyons, evidence of decreased regional trade relations, and the introduction of the kachina cult prevalent during the historic period among the Pueblo peoples are all indications that Anasazi society was undergoing significant change.

Archaeologists argue about what caused these cultural shifts and the subsequent abandonment of the San Juan drainage area. Some people attribute the changes to environmental factors such as prolonged drought, cooler temperatures, arroyo cutting, and depleted soils. Others in the past suggest that nomadic hunters and gatherers, precursors to the historic Ute, Paiute, and Navajo people, invaded the area, although no concrete proof exists to suggest large-scale warfare with outside invaders. No single explanation satisfactorily answers all of the questions, but by 1300 AD the Anasazi had left the San Juan drainage on a series of migrations that eventually took them to their historic, present homes along the Rio Grande (Eastern Pueblos) and to the areas where the Acoma, Zuni, and Hopi villages (Western Pueblos) now stand. There they continued to evolve through the Pueblo IV and Pueblo V periods of the Pecos Classification system.

Traditional Navajo teachings care for little of this. Rather than worrying about physical changes in lifestyle, they have a detailed understanding of what they believe happened to the Anasazi spiritually and why. Indeed, they were neighbors in the world beneath this one, shared food and information, emerged into this world around the same time, and had a generally peaceful relationship. Yet they were different people who eyed each other with suspicion that broke out in occasional hostility. Most of the teachings about this bygone era are found in the songs, stories, and ceremonies that the Navajos have.

This ruin, photographed near Oljato in 1910, today shows the wear and tear of heavy visitation. Small rooms for living, storage cysts, and a few kivas characterize this type of dwelling found at a distance from major Anasazi populations. (Courtesy Special Collections, J. Willard Marriott Library, University of Utah)

Fred Yazzie—A Navajo Perspective of the Anasazi

Fred Yazzie, a man born and raised in Monument Valley, in a series of interviews, shared his extensive understanding about these people and how the living are to interact with those who have gone before. He began:

> My grandfather on my father's side, three generations ago, told me about the Anasazi that once lived here. So did my grandfather on my mother's side, who used to live near Blue Mountain where Comb Ridge begins. When he talked about the Anasazi, he felt that they were a fallen people who fought among themselves. That is why their arrowheads are naayéé' (contain evil). The Anasazi were small and probably more round than tall. They were not made properly, and ate mostly corn and dried meat as well as sumac berries and other plants, so they became strong that way.
>
> They lived in places that were very hard to get to. Some say there were prehistoric reptiles like giant snakes and great lizards that they feared. Because of these creatures, the Anasazi moved up into the cliffs. Their diet was mainly corn, the remains of which are still found in their

sites. That is how they lived. The Anasazi were doo bił ndahonitł'ah da, meaning that they were a gifted people for whom nothing was difficult. Since they built their houses in cliffs, we know they mastered rock climbing without any problems. They carried stones on their backs to make their homes. Maybe their feet were sticky, while others say they used hał (a very shiny, smooth rock) to slide up and down the cliffs. The people say that they were great thinkers and so learned how to travel in the air. Everything turned into a big competition with them, which caused jealousy. As their population grew, they fought serious wars that broke out among them and that is why there are lots of arrowheads lying around.

But this was not the reason they disappeared. They refused to keep things sacred and continued to toy with holy things. For instance, the Anasazi copied the great wind and used it, just as Anglos design new things today such as big guns, poison gas, and other weapons that harm humans. I am relating the past to what is happening now. It was all in the thinking. They were so inventive that they worked themselves out of existence ('ak'eeda'iich'ąą'). Because they copied the Big Wind, it became offended and wiped them out by taking away the air they breathed. Some Anasazi are found in a sitting position, while others are sleeping, killed quickly by a lack of oxygen. After the great wind, it rained very hard and the water eroded the surface of the earth and made canyons and valleys. That's how my grandfather told about the Anasazi.

Another thing that angered the holy people was when the Anasazi reversed sacred symbols on their pottery and used them too much, causing them to become less holy. They did not believe they were being overly inventive and profaning the sacred and so were destroyed. Now Anglos are traveling to the moon and other planets regardless of obstacles in their way. Some are killed doing this while others return from their quest. Do these people understand the holy people or God? Whoever really believes in their prayers will return from their travels, but if they do not believe in anything, they will perish trying to get off or back onto the earth. Just as the people who made the atomic bomb over-invented that destructive weapon, the Anasazi were killed by their own creations, because the holy people did not like what they were doing.

I remember when I was a little boy, I herded sheep with my sister, who used to give me piggyback rides. We sometimes went to where there was a large ruin with perhaps as many as one hundred rooms running beside a long rock front. The buildings were like new with well-plastered walls and lots of objects left lying around. Even the writing on the rock wall appeared fresh. They had drawn pictures of themselves standing about—some of men, others of women, still others of goats. There were also many handprints and other designs. My older sister and I herded sheep near there and picked up beads, stones, and pottery. One is not supposed to do things like that or be in the ruins, but as a little boy, I did. I also put my hands on the large painted handprints, saying, "Look how big." This is also forbidden because the person who made the print will haunt you. Still, as you can see, I am very much alive. I might pick up a grinding stone and pretend to grind something on it, or arrowheads and think they were special because they were used in war. I would inhale on it four times to bless it and make it mine. This serves for protection as I thought, "This is a very special, sacred, holy thing that has come into my possession. It was once used by the Anasazi to ward off fearful things like animals and enemies, but now it is my shield." My father performed a ceremony for me and tied the arrowhead in my hair to serve as a holy protector or shield (doo bééshee hodéélnii da). The point remained there for four days. Also, a fire poker and corn pollen can serve as a shield against evil.

Anasazi pottery can be used as a drum in the Enemyway (Anaa'jí) ceremony. Some people consider Anasazi objects to have belonged to an enemy (anaa'bihii) who could also war against them if not respected. On the other hand, they had rattles that had the same symbols as our own. Big Star or the Morning Star (Venus—Sǫ'tsoh), the Big Dipper (Náhookǫs Biką'ii) on the handle, and Dilyéhé or Pleiades, a small cluster of stars that come up in the very early mornings, are found on it. Someone having a five-day ceremony can pick up the rattle and see the sacred designs on it. Black jet, turquoise, and abalone shell are also found inside the rattle and are used in our medicine bundles. Today, some Navajos and Hopis claim an ancestral relationship to the Anasazi.

There are two different views about entering Anasazi ruins. Some Navajos believe that they should treat it like a gravesite and not even walk into it. If one goes in, there may be a spirit that will attach itself and take hold, bringing your spirit to ghost land (ch'įįdiitah). This is true especially if you are afraid of these types of things. The ruins, like a cemetery, may seem haunted, but if you do not believe in these things, it may not bother you. This is real for those who do believe as it starts to attack them (shi'niiłhį); they say, "This spirit is killing me." Others will comment that this person is already dead, so his spirit will soon be gone. He has committed suicide for the Anasazi and will feel a gnawing in his thoughts. It is said that some people use the powers of these ruins as part of their witchcraft practices and leave their evil medicine there.

Once white men started living in Monument Valley, Anasazi sites started to be disturbed. When I was about nine years old, my sister and I herded sheep in the area of some of the ruins. There were round balls of mud—some were yellow, some black, others white. We picked these up and put them in water, then formed horses and other play objects, using pebbles to represent sheep placed in a corral. This was all set up in a canyon near the Anasazi ruins. I then noticed that Anglos had by this time moved into these sites and taken all of the property of the Anasazi and excavated the remains. My father also talked about this. One of the white men doing this was called Jaan Sání (John Wetherill) and another was Bilagáanaa Nééz (Tall White Man—Clyde Colville); both were looking for pottery throughout this area. Wetherill was young at the time, tall, and somewhat heavyset. He built a trading post in Oljato, where he remained for a number of years (1906–1910) before moving to Kayenta. It was said they had Navajo ceremonies like the Blessingway (Hózhǫ́ǫ́jí) performed for him and his wife (Louisa) for protection. All of them were interested in the Anasazi.[2]

Ada Black—A Woman's Perspective

Ada Black lived most of her life in Monument Valley, raising a family and participating in many historic events spread over eight decades. The topic of the Anasazi is often more in the domain of men, because of the ceremonial nature and teachings associated with this ancient Puebloan people. Ada, as a medicine woman and assistant in many healing ceremonies, understood the importance of explaining who these people were, so she shared her experience encountering their remains. Of particular interest here are her feelings about archaeologists in the old days.

As I grew older, my grandmother warned me about the future and compared it to what happened to the Anasazi, some of the first people who lived on this land. They clustered together and grew in knowledge, inventing things through spiritual means and understanding that controlled many of the powers in the universe. It is said that they learned ways to use the wind, lightning, and forces of nature. They carved in rocks and alcoves, painted on pottery, desecrated stone axes and arrowheads, and used designs that symbolized these powers. Every way that is known by the wind came out in their patterns. Since they understood the wind's powers, the Anasazi turned this into the ability to fly, just as Anglos use these principles today in airplanes. That is why their homes were in the cliffs. They harnessed the same powers of electricity as seen in their paintings of lightning and rainbows used for flying or protection. Their ruins are all over the land, and broken pottery lies on the ground, painted with the holy symbols of wind, lightning, and rainbows. The Anasazi became proud of their accomplishments, ignored the holy people, and turned the sacred into the profane by not praying and giving offerings. They were a blessed and gifted people caught up in their own greatness.

The holy beings watched, saw that this was not good, and met to discuss the problem. They were offended by what they witnessed and so decided to perform a wind ceremony that would destroy the Anasazi and leave a lesson not to be forgotten for future generations. The wind began to blow, sucking the oxygen out of the air, hurling fire and rocks about in Anasazi communities and destroying their means of livelihood. Now there are only handprints and worn pictures, carved footholds and ruins, arrowheads, and broken pottery to serve as reminders of what happened to them and why. The Navajos, unlike the Anasazi, have to keep their population under control and maintain a humble life through the Blessingway ceremony.

Navajos did not bother these places, knowing that Anasazi spirits and powers were still in those sites and rock art. It was the white-skinned people who excavated their remains, took their pottery and stone objects, and exposed them to the world. Before that they were treated with respect; they should be left alone as a deceased population. We hold a high regard for them and do not disturb things concerning the supernatural. The white man has exposed them, removing the rocks that hid them and the sand that covered their houses. There were rocks that closed their entrances that are now opened. The Anasazi used to live in those places. Their bodies are found in sleeping positions with pots beside them, just as they had died.

When I was living at Navajo Mountain, there was a group of white people [archaeologists] who were digging in some ruins. A water reservoir was close by where they were excavating, with a flat-surfaced rock and a white rock exposed in the ground next to a building and a stack of rocks. The stones had been used to make walls and a pile of white sand rested nearby, while groups of rooms composed the site. These had doorways that led to different spaces. The whites were gathered there, putting things in gunny sacks and boxes. It was a harmful feeling that came with what they were doing to the dead and their possessions. It was a sight. I was six or seven years old at the time, herding the sheep back to water

A Navajo person, unless a medicine man who knows how to control the powers found within, should not enter an Anasazi ruin. Many traditional Navajos looked on in horror and disbelief as Anglos not only entered these sites, but dug in them looking for artifacts. (Courtesy Special Collections, J. Willard Marriott Library, University of Utah)

at the reservoir. There were piles of gunny sacks, some not even covered, with bodies sticking out, their heads still attached. It was a harmful sight to see but I did. It is said their spirits will overtake and can kill a person unless they have an Enemyway ceremony to ward off and exorcise those evil forces. That night I had a nightmare concerning what I had seen that woke me up. I told my relatives about it and they warned that I should not be looking at the remains of the Anasazi. The darn goats kept going back to that site, forcing me to go through it to round them up and get them out of there. They required me to go among the remains of the Anasazi. The white men were there for a number of days, maybe even a month. They brought many boxes and sacks to put bones in, then stacked them.

Some Anasazi rock art can be used for witchcraft. People say that those who know the Enemyway can do bizarre things with witchcraft against others. This uses the power found in it to curse instead of heal people, my maternal grandmother would say. It is believed that a person who is envious of another, can call out an individual's name, draw their image, and curse it. This is why one does not bother rock art images or Anasazi dwellings; it is dangerous. Do not get involved in their places or with their objects or trace images because they are connected to and remind one of the bad things those people did. If one listens to what is told, they will be alright but some who are foolish ignore these warnings.[3]

Medicine Men Share Further Insight

Four elders, mostly medicine men involved with the Enemyway, add insight as to how the Anasazi are viewed. This ceremony is used to rid a person of the ghosts of a non-Navajo enemy while the Evilway (Hóchxǫ'íjí) rids a patient of spirits or evil influences brought on by a Navajo. The Enemyway destroys that spirit while the Evilway casts it away. The distinction here is important. Some Navajos claim through heritage that their clan originated from Anasazi roots, anthropologists suggesting perhaps as high as 40 percent.[4] Thus, which ceremony will be used to expel a ghost-like influence depends on how the individual being healed is connected to the Anasazi—as a relative or nonrelative. Billy Yellow, a medicine man who lived near the base of Eagle Rock in Monument Valley raises this issue while confirming much of what Fred Yazzie said. Billy starts at the time of creation and brings the reader to contemporary practices.

> In the beginning, water was everywhere. The holy people prayed and asked for it to depart as the earth was plowed and the water drained out to the ocean. The water subsided, exposing the sandstone that remained standing as the winds dried and carved the rock through different kinds of erosion. Later the Anasazi appeared, but because of their actions, they were killed when the air was taken away from them. They progressed only so far, making their homes and pottery out of mud, but when they became too creative, Big Wind extinguished them. Now they are found in a sitting position, covered up with sand by the wind and surrounded with broken pottery.
>
> What is left behind is taboo (baa hásti') and should not be bothered. It is frighteningly dangerous; Navajos fear anything that is gone from life. We even treat each other like this when one of us dies, just as we do with the Anasazi. People say that if one walks among the ruins, that person can become deaf or blind. This is what they say and this frightens them. The spirits there could harm you by attacking your legs so that you cannot walk. Finding an arrowhead is different; it may be picked up without hesitation. The horned toad makes small ones. He does this by facing a piece of rock, blowing on it, chipping away with its breath, walking around the point to form beautiful arrowheads. This has happened

since the beginning of time. A story tells of how the horned toad could not be struck by lightning sent by one of the monsters living on the earth. Lightning tried to hit him as he made these points, but to no avail. As hard as the lightning tried, it just could not harm the small reptile who continued making arrowheads. If one finds pottery, this also can be picked up and used. Today pot shards are ground into powder and added to clay that is mixed to create another piece of pottery.

Anasazi bones, however, are treated far differently. They are used in the Enemyway ceremony, when a person is haunted and feels like they are being killed by an Anasazi spirit. The individual has ba'alíí on them because they went to an Anasazi ruin and their act later caught up with them. A person who has had an Enemyway ceremony performed for him a couple of times is immune from being bothered and so can go to a ruin to obtain a bone for a pending ceremony. In the past, some people said that the Anasazi were once Navajos and that we should not have the Enemyway done against them, but should keep the ceremony at the level of a dead Navajo spirit [Evilway]. We are like this when we pass on; some people might dream of a dead person. If you are sleeping, you may suddenly feel swamped, have nightmares, end up kicking and moving about restlessly, or die from a heart attack. These are all signs that something is bothering you. A spirit or ghost is present and doing this to that person. This is caused not only by the Anasazi but even our own people who have passed on. If this happens, then the individual would have an Evilway and be blackened during the ceremony.[5]

Guy Cly, who lived near the entrance to the Navajo Tribal Park, was highly offended by the things that archaeologists did in unearthing the remains of the dead. Like Billy Yellow and Ada Black, he explains the results of behavior filtered through the lens of traditional teachings when he said:

When these Anglos were excavating some ruins, the dirt and sweat that caked on them was like gray ashes. They dug up bones and even though I was quite a distance away, I could smell them. They smelled like a hole in the ground where corn is stored. It is like that in the Enemyway, where the songs are about lightning and rain. Sometimes lightning strikes the earth, a home, horses, or sheep, and if that happens, it starts to bother you. This is also true with Big Wind, who leaves trails in the sand where a person should not sit or lie down or get in its path as it moves about. A Windway or Lightningway ceremony can help cure this. Just as with the Anasazi being disturbed, these supernatural powers start to bother a person. This type of illness can also be cured by ceremonies like the Yé'ii Bicheii (Nightway) dance and the fire dance of the Mountainway. These ceremonies remove what is bothering the patient, but if they are not performed, that person will continue to suffer. They are very powerful.[6]

John Holiday mentioned that during the Enemyway only one person is chosen, at a certain point in the ceremony when the singing stops and all is quiet, to shoot the bone being used to represent killing the enemy spirit. As with burying a Navajo person in the old days, that person responsible for the actual interment was dressed only in a loincloth. Ashes are placed on the weapon used to kill the spirit. Firing the gun concludes the ceremony and the ghost is vanquished. That is the end. This ceremony is the opposite of the Anglos who dig for skeletal remains, some of whom have died because of what they do—probably caused by inhaling the essence from the bones of the dead, which sticks to the offender.

As a medicine man, John used elements from Anasazi culture, such as an arrowhead, for protection. He explained, "The arrowhead is a shield. I say, 'From behind this arrowhead (béésh yist'ogí) the bad ailments will go ("Bééshdiłhił t'áá díígóó shináhiníláa doo"). In the four directions black arrowheads will protect me.' These prayers refer to the arrowhead, casting back the bad ailments to where they had originated. When I use it as a medicine man, I am only looking for the good things in life. I also use a hał, a sharp, very smooth rock in my prayers for protection."[7]

Don Mose—Tying it All Together

To many Navajos, the Anasazi were a gifted people who abused their talents and spirituality to the point that the offended holy people destroyed them. This is the message. It is reinforced by every ruin, petroglyph and pictograph, piece of pottery, and burial site encountered. Don Mose, a Navajo curriculum specialist, hand trembler, and traditionalist, provides a final summary of who these people were and why they are so important. Much of his information comes from his grandfather, who not only taught about these ancient people that "disappeared," but also about what lies in the future for the Navajo. This sobering look ties past to present to future in a spiritual universe that unites the entire world—a world that Don concludes still holds great power for the here and now. He begins:

The Anasazi controlled a great amount of spiritual power, to the point where they could transport themselves through the air by what Navajos call álílee k'ehgo, meaning the "supernatural or spiritual power by which things are done." This channel of power allowed them to accomplish things that would otherwise seem impossible. When people wonder how they climbed or flew into places that today are inaccessible, it was through álílee k'ehgo that it was performed. Their ability, however, eventually diminished so they could no longer control the rain or other aspects of the universe as they once had. Even Mother Earth turned against them so that there were no longer plants and food for them to rely on. They began to draw on rock walls, leaving their last messages, outlining their problems, and divulging many of their sacred symbols. Everything became profane as these pictures were used more as a form of art than an appeal to power. The Anasazi realized their hopeless situation but persisted as they destroyed the sacredness of life (ak'eehiidlá).

Their actions were comparable to a Navajo taking a sandpainting used to heal the sick and creating an imitation to sell or display. That is what we are doing today. This is what happened to the Anasazi—all they were interested in was competing with their neighbor. Powerful symbols were abused and misused, transforming the unique and sacred into something ordinary, while at the same time, these people demanded more and more ease and power. The holy people stepped in and stopped it. When one finds an Anasazi bowl, for instance, there is often a design on it. Perhaps it is lightning or raindrops used to call out the thunder god or one of the female holy people who control rain in the black clouds. These same symbols are also found in Navajo sandpaintings. To my grandfather, a number of these designs were actually learned from the Anasazi, who received them from the holy people. Some medicine men include the Anasazi as part of a generation that called upon the holy people and were the first to be taught some of the things we use in today's ceremonies to heal people. Understanding all of this must be interpreted through spirituality. The things that the Anasazi left behind tell us that there is power that can be called upon to bring the rain, help people, and tie the physical world to that of the spiritual universe in a good way.

However, the Anasazi refused to take this good path. Witchcraft was an aspect of spirituality they used because it is a fast way to defeat an opponent. Álílee k'ehgo, in addition to being a positive force, can also be used to destroy people who are good, even though this power was a gift from the gods. The Anasazi were able to visualize through spiritual means what they were to build or create, where and how to find water, where to move for resources, how and where to plant crops, and what the stars knew about the future. They were taught that if they were respectful, Father Sky and Mother Earth would provide for them. But it was all based in keeping the holy sacred. If they ignored the principle of being thankful and reverent, hardship would follow. This is exactly what happened to the Anasazi, who became prideful and corrupted because of their accomplishments. Instead of helping their own people, they fought amongst themselves, stole property, and abused their power.

As in today's society, the Anasazi turned against what they knew was right. They lost respect for the sacred, had improper marriages, became promiscuous, practiced bisexual behavior, and embraced jealousy, angering the holy people. As they became more powerful, they stole children, committed fornication with their own offspring, and practiced evil (bóhodoshzhéé') through witchcraft. An example of their corruption, it is said, is when they would have a man and woman perform sex in a ceremony to obtain their bodily fluids, then mixed them with other substances to form an evil substance used to curse others. This is directly opposite of how corn pollen is used to bless a person for good. The same act is said to be performed by those who practice Navajo witchcraft today. This is what my grandfather said. He warned that when there are too many pinto horses, we will recognize this as a sign that there is too much integration. There will be no more purebreds, whether we are talking about people or animals. When dogs begin to speak, the end is near and we have gone beyond what we are supposed to do. Just as the Anasazi overdid everything, we too are killing ourselves with evil.

One day, I went with a group of friends to explore some rock art sites at the place of Navajo emergence (Hajíínéí) near Farmington, New Mexico. There are both Navajo and Anasazi petroglyphs there to study and learn about one's heritage. Navajo sites are often marked with red ochre. But I remember my grandfather telling me about some of the petroglyphs, saying, "The Anasazi are not the only people who created drawings on the rocks. We also had our symbols," many of which were connected to Father Sky and Mother Earth. We think of these as having spiritual messages, just like writing on paper. Once the group reached the site, they smoked mountain tobacco to spiritually prepare for what they wanted to do. One of the leaders said, "I think this is the place to go ahead and light up our mountain tobacco and have a smoke." I was quiet and just observed. A medicine man named Robert Johnson wanted to show me a particular petroglyph, so he said, "Let's hurry up and go before the group gets there so that we can see it without being disturbed. The sun is in the right position now so that we can actually see the symbol." We made our way to the petroglyph but it was hard to understand. As the sun traveled across the sky, there were times when I could see the image, but later it appeared to have been removed from the rock. Robert said, "Later on, you'll notice that after we have been walking around and return, you will not see it anymore." He was right. I could not see any trace of it.

To Robert, this was an indicator that this was a place to perform ceremonies, because the symbol was physically visible but then faded from view, just as spiritual things may have both a visible and invisible manifestation. He indicated, "This is the place where they should have lit their mountain tobacco for self-purification and this is where we will sing a song. We will visit other spiritual places where groups of people once lived and introduce ourselves to them. Although we can't see them, we can reach out to them as human beings to feel a spiritual uplift as we go through these little canyons." As a medicine man, he was allowed to see and sense these kinds of things, to open the doorway to the place we needed to visit. His understanding of sandpaintings helped him to know these things.

As we toured through that area, I noticed a Navajo lady addressing some rock art handprints. I stood back and watched her make her way down to some prints, then place her right hand next to, but not on, them. She stood there for a few minutes, then suddenly her left hand raised up to her shoulder as though she was touching herself while assessing what was taking place. She brought down her hand, then began motioning again, as though blessing herself, much like it is done in a ceremony, but with fetishes or objects like arrowheads and certain stones found in the ruins. Now I understood what she was doing with her hands, but did not say a word until she climbed back onto the trail. I said, "That's the first time I've seen anybody do that," to which she replied, "You need to go do it." So I did. Climbing down to the petroglyph, I repeated her actions. Since I was a hand trembler at one time, I recognized the same tingling sensations running through my arm, then brought it down and began to massage myself. I felt in my leg the same type of sensation one feels when one's feet fall asleep. An intensified feeling of the heat from the sun penetrated my back while a small breeze remained swirling around me. I thought of my grandfather, who pointed to the common coil symbol composed of concentric spirals, saying that they represented the wind moving and talking. Gentle in its movement, the wind encircled me. In a matter of seconds it was over and I climbed back up to the trail.

The woman was waiting there. "Did you feel anything different?" I said that I had but that I found it difficult to explain. She then told me

Rock art, artifacts, and sites are still inhabited and controlled by Anasazi power from the person who created them. By picking an object up or touching the rock art, that individual is inviting the deceased to interact with him or her, often in a harmful way. (Illustration by Charles Yanito)

that she does it every time she goes to a ruin; in fact, that was why she went to them, to get an energetic feeling that let her know she was alive. "I want to be educated. I have problems at home and a lot of stress, but when I go to places like this, it regenerates me." I agreed, saying, "I felt that same energy, the sun on my back, and the wind trying to teach me something, as I stood on holy ground." My grandfather had said that those signs, if respected spiritually, are allowed to speak to a person.

Remember that I did not put my hand on the symbol but next to it. If I had put it on top of it, that would have been offensive to the spirit of the person who made it, but next to it is like an invitation. It is the same concept used when picking medicine plants. When I was learning how to obtain herbs to heal, my uncle said, "This is what you need to do" after saying a prayer. At the time, I had a kidney infection and he wanted to make medicine for me, so he instructed, "Go to the plant and make an offering. Speak to it just like a human being." When we got there, he said, "Naaniidzá, we have come to visit you, plant of the earth. Nanisé, that grows on the earth. We have come for your help. Ne'azee', we have come to have you provide us with your medicine. This person wants to be healed. I am talking to you, so come here and heal. There are pains in the back, the kidneys are not functioning very well, and he wants to be made whole again. Can you help?" That was it. Then, instead of cutting a piece from the plant he addressed, the one I was readying to cut, he said, "No, no, no. Don't go to that one. Go to the next closest one to it. You take the one from there because you have prayed to another one that holds the request and has the power." The same is true of the rock art image. If a hand is placed over it, then it becomes blocked, disconnected from you. It has to be respected. Placing my hand on it would mean that I think I have more power than it does and so I place it to the side.

My grandfather and uncle taught me this way, but until I had a real desire to experience it for myself, it was all just words. Once something like this happens, it becomes a part of you, and you understand. One's respect becomes real. The medicine man that I went with honored the land, petroglyphs, and the people who had gone before. This is why the elders teach not to go racing through Anasazi sites, no spitting, eating, and urinating in their areas, but rather just enter to observe and be polite. Even when I was a child living in Piñon, I knew that I should not yell and disrespect these sites. We used to have to herd sheep through a certain area called Nay' guun [?], which means where people at one time lived. There were ruins there and perhaps someone had killed a deer and feasted or held a ceremony, thus making it sacred ground. There was not a lot of explanation given by the adults, but we knew as children we needed to be respectful. As we herded sheep, there was no talking, spitting, or rough play—we did nothing until we were past there. That was how we honored that sacred ground, treating it as a burial place.

This same kind of behavior should be shown to elders as they teach about the Anasazi. You should never make fun of the old ones. When they say that they are talking about the Anasazi, respect them. Even though they are gone, they left behind symbols that we can use in ceremonies to heal. They also left great knowledge and learned how to develop great spiritual power. When used properly, one can perform similar miracles.

They have also provided an example of what happens when people go astray, show no respect, profane the sacred, and ignore traditional teachings. They took the most sacred things they had and began displaying them. Grandfather said that the symbol for this was a snake who was a destroyer. The main lesson is that the Navajo should not follow the same path as the Anasazi. If we choose not to see life, disrespect Mother Earth and Father Sky, do not pray to plants or ask permission to use its root to heal somebody, and say that spiritual things are nonsense, then we will become like them. When that generation has no more faith, does not understand these principles, and knows nothing except how to kill and do evil, then there will be destruction. Losing contact with spirituality will destroy them. That is what happened to the Anasazi and what may happen to us.[8]

CHAPTER THREE

Violence in the Valley

The Long Walk Era and Aftermath

E very culture around the world has hallmark events etched into their historical conscience that define who they are and how they have encountered a changing world. The Navajo are no exception, having two—the Long Walk era of the late 1850s and 1860s and livestock reduction of the late 1920s and 1930s—events that redirected their historical trajectory. The first is the topic of this chapter. Prior to the 1860s, the general Navajo population lived south of the San Juan River in New Mexico and Arizona. Small family groups did live to the north, but generally, this was the domain of the Utes in Colorado and southeastern Utah and the Paiutes farther to the west in southwestern Utah and Nevada. The former was a force to be reckoned with as Navajos first bumped against, then entered into their territory. The San Juan River provided a permanent source of water for agriculture while the mountains to the north held bountiful game and plants for hunting and gathering. Many of those Navajos who lived in Ute territory had intermarried or carried on extensive trade relations that led to cooperation and a fragile truce in hostilities. But for the most part, constant across-river raids and ambushes, strengthened by shifting alliances with first the Spanish and later the Mexican military, added fuel to the fire. With a few noteworthy exceptions, the Utes formed alliances with these Euro-American forces against their traditional Navajo enemies. When the United States assumed control of territory in the Southwest after the Mexican War (1846–48), it continued the conflict with the Navajo. A series of treaties in the 1850s were short-lived, adding more reason for distrust. With events in the East leading up to the Civil War, the federal government withdrew much of its full-time peacekeeping force, assigned newly raised civilian armies to maintain control of the Indians, and encouraged Native American allies to join forces to quell any uprisings. Conflict proved inevitable.

By the mid-to-late 1850s, the Utes had become the tip of the spear-point aimed at the northern part of Navajo lands. Knowledgeable about where their enemy lived, how they obtained food, and how best to defeat them, the Utes became highly effective in locating small homesteads; killing the men; capturing the women and children to sell in the slave markets of Taos, Abiquiu, and Santa Fe; spiriting away all of the livestock to their homeland; and receiving pay and weapons from the U.S. military. Soon every Navajo family had their own tales of woe, abandoning large portions of their traditional lands, fleeing to inaccessible terrain on the periphery, maintaining constant vigilance, and swearing vengeance if the opportunity arose. Some families joined larger groups for protection while others were captured, killed, or sent to Fort Sumner, aka Bosque Redondo, on the Pecos River in southeastern New Mexico. Eight thousand Navajos who were either captured or surrendered made the "Long Walk" over a series of trails to live there in impoverished conditions between 1864 and 1868. A lot has been written about this totally traumatic era.[1] However, perhaps as much as half of the tribe never made the "Long Walk," but chose to live in the hinterlands to avoid detection and eke out an existence.

In this chapter, a variety of experiences of residents of Monument Valley are shared. Wolfkiller tells what it was like as a young boy, his family's fear, eventual surrender, and their experience at Fort Sumner. Not so for Hashkéneiniihii, who fled the advancing troops and hid at Navajo Mountain. When the captive Navajos returned to their newly defined reservation and Monument Valley in 1868, in particular, he was there to greet them as a wealthy person and prominent medicine man. There were also those who stayed in the canyon system near Oljato and remained there the entire time. Susie and Fred Yazzie share part of their family stories, telling of their challenges to survive. For all who were involved, who teetered between triumph and despair, this was one of those formative times that is still discussed to this day.

Wolfkiller and the Road to Fort Sumner

Sometime after 1910 and over the course of several years, Louisa Wade Wetherill recorded the experiences of a Navajo man named Wolfkiller who came from Oljato and worked for her and her husband, John, at their trading post in Kayenta, Arizona. John's great-grandson, Harvey Leake, gave permission to use what Louisa recorded, offering one of the best accounts of what the Fearing Time was like. During that era, roughly 1857–68, this Navajo elder endured the beginning of hostilities that resulted in his family spending four years at Fort Sumner. His detailed narrative captures the surprise and fear experienced by so many. Wolfkiller began:

> The winter passed quickly, and it was soon time to plant corn again. The men started getting the fields ready. Late one afternoon as my brother and I sat watching the sheep, we looked up and noticed a thin line of smoke rising toward the heavens. It came from the top of a high rock far away. The air was very clear, and we could see it plainly. After a very short time, it disappeared. As we were discussing what it might mean, we saw it come and go again. Then we saw it a third time, and then a fourth. We watched for a long time, but did not see it again. We talked a great deal about it. "We will ask Grandfather about it tonight," I said.
>
> That night when everyone was sitting around the fire, we told the older people what we had seen. They were startled, and then I saw sadness come into their faces. For a while no one spoke. They were very quiet, and I began to be frightened. Then Grandfather spoke. "My grandson, it was a signal fire—the warning of trouble. I fear the evil spirit of war is coming. There has been some unrest ever since the raiding party I told you about some time ago went out and brought back the sheep and girls, but we had hoped the war would not come. We must still try not to add to our thoughts the thoughts of the ones who are causing us trouble. We must pray and work as before. Pray that the evil will miss us. We have done nothing to cause it, so we must let the ones who want war go their own way. We will stay at our own hogan and plant our corn and not worry about what is going on about us."
>
> Some of the old people said, "If we go about our own business, it will not bother us. But even among us there may be some who secretly hope that they will see war. We hope not, and we must pray that their thoughts will change if they do have these evil thoughts."
>
> At this, our visitors silently left the hogan and went to their own homes. When they were gone, Grandfather said, "My grandson, tomorrow I want you to watch the point on which you saw the smoke today. I want to know what the next signal will be."
>
> "We will watch it and tell us what we see," I promised. "But will you tell us how they can make the smoke go up in such a thin column, and then stop, and then come again? And why was the smoke so white?"
>
> "It is done, my grandson, by building a small fire and putting damp bark on it. Have you never noticed how white the smoke is from a damp

fire and how it goes straight up? Then, when the smoke goes way up, they hold their robes over it for a while. Then they put more bark on and take the robe away. This they do four times. If it is dark when they want to send the signals, they do it with a blaze."

Before breakfast the next morning, Grandfather and some of the other old men met in our hogan and talked about the smoke. It was not as clear that day, and the people were worried that they would not be able to see the signal. They decided that someone must do nothing but watch for it all day, so they appointed one of the older boys to go to a high point to do this. They asked my brother and me to watch as well. All through the forenoon we saw nothing, but as the sun dipped toward the west, the sky cleared in the east and we saw the signal. This time it was two slender columns of smoke side by side. They came and went four times as they had the day before. When we reached the hogan that evening, the people knew about the signals, as the sentinel also had seen them. They were all talking about what to do when we came in. We asked Grandfather what the two signals meant. He said that it meant that they were calling a council. That night the people decided to send some of the old men to attend the council the next day. That morning we were all up early. The women fixed lunches of dried meat and corn bread for the men to take with them. They must not let themselves talk or think too much about trouble.

For two days, we all went about our business and tried not to think about the fact that what we feared was coming to us soon. After we returned to the hogan on the second night, the old men came in. They were very quiet. The rest of the people were quiet, too. We all waited for what they would tell us about the council. We were very anxious for supper to be over so we could sit down and hear what they had to say. As soon as everything was finished, the people began coming into our hogan. When we were seated around the fire, Grandfather spoke.

My children, it is as we feared. The spirit of war is trying to walk into our land, but we must try to stop it. We do not want war, as I said before. We have done nothing to cause this thing, but some of the people have made an-other raid, and our chief, at what they call Washington, has sent us word that we must leave our land and go with the soldiers to a place far to the east. They say they will take care of us. Now I think the people who have brought this on themselves should be taken, but we who do not want to have trouble should not be taken away from a land we know and are contented to live in.

We will go on with our planting and try to raise as much corn as we can. Then we can go back into the canyons west of us and live there as we have lived for many years. We will still fight for peace and try to stay in the path of light. Some of the people who called us to the council feel as we do about this thing. They do not want war, so we have decided to plant our corn, and then leave our fields and scatter our camps in the rock-walled canyons. We will have to appoint some men as scouts and keep sentinels out to watch for signals—not for the same purpose as we sent out our scouts and kept our sentinels on the hills in years gone by, but for our protection. In times gone by, when we were at war, we kept the sentinels and scouts out to let us know when it was the best time for us to make an attack—to tell us where our enemy was and when they were off their guard. Now we will send our scouts and sentinels out to keep us posted so that we can move when the soldiers come near to us. We will hide so they cannot find us. We will continue to pray for peace as we have been praying ever since the rumor of war first started.

Now, my children, I have told you what the council was. A number of men who were there feel as we do, but some of the other ones want war. Our war chief thinks we should fight. He thinks that we are strong enough to fight as many soldiers as the enemy could send against us if we fight here in our own land. But we old men know that we are not as strong as they are—not because we have not the strength in our bodies, but because we haven't the guns and ammunition of the white men. Many of us have only bows and spears with which to fight. The war chief has told the people that, though the white men have many guns and cannons with which to fight us and have many soldiers, our people know the country. By sneaking up on these people we can steal their food and horses and leave them in want so they will be too weak to fight. Another advantage we have over them, is that we know where the water is and they do not. He says we must cause as much trouble now as we can so they will come against us in the summertime, because in summer there is not much water except in the springs and tanks in the rocks. Now, my children, we who do not want war must hurry and get our corn planted. The Seed Basket is now in the heavens, so it is time to plant. We must work until late at night and grow as much corn as possible. We do not know how long the war will last, and we must have food laid by for a siege.

For many days, the people worked until it was too dark for them to see. They planted large fields that year. One evening the people were talking about the news of the day when one of the men spoke.

At the place we call Bear Water, a council has been held. The men who told us about it say that a man who is the chief of the soldiers from Bear Water has been talking to our people. He told them that if we will come in and go peaceably to the place they want us to go, we will not have to fight, but if we do not

Wolfkiller, a friend and confidant of Louisa Wetherill, shared with her one of the most complete accounts of the Long Walk period in Monument Valley. He died in 1926, leaving a legacy of Navajo thought and history that stretches back into the mid–1800s and earlier. (Courtesy Harvey Leake, Wetherill Family Archives)

go peaceably, they will send many soldiers and many big guns against us. Some of the people say they think it would be good to go, but others think as we do.

Since we have not done anything to cause the evil spirit to walk in our land, we cannot see why we should be punished. Of course, our past record is against us, as in years past, our entire tribe approved of going out and raiding people's villages. The raids that have been made in the past few years have not been with the consent of most of us because we wanted peace. We still want it, but it remains to be seen whether we can have it. If in the end we have to go, we must do it with peace still in our hearts. We have planned to harvest as much corn as we can and keep away from the ones who want war. Our war chief is all for war, and he has many of the young men with him. These young men have never seen the sorrows of war, so they do not know what it is.

Then Grandfather spoke: My brothers, you feel as we do. I am glad there are others among us who are still fighting the evil thought. We are planning to move into the canyons west of us as soon as we finish planting our fields, which will be soon now. We hope the enemy will not find us. We hope our young men will not get the evil thought in their hearts and join the war chief. If they do, it will mean that we will have to help them if they need us. But we must not think of such things. We must still hope and pray that this evil will miss us. We must not talk too much about our fears, for if we do, we will put the evil thought into the minds of some of our people who do not think much about it now. We must all work together and try to stay in the path of light. We will let our war chief and his band of men go to the place they want to go without us, as it is now too late to do anything for them. I do not feel anger in my heart against our chief who is at the place they call Washington. Some of our people have brought the trouble on themselves and all the rest of us, as we who do not want to fight will have our troubles keeping out of the way of the ones who are for war, and out of the way of the soldiers. But we will try to keep out of their way as long as we can. The stars are dipping toward the west. It would be good for all of us to rest now, as we will have our work to do tomorrow.

We all went to bed, but I could not sleep for a long time. I was thinking about all of the things the old men had said. I again thought of what Grandfather had said about the raids in the past being needed to save the life of the tribe, and now this other old man had said the same thing. I wanted to know what they meant by this and hoped that I could get my grandfather or mother to tell me the story sometime.

After our corn crop was established, we moved to a place where we would be among the rocks. Soon after we moved there, we saw some signal fires one night, calling a council. The next day Father and Grandfather went to it. When they came back after three days, they told us it was as they had feared. The soldiers were going about in our land and had had some fights with some of our people. A number of the war chiefs had been killed or wounded, but the rest had gotten away into the mountains.

"Now we must keep our sentinels and scouts out," Grandfather said. "We will try to stay away from this trouble."

For many days we hid in the canyons where we could find feed for our sheep and horses while the men went to the cornfields from time to time. The rain came and made the corn grow very fast. The women wove blankets and gathered grass and weed seeds to store for the winter, as this year the men would not be able to go out to hunt as they had each year before. They would not want to leave the women and children alone long enough to hunt. From time to time, the scouts came in with the news of more and more trouble.

The summer went by, and it was again time for the harvest. Everyone worked very hard to get the harvest over as soon as possible. The corn was taken to the box canyons some distance to the west of us. We had also grown some pumpkins, and the women dried and stored them in buckskin bags. We were all as happy as we could be at a time like this, since we had food enough to last us a long time. Soon the winter came again. We lived in the canyons and moved from one place to another. I now saw what war could be. We could not have our nice, warm hogan because we were moving so much. Then the heavy snow came and we were not as afraid. Grandfather said we could build a hogan now, but it had to be among the rocks so that it could not be easily discovered. The rocks would serve as a chimney to carry the smoke up to the top of the mesas so anyone in the canyon would not be able to smell it.

From time to time, the scouts went out. Each time they came back they told us that there was no news. The winter went by, and when spring came, the people planted again. We had much food left, but we knew we must keep up the supply. . . .

When the summer rains came again and the corn was growing well, the scouts began to bring in news of the many soldiers who were coming against us and the efforts of our people to fight them. We still hoped that we would be spared this trouble. One day a scout ran into camp and fell down exhausted. We waited as he caught his breath and was able to speak.

"We are lost," He said. "The enemy has brought Utes to help them track us down, and they are coming nearer. They are cutting down the cornfields and killing the old people who cannot travel. They have taken many of the people out."

After hearing this, Grandfather and the rest of the old people sat with their heads bowed for a long time. They were very quiet and sad. Then Grandfather spoke. "We will try for a while longer to keep out of this trouble, but if the time comes when we think there is no other way out, we will surrender and go quietly with those people. They will be decent to us if we do not fight. After all, we have brought this on ourselves."

For a few days we did not get much rest. As we moved farther and farther back into the canyons, the soldiers and Utes came nearer and nearer. The sentinels came in and told us that they had seen the dust of many people moving and could see their campfires. As we moved, the men sent the women, children, and sheep over the rocky ridges. Then they came along behind them, walking backward and brushing out their tracks with boughs of trees at places where we crossed sand. They hoped that by doing this we could avoid being discovered. Each night the men climbed to the top of the mesa to watch for signals. One evening I went with them. The stars were dipping far toward the west before we saw any signals. When they came, there were four fires in a row, and they came four times. Then we all started for the hogan. Everyone went quietly. No one spoke. When we reached the camp, it was nearly dawn. Grandfather awakened the women and children and told them that it was no use to hide any longer, as the four fires meant that we were surrounded. The men sat down and talked while the women cooked breakfast. They decided that three of the old men would go up that night to the camp of the soldiers and tell them we were ready to go with them. They said that the camp was not far from us.

"We will start as soon as the night comes," said Grandfather.

"Why do you go at night?" I asked.

He explained that they were afraid of the Utes who were with the soldiers. The Utes would welcome the chance to kill as many of our people as they could if we came while it was light. The sheep were corralled in the rocks all day, and some of the men slept while the others kept watch. It seemed a long time before the night came. Everyone was quiet, and no fires were built. We ate bread and dried meat that had been stored for a time like this. As soon as the night came, the three old men stole silently out of the camp and were gone. We did not sleep much since we were all nervously waiting for them to return. They did not come until the afternoon of the next day, causing us to fear that the

Utes had killed them. Once they came in, some soldiers were with them. This was the first time that I had ever seen a white man. They looked very strange to me, but I was not as afraid of them as I thought I would. They did not seem so bad. They had no Utes with them.

We were told to get ready to go with these people and to take everything we wanted. We were all busy for the rest of the day. The men got the horses and put them in the rocks for the night. The next morning, we saddled the horses and packed them with food and robes. We could not take the corn we had in the pits, but the white men told us we would not need it because they would give us plenty of food. One white man who was with these people could speak our language pretty well, but we could not understand anything the others said. The man who could speak to us told us that we would have no trouble from now on. We went with them without fear in our hearts, but we all felt sad that we would be leaving the land we knew and loved for a strange place.

For the first few days everything seemed strange. The soldiers sounded like a flock of birds in a tree when they talked, and their clothing was odd. They did not wear robes like our people. I was interested in their blue coats and pants and the strange things they wore on their heads. They did not wear headbands. I thought, as we rode to their camp, that this would be a strange life, but I was not going to complain. We were not suffering, and I knew that it must be for the best, or it would not have come to us. When we reached their camp, I saw a wagon and a big gun. I asked Grandfather about these things and he told me what they were. I said I would like to see the soldiers shoot the big gun. He replied that he did not want to hear me say anything like that again, and hoped I would never see them shoot it.

We stayed in the soldiers' camp that night. Grandfather told us how the three old men had slipped into the camp two nights before: "When we came near the camp, we saw some Utes and one white man with the horses and mules. We crawled up as close as we dared to, but we were afraid to get very near them. We looked at the stars. I was wishing the people who were herding would soon get tired. We could hear the Utes talking to each other once in a while, but most of the time they sat quietly on their horses and watched. I started up over some rocks, and a small stone broke loose and rattled down to the bottom. I saw the Utes raise their heads and listen. I lay very quietly, but one of the Utes started toward me, so I crawled farther away and hid behind the rocks. The other men who were with me had slipped around on the other side of the horses to see where we could get into the camp most easily, so I was alone.

I was afraid the Ute would find me. He came very near, but I was in the shadow of the rock so he did not see me. He hunted around for such a long time that I was afraid the other men would come to where I was. It was very dark among the rocks, and I thought, if they come to hunt me and did not know the Ute was there, they would surely be killed. So I began to pray that they would not come. After a time, the Ute started back toward the horses and I could breathe again. Soon after this, the other men joined me. They said they had been near some of the horses who did not pay any attention to them. By this time, the stars were dipping toward the west. We crawled away some distance so we could talk to each other.

We decided that if the Utes did not sleep, we would go back to our camp. We waited until the stars were dipping far to the west, and then we crawled back near the horses again. We saw that the Utes were resting. We waited just a little longer and then slipped in among the horses. We were afraid they would make a noise, but after a while they did not pay any attention to us and kept grazing as if we were not there. Once we got close to the camp, we saw a guard standing near us with a gun, which frightened us and so we lay quietly for a long time until he walked away; then we went on. We were almost up to the tents when I passed one of the Utes who was sound asleep. I did not see him until I was very close as I went by. I was so near that I touched his braid as I passed. He did not stir, so I knew he did not hear me. It was getting darker now, and I knew it would not be long before the dawn would come. We were almost to the tents, and I was glad and hoped the soldiers would soon be awake. We crawled up to one of the tents and lay down. We were very tired and were glad to be safely in the camp.

I was relieved when I saw the first white streak of dawn. A little while after that, the bugle sounded and the soldiers began to stir in the tents. Soon a soldier came out near us. We went up to him and tried to tell him what we wanted, but he could not understand. By this time, many of the soldiers were about, and they called the man who spoke Navajo and had been at our hogans the day before. He asked us what we wanted, so we told him that we were tired of hiding and wished to go with the soldiers to the place they wanted to take us. Soon the chief of the soldiers came out, and the interpreter told him what we were there for. He thanked us for not causing him anymore trouble. He was very good to us and soon the soldiers gave us food. We told the interpreter to tell the chief that we never wanted to fight and only wanted to lead our lives as we had in the past. I said that we knew our record was against us and that some of our people had brought the trouble on themselves and deserved the punishment they were getting, but we who did not want trouble felt that we did not deserve to be punished for the sins of someone else. Now we had decided there was nothing for us to do but surrender. I explained that we would have come in to the soldiers' camp before, but we were afraid of the Utes. They had always been our enemies, and we knew that they would welcome the chance to kill as many of us as they could. I asked him to send some of the soldiers with us to our camp and not take any Utes to which he agreed. He said he knew he could trust us, not to be afraid, and that we would be treated well."

The next morning, we started on our long journey with about fifty of our people. Some of the soldiers went with us, but others started in another direction. I asked Mother where they were going. She said they were going to hunt down more of our people. The soldiers who were with us took one of the wagons and one of the big guns. I was very interested in watching these things being drawn by horses and mules and to see the wheels go around and around all day long for several days until we reached a place where we stayed for a while. There, for the first time, I saw a white man's house. It was different from our hogans or the stone houses under the rocks that the ancestors of the Hopis (Oozéí) had built. Grandfather said there would be little for me to do for some time and to look around to see what was of interest.

Time passed and every day more and more of our people were brought in carrying heavy packs; some were driven like sheep and could not use their horses. These were the ones who had wanted to fight. Others had come in peaceably as we had done. The soldiers said that some Navajos were still fighting and that our war chief would not give up. Grandfather told the ones who complained that it was their own fault. He said they had not tried to control their young men, so the whole tribe must suffer.

As days went by, the war chief and his band continued fighting. Our people who wanted peace hoped every day that the next party to be brought in would be the warriors. We were all very glad when they were at last captured and wanted to see how the war chief would act now that he was in camp. The soldiers tried to treat these people well, but they were sullen and would not eat, keeping the spirit of war in their hearts. The old men talked to them, but they would not listen.

We finally resumed our long walk, and, after many miles, the day came at last when we reached the place where we were to stay. The winter came very soon and we had nothing to do but visit among ourselves.

Grandfather talked to us more than he had been able to when he had his work to do. For some time, everything went well, then some of the people died. The old ones said they could not stand the meat the white people gave them. It was bacon. They did not know how to make bread with flour. Many of the people died during the winter, most of whom would not try to learn how to cook the food they had to eat. We who tried were well most of the time.

When spring came, some of the old people asked the soldiers to let them have some land to put in cornfields. We received land a few miles from the fort, so moved our camps there. Soon most of the people were busy putting in corn and were content. There were still among us those trying to cause trouble, but they were too few to make much headway. Of course, we were not as happy as we would have been if we had been in our own land, free to do as we pleased, but there were many flowers as summer arrived and Grandfather began to teach me about them. He showed me many plants that grew in our own country. I was very interested in them.

We did not have many ceremonies, as the white doctor took care of us when we were not well. Grandfather said that we would be allowed to go back to our country when all the people got the thought of war out of their hearts and tried to do as they should. Our war chief spent most of his time making arrows. Some of the old men told him that if he would get evil thoughts out of his heart, he would not need so many arrows. "You have heard what the white chief in Washington has said," one man told him. "If we promise not to make any more raids on the people of the towns and the Indians of the villages, we will be allowed to return to our own land, and they will protect us against our enemies—the Apaches and Utes."

"We have heard all of this, but I do not believe it," the war chief replied. "They have made promises to us before, but they have not kept them. I am going to continue to make arrows."

One day my brother and I went down to the creek that was near our camp. We were searching for plants that I wanted to learn about. While we were looking around among the willows, we heard a terrible noise in the camp. We thought our people were fighting, but when we reached a place from which we could see, we saw that our old enemies, the Comanches, were making a raid on the people. We were frightened so lay down in the grass and watched the fight.

Soon we heard the bugle at the fort and saw many soldiers coming to help us. When the Comanches saw the soldiers arrive, they started to run with both the soldiers and our people following them. When they returned, they said they had killed several of the Comanches, but several of our people had also been killed. There was a man in our camp who had been with us since he was a little boy. He was a Mexican who our people had stolen when they made one of their raids some years before. Not being one of our people, he was not afraid of the dead and so came into camp with the scalps of three of the Comanches tied to his belt. When our people saw them, they made much fuss. They told him that his actions would cause us all trouble, and that he would have to bury the scalps and be ceremonially cleansed of the blood, or else leave the camp. He buried the scalps, took a sweat bath, and had some prayers said before any of the people, except the medicine man, would go near him.

The soldiers buried our people who had been killed. One of our girls was missing. We knew that the Comanches had taken her, and some of the people wanted to go after her, but they decided it would be of no use to take the risk of entering enemy country to fight. We had no guns or ammunition, were not allowed to have anything to use fighting, and that it would not be right for the families of the ones killed to go anywhere until the spirit of the dead had time to make the fourth circle. One of my father's brothers had been killed, so we had to stay at our hogan for four days. On the sixth night after the battle, the girl who had been stolen came in just before dawn. She said that one of the women in the enemy's camp had cut the ropes with which she was bound and gave her a horse to get away on. She rode for two nights and rested for a short time during the day. None of the enemy had followed.

After four winters of this life, our war chief said that he would agree to signing the papers that the white chief at Washington wanted our people to sign. We were all so glad because now we would be allowed to go back to our country. The time soon came when we at last started back over the road on which we had come. The soldiers took us to the river we had crossed on our way there and helped us over it. They said we might need something to fight with because an Apache war party might attack us if we were not armed, so they gave our men their spears and shields and some guns and ammunition. They also provided food, clothing, and blankets and then we were on our own. It did not seem long before we were in our own country and very happy.

Grandfather said we would have to start to work to get a supply of food so we began to gather various kinds of grass seeds. My brother and I were now old enough to work with the men, who told us we could go on their next hunting trip. We were very anxious for that time to come, but we worked to gather as much food as possible. Grandfather went out with me every day, and, as we gathered seeds, he told me many things about the different plants—how they were used for food or medicine, how they must be gathered when used for medicine, and what chants they were used in. I grew more interested in them as the days went by.

We saw many of our people who had not gone with us when the soldiers took us prisoner. They said they had had it very hard at times while we were gone. We told them that it had not been so bad where we had lived, but we were glad to be back again so that we could live our own lives as we wanted. The old people said it would have been better to have listened to the man who said that if we would go peaceably, we would have no trouble. I now knew what war was and hoped I would never see any more of it. Grandfather told the people that the way to avoid war was never to think of it. He said that we should get rid of all of our spears and shields, as they were implements of war. Now that we were at peace again, we should not have anything around to remind us of fighting. Many of the old men agreed with my grandfather, so we decided to bury the spears and shields in caves in the canyons.

Some of the white people came to a place we called Big Meadows. They told the people that they would have food and clothing for them there. A good many of us went in and received what they had to give. Sometime after this, they called us in again and gave us sheep so that now we could start anew our flocks. We were grateful to the chief in Washington.[2]

Those Who Stayed—Fred and Susie Yazzie

There were also Navajo people who remained around the Monument Valley area and had their own family stories to share. Fred Yazzie and his wife Susie Laughter Yazzie each have tales to tell. Fred shared from his mother's side this narrative.

Perhaps two generations ago near Mystery Valley where the black volcanic rock stands, her family lived in a very secluded place, because of enemies lurking about. When the soldiers and Mexicans came to capture them and take them to Fort Sumner, the number of enemies grew huge. They defeated some of the Navajos who then laid down their weapons and surrendered. Next, the soldiers, Mexicans, and Indian allies rounded up the Navajos and marched them off, but my great-grandmother never went with them. On one of these mesas, there was a rope made out of yucca on which my great-grandmother's family escaped, climbing atop and hiding. In 1925 when I was a boy, I observed some of this rope and used it to climb part of the way to the top of the mesa. Now, much of the side of this formation has since eroded away, the gentler incline becoming much steeper. This braided yucca was there before the Navajos, who did not make it, so I think the Anasazi did.[3]

Susie Yazzie also talks about the mesas and rock formations serving as defensive positions to protect the Navajo. She said:

My grandfather, Son of Giving Out Anger (Hashkéneiniihii Biye'), told us stories about this when we were children. From what I know, four generations have lived since the Long Walk took place. Our great-great-great-great-grandfathers and grandmothers went on that journey. They say the Diné were gathered up from all around this area and other places on today's reservation and taken to Fort Sumner. Some people ran and hid in Tséyi' Valley, about ten miles west of Kayenta. They said that our people fought off their enemies from on top of the mesas to the south of the Navajo Tribal Park, that long formation [Mitchell Mesa] behind Mitchell and Gray Whiskers Buttes. You can still see some rock walls on top of it. The Navajos had all sorts of enemies back then; some were Indians and others were white men. The plan was to kill off all of the Diné, so those against us banded together to fight and destroy the People. While the Navajos were in hiding on top of the mesas and among the rocks along the valley walls, they never built fires, fearing they would be discovered. They slept in alcoves and crevices, staying hidden, because once discovered, they were attacked. The Navajos knocked down walls of boulders on the advancing foe. They had no guns, only bows and arrows, so they killed them with rocks, turning them away and giving the people a chance to find new hiding places.

The Mexicans with their Indian allies searched ahead of the white soldiers. There is a story about a family living in these rocks when Indian and Mexican scouts arrived. Those hiding had small children and infants. One Navajo woman had a baby who would not stop crying and so she ran farther into the rocky area to keep the enemy from hearing the infant. She went as far as she could, but the baby still cried and so she put it under her to cover the sound. This did not help; the baby continued crying. In the meantime, the rest of the family, along with others living close by, had also run up into the rocks to hide, leaving their flocks of sheep. The

In the northern part of Navajo territory, there was no more implacable foe of the People than the Utes. For decades, they pushed the Navajos south of the San Juan River, although there were small groups who moved across and lived in Ute territory. The inflamed relations heated white-hot when the United States military encouraged the Utes to conduct unconditional tribal warfare. Wolfkiller, Fred and Susie Yazzie, and many others testified of their effectiveness in tracking and finding Navajos in hiding. (Courtesy Denver Public Library)

scouts came to their homesteads and set fire to the vacant hogans and shelters. The woman observed all this happening, while she continued to quiet her baby. She did not know where her family or the other people had gone. Everyone was running for their lives, as the scouts came on too fast. The fleeing Navajos could not help the little children, so they stuck two of them in a crevice between a couple of boulders, telling the little ones to sit still and be quiet. The woman in hiding did not know that an enemy had made his way to a point above her where he had heard the baby's cry below. He quickly alerted the others who found the woman and infant. After killing her, they took the child with them, something they often did. The other families went into hiding farther up on the mesa, but were able to see the scouts killing the woman. As the enemy descended, the little children in the crevice came running out from cover, thinking that it was the mother bringing her baby home. The enemy grabbed the two little children and took them also. The hidden families saw their homes ablaze and watched their children and sheep taken away.

Other families, lower in the valley, had been killed before they had a chance to escape. Some Navajos living closer together in makeshift homes in the rocks were attacked, overcome, or killed in ambush—that was how the people described the conflict. Their children were taken amidst the fighting, killing, and screaming that grew so loud that it frightened the goats, causing them to jump over the corral fence and flee to the rocks and mesas. The scouts rounded up only a few to take with the rest of the stolen herds. At another place called Chased by the Mexicans (Naakai Ch'íhoniítkaad), which is the name of a site northeast of the entrance to Narrow Canyon (about eight miles southwest of Oljato), some Navajos escaped up on the mesa, giving that name to the landscape.

The aftermath of all of this was horrendous. The Navajos came out of hiding, calculated their losses, and found their slain people with those who had been hiding among the rocks. All of the dead, who had worn their long hair in traditional buns, had been scalped by the enemy, who put their trophies on their long sharp weapons and guns as they sang and rode away from this scene of carnage. Those who survived remained in hiding for many, many days, going without food and only a little water, until things quieted down. They returned to the ashes of what had been their homes, now burned to the ground. One homestead on the mesa had remained undetected. A group of survivors stumbled upon it, gathered the nicely tanned sheepskins and took them to use for bedding and blankets; there was also a piece of burning firewood they used for their future cooking fires. This temporary shelter was made from a couple of posts with a crossbeam supporting a bunch of sticks and branches leaning against it; this was a small shelter, about the size of a sweat lodge. Another story tells of the people finding a little dog that had somehow managed to get to a ledge on the face of a sheer cliff wall. The people heard the animal barking and saw it high above them. They thought that someone might have been hiding on that ledge. This took place in Tsegi Valley west of Kayenta. The aftermath of the massacres was too much for many of the survivors, with bodies and blood strewn about the desert floor and in the rocks everywhere.

Our family experienced much of this. I have mentioned that some people hid on top of Mitchell Mesa. You can still see the walls that were built along the edge of the cliff and various narrow passageways, so that if the enemy tried to enter, rocks could be pushed down on them. My husband's [Fred Yazzie's] father, Frank Adakai Yazzie, said that his great-great-great-grandmother hid from the enemy up on that mesa. She and her family were never captured; they survived. It was said a handful of people from El Capitan joined them and remained hidden on it. Their defensive wall of rocks is what saved them. My paternal grandmother's great-great-grandmother was captured and killed while she tried to save herself and her baby. These stories came from her great-grandmother and then she told us. These are the only ones that I have heard about the people who survived without being captured.

It was said that one of our great-great-great-grandmothers escaped from her Paiute and Ute captors and later returned to her people. She was just a little girl when her mother was shot and killed and she was taken away. Different tribes like the Utes, Hopi, Zuni, and some Plains Indians from Oklahoma came to our area to kidnap and kill our people, take the children and livestock, and burn our homes. This grandmother, after being captured, grew up among the Paiutes and married one of them. She became pregnant and ran away from her abusive husband. These Paiutes had been hostile to her saying, "You don't have any parents, because they are dead and we can kill you, too. We have taken care of you for no reason." Because of this kind of treatment, even though she was pregnant, she decided to escape. While she had been in captivity, she had occasionally heard news about the Navajos. Fleeing from the Utes and Paiutes, she hid in the bushes, shrubs, and tree roots along the washes as she traveled toward Navajo land. The enemy on horseback tracked her and found where she had been, crawling under objects and over rocks to avoid detection. She stayed ahead of them and one day met a couple of people also heading to Navajo land. They decided to go up on Black Mesa to avoid their enemies, where they survived primarily on cactus bulbs cooked in ashes. Eventually the small group traveled on and found some Navajos camped close to what would later become reservation lands. She became reacquainted with her people and raised her Paiute child, living to an old age. That is why our family has Paiute blood. The Utes and Paiutes are two different tribes. Our great-grandmother was part Paiute and Navajo. After several generations, we outgrew our Paiute bloodline.[4]

Those Who Fled—Hashkéneiniihii

In April 1939, Utah historian Charles Kelly interviewed an old man named Hashkéneiniihii Biye' (Son of Giving Out Anger) living in Monument Valley, who as a young boy fled with his father Hashkéneiniihii (sometimes spelled Hashkéninii) to Navajo Mountain. This Navajo's firsthand account

tells the story of their successful evasion of the enemy and how they pros-
pered during four years of exile, while others had to endure Fort Sumner.

At that time I was five years old and my family was living at Kayenta.
Monument Valley then belonged to the Utes, and the rock called Agathla
(El Capitan) was the dividing line between Utes and Navajos. We had
heard of the trouble between the Navajos and white soldiers, and some
of our family had been arrested or surrendered, but we lived so far north
we thought we would be safe. One of my uncles tried to talk father into
surrendering and going to Bosque Redondo with the others, but father
became very angry and said he would die before he went to any prison
camp. The rest of the family agreed. My father at this time was not a chief,
but he was a strong man, about 35 years old, and the people looked on
him as a brave leader.

One day a rider came in from the south and shouted that the soldiers were coming for us. They were so close we could see their dust. We
had no time to get our horses nor prepare for a journey, so each person
grabbed what he could and we ran north toward the Ute country. There
were some Ute scouts among the soldiers and we were more afraid of
them than the whites, as we had always been at war with them. We scattered and hid on the desert so the soldiers could not find us. When it was
dark we started traveling and walked all night to avoid being seen by the
Utes, as we were then in their territory.

In this party which escaped, there was my father and mother, mother's two sisters whom father later married, two Ute slave women, two
uncles, grandfather and grandmother, and other relatives to the number
of seventeen. Later a few other stragglers joined the group. Father had
a horse and an old rifle; otherwise, everyone was on foot. Mother had
rounded up twenty sheep and it was my job to drive them while she
hunted for food. Father rode ahead to find a trail and watch for Utes.

We traveled many nights and slept during the day. Everyone was
footsore and hungry, because we had not brought food, so lived mostly
on grass seed and an occasional rabbit. After traveling north for a while,
father turned west toward Navajo Mountain. It was also Ute country,
but they seldom lived around there. The land was very rough and we
became worn out climbing down into deep canyons and out again while
water was very hard to find. Finally, we reached the south end of Navajo
Mountain and came to a nice little stream with grass. Mother sat on the
ground and said she would go no farther. Father tried to make her go on
but she refused, so we made camp there, and lived in that place for six

Hashkéneiniihii fled the Monument Valley area by taking a circuitous route to Navajo Mountain, where he remained undisturbed for four years. He returned to the Monument Valley region, where he and his son served as medicine men and provided strong leadership for the local people. A number of geographic features have been named after him. (Courtesy San Juan County Historical Commission)

years. Only one Ute ever visited us, and he came to trade. When we got to that place, all twenty sheep were still alive, and father issued orders that none were to be eaten; we would keep them to start a new herd. Later he and my uncles went back to Kayenta and found a few more sheep and some horses that the soldiers had not killed.

By that time the weather was cool and winter not far away. We had no meat and could find no game on the mountain, so father made everyone go out and gather grass seed and pine nuts to store for winter use. He drove everyone all day long and would never let us rest, knowing that we might starve. He always seemed to be angry with everyone for being lazy and that is why he received the name of Hashkéninii, meaning "The Angry One." The food he made us gather was stored in many different holes in the rocks where the Utes could not find it, so no one died that winter. You must remember that no one knew where we were living, or whether we were even alive. We had no bullets for the old rifle so hunted in the old way and never went to a trading post. The rest of our people, except for a few on Black Mountain, were all in the prison camp. We saw none of our people, no whites, and only one renegade Ute, who did not betray us. It was lucky that we had this friend named Gray Hair, but he was a very bad man who had been driven from his own band because of woman trouble. He pretended to be our friend only in order to spy on us. When our flocks began to increase, he organized a group of young warriors and started for Navajo Mountain to kill us while also getting revenge on the people who had thrown him out. At one point, he stopped to visit some Utes, but he was so bad they killed him and his nephew. After that, all the Utes moved away from Navajo Mountain and we had no more trouble.

One day while my father was riding on the mountain he found silver in the rocks and brought it home. He found that he could shape it without melting and so he and six other men went back there and took out more silver to make into ornaments. He never let anyone else see where it came from. In those days all silver was made smooth, without designs. Our people learned to ornament silver from a Mexican at Bosque Redondo.

We lived at Navajo Mountain for six years. During that time our sheep and horse herds increased so that we had plenty of meat and many blankets as well as lots of silver. When our people returned from Fort Sumner, they were each given two sheep and some seeds, but otherwise, had nothing else. Even their peach trees had been cut down. When we came away from Navajo Mountain, the people were surprised to see us and all of the wealth we had. We moved to our home on Hoskininni Mesa, while the Utes had abandoned Monument Valley. We were the strongest band and the richest Navajos in the whole country. The grass was good in those days and every year we became increasingly wealthy. Father had given me sheep and horses of my own and a lot of silver, so that even as a very young man, women began laying hold of my belt (an offer of marriage). Some of the people said to themselves, "Hashkéninii must have found a rich silver mine." When the whites heard about it, they all wanted to come into our country and hunt for it, but father would not let them, and none of those who knew about it ever told a white man or even another Navajo how to find it. I do not know where it is myself, because when the whites began looking for it, father never went there again.[5]

Aftermath—The Myrick (Merrick) and Mitchell Affair

Hashkéneiniihii Biye' ended his story of the Long Walk period, but he knew of more violence that occurred later, much of it centering around the silver mine his father had discovered. Word eventually spread of its existence, encouraging white miners to begin searching. The Monument Valley–Navajo Mountain area saw different parties crisscross over the land with hopes of discovery, but the Navajos, Utes, and Paiutes in the area wanted nothing to do with them. The best known of the hopefuls were two men—Charles S. Myrick (usually incorrectly spelled Merrick and sometimes Merritt) and Hernan D. Mitchell, for which two large buttes in Monument Valley are named. A number of versions of the events that led to their demise have, over the years, taken twists and turns in accuracy, but much of that misunderstanding has since been clarified by James H. Knipmeyer in *Pish-la-ki, The Lost Merrick and Mitchell Silver Mine*.[6] Only part of that story is told here about how a handful of Paiutes managed to immortalize these two men.

Hashkéneiniihii Biye' provided an account as a bystander of events to Louisa Wetherill, who recorded them some years after. She wrote:

It was from the old chief's son that Asthon Sosi (Asdzą́ą́ Ts'ósí—Slim Woman—Louisa) heard at last the full story of how Mitchell and Merrick had been killed. They had stopped at Hoskininni's [Hashkéneiniihii's] hogan and demanded mutton. When it had been killed for them, they were directed to water. After watering their horses and filling their canteens, they rode to the foot of the monument that was later named for Mitchell. In the morning they were ready for a fresh start.

A band of Paiutes had planned a surprise attack at daybreak, but when they came to the men's camping place, they found them already mounted. The Paiutes told them that they had been using Paiute water to which they had no right. "We were sent to that water," replied the white men calmly. The efforts of the Paiutes to make them angry and pick a quarrel were fruitless. "Give me a chew of tobacco," demanded one Paiute [later identified as Big Mouth Mike]. Mitchell reached into his pocket for a plug of tobacco. At the same time, the Paiute grabbed for the gun on the [white man's] hip. A moment later, Mitchell lay dead on the ground, killed by a bullet from his own six shooter. Merrick whirled at the shot, and seeing his partner past help, put spurs to his own horse and fled, firing as he fled.

For three miles he rode, to the foot of the great rock which later was to be named for him, Merrick Butte. There, knowing that he had been wounded, but fearing that he might have cartridges left, his pursuers turned back. Alone among the rocks he died.[7]

Because this occurred in Navajo country, they were automatically implicated, but after Navajo scouts, sent by Agent Galen Eastman, investigated the incident, they determined the culprits were of Ute-Paiute ancestry. In the meantime, search parties went looking for the two men, who were long overdue to be back at the trading post owned by Mitchell's father, Henry L. Mitchell, at present-day Aneth. On March 13, 1880, the *Dolores* [Colorado] *News* reported one of the party's discovery.

Mitchell's body was found near an Indian sheep herd, but was so mutilated and destroyed that he could only be recognized by his wearing apparel. The wolves had eaten all the flesh they could get at. The flesh was eaten and gnawed off his bones as far in his boots as the wolves could reach. One bullet hole was found in his body. Merrick was found about three miles from Mitchell and it seemed that he had been separated from Mitchell by the attack of the Indians, and had had a running fight with them, as he was shot eight times through the body, and once through the head, which latter shot was doubtless the final, though it is stated that the greater number of the eight, even alone, would be fatal. He had crawled and dragged himself a distance, between two and three hundred yards, in a deep sand arroyo or ravine, and about every twenty or thirty feet, pools of blood—dried up—were found. He had crawled under a large overhanging rock; his watch remained in his pocket, and his hat and smoke-pipe were found nearby. Also, a lead pencil and some pieces of paper were found near his hands, but no writing had been done. He perhaps intended writing, but lingered too long, awaiting recovery from the stupor caused by loss of blood. He died a most horrible death, far from friends and without any hope or source of recovery.[8]

As for Hashkéneiniihii's mine, it is still "lost." Rumors grew, and discovery efforts increased, but to no avail. This incident ends much of the violence characteristic of the nineteenth century in Monument Valley, although there were other events at Navajo Mountain, Kayenta, and places nearby in the years to come.

Perhaps the best way to close on this time of chaos and death is to turn to Ralph Grey, a longtime resident and livestock man of Monument Valley, who shared some final thoughts about this era, when "the enemy sneaked right up to our feet somehow." Speaking of the Navajos' return from Fort Sumner to their homes, he mused,

It is said that the white men felt very wrong about the whole thing at Hwééldi. They said, "You (Navajo) never killed anyone, right to this day, so none of you will be killed. Let them move back to their land where there are mountains standing and where the river flows." So the people started moving back from there, some walking with their belongings. The horses helped others. . . . They [military] said, "You will go back to your own land where the people, horses, and the sheep will multiply, and the corn will always reproduce itself. Plants of all kinds will always grow. All things will happen, and it will rain on it. So, go and move." This is what my grandfather used to say to me. . . . There is a prayer that goes with it.[9]

CHAPTER FOUR
Childhood in the Early Days
Making a Living

Most of the chapters in this reader examine specific topics that are important and often unique to the land and people of Monument Valley. The other side of that coin is the day-to-day life of traditional Navajos making a living and going about activities that support their physical needs and cultural values. For those raised in the first three decades of the twentieth century—before livestock reduction and World War II escalated change—patterns and teachings for raising children, performing marriages, and maintaining cultural responsibilities were derived from role models provided by the holy people. Changing Woman for females and the Twins—Monster Slayer and Born for Water—for males were the examples that an individual followed. Lessons learned from historical events such as the Long Walk and local conflicts encouraged Navajos to be ever vigilant and circumspect in a world that continued to shift. Wisdom from the past translated into learning to survive as a member of a family that needed to eke out an existence. Here, an overview of daily life in those early days gives a glimpse into activities and concerns for those living over a hundred years ago.

A Girl's Tenor of Life—Susie Yazzie

Susie Yazzie shares her experiences as a child and young woman, touching upon many of the mainstays of her culture—the importance of agriculture, livestock, weaving, traditional skills, and family cooperation. What she discusses was very much a part of most girls' training as they prepared for the rigors of adult life. Female roles were clearly defined in Navajo culture and strictly adhered to. The successful woman was the one who carefully and skillfully performed the domestic activities within her domain—the home, agricultural fields, and herds of sheep and goats upon which the family depended. Susie was successful in each of these areas.

All families moved around a lot, not living in one spot as we do now. They moved up and down along the riverbed or by the washes that extend all the way from Kayenta eastward to T'iis Haaz Áhá and then northward back to the San Juan River. The people constantly searched for good vegetation, abundant water, pastureland for their livestock, and fine soil for farming. Some planted gardens wherever they lived so one would find corn and melon patches here and there at a site nobody claimed; everyone shared the land and produce at harvest time. Some even planted corn and melons inside their sheep corral due to lack of fencing to keep the animals away. According to my mother, everyone moved about freely. That is how it was.

I was born at our family homestead called Where the Cows Grow Up (Béégashii Nit'ání) beyond No Man's Mesa in a canyon about twenty miles from Oljato. When I was small, I herded sheep with a young aunt. She used to carry me piggyback after the flock; when I was a little older, she would hold my hand and we would walk after the grazing animals, even during the winter months. This aunt would say, "If a child stays home with nothing to do, they will be irresponsible." We did not have shoes like those available now because there were no stores or trading posts close by. The winter brought a lot of snow—knee-deep on adults—and it lasted a long time. It seemed like winters were longer back then. In the summer, we wore homemade moccasins that my father knew how to make. He also taught his three wives how to sew them after dyeing the leather in boiling water with plants that gave the skin a reddish color. After butchering the cow, they would take the hide and spread it out to dry. Next, they tanned the leather to make it soft, cut it into pieces, and then formed the moccasins. Sometimes the soles were rinsed and reused several times before being discarded. We never complained nor asked for store-bought shoes or clothes. No one said anything about buying shoes because it was unheard of back then, and so all the children had homemade moccasins and clothing. Mother made one skirt and blouse for each of us girls, which we wore for almost a year. The hems of our skirts would be tattered and torn, as if someone had beaten them with a stick. There were no coats, so we wore a blanket folded lengthwise and secured with a belt around our waist during the cold winter. That is how we dressed while herding sheep.

We always wore our hair in a knot (tsiiyééł), and as children, we never had it cut. It is good to keep your hair clean with yucca root shampoo and brushed so that it grows better. My hair got so long that it touched my ankles. Now I occasionally trim the ends, but wearing a knot looks good on women and men, so I still keep that style. There are also a lot of teachings about the care and importance of hair, but I guess they are like everything else in that they teach about discipline, respect, and thoughts. As we get older, even taking care of one's hair becomes a chore. They used to say that if a person believed in traditional ways, they would not cut their hair. If you respect and think in a holy way about the four sacred mountains, you will not do the forbidden. Everything was considered holy. Legend says that sometime during the early part of creation, the mountains went crazy. One mountain, namely Furry/Fuzzy Mountain (Dził Ditł'oi) shaved one side of its head because it became jealous. Some mountains burned; others did not. From these events came the mountain smoke ceremony used to calm and quiet people who do foolish and crazy things. It is said that in the future, when all of our people have cut their hair or shaved their heads, that will begin the end of our era because we will have failed and been overcome by the white men and their ways.

Livestock was a vital part of our existence. We grew up surrounded by sheep, horses, and cattle. Even to have one or two sheep now makes where you live feel like home. It gives one peace of mind, even if a person is unable to take care of them as we used to. To give this way of life up and live without animals—I do not know what I'd do. This is especially true for those who grew up with livestock and have been with them for as long as we can remember. It would be hard to be without them. I was raised in a home where we had sheep and cattle, which consistently provided our livelihood. When we lived above Narrow Canyon at Where the Cows Grow Up and higher on the mesa at Tall Mountain (Dził Nééz), my paternal grandmother, who was homebound, always had sheep and goats. They used to separate the rams and billy goats, sometimes leaving the sheep and their lambs with the goats and kids. When they grew bigger, she butchered them for meat. She used to milk the goats that always seemed to have plenty to share.

I must have started herding sheep with my aunt at age four. Later I was able to go alone. Back then we had good meat. We were constantly in search of plentiful pastureland no matter what the season. Our livestock had lots of natural vegetation and water so they were nice and fat. We herded the sheep all the time to springs with clean water that came down year-round from the mountain. I have heard lately that these springs have stopped flowing in the summer. My aunts sometimes took the sheep past Tall Mountain and toward Shonto, where there were only a few homesteads scattered about. This gave us plenty of grazing land, water, and a good place for lambing in the spring, when the weather was warmer.

Two of my aunts had the responsibility of moving around with the animals, looking for pasture, and so I went with one of them to assist. My aunts taught me many important things, such as how to keep matches dry and how to build a fire under any condition. I would gather the dry limbs from under the trees along with some dry bark to build the fire. During the winter months, we had to care for the newborn lambs. We would clear a dry spot and build a fire for drying and warming them. Sometimes two or more sheep had their babies at the same time, but once the lambs were dry, we would herd all of the animals home together. I remember doing this with my aunt, who took really good care of me. In the winter, I wore goatskin moccasins with rags wrapped around my feet for socks. At that time, most Navajo people did not have socks. I would stay by the fire to keep warm, while maintaining the sheep close by. We lived near a mountain, so the weather was very cold with deep snow and heavy fog. At times, it was easy to get lost, but when you have been out with the sheep a lot, you can find your way around. There were some deep canyons too, where we used to herd the livestock. I remember carrying newborn lambs up those steep canyon slopes. Often, I put a lamb inside my blanket on my back, then carried it home with its mother following me all the way. Once I got the baby home, I'd make sure it was fed and put with its mother. It does not pay to be lazy; if you do not take care of sheep properly, you are liable to end up feeding more lambs that now depend solely on you. Sometimes the mothers would abandon their babies, creating more work. There is a lot to learn when caring for livestock, which also provides excellent lessons for a child. We learned from our experiences.

This was also a time when we had plenty of goat's milk. Grandmother instructed me and my younger sister, Lois, to be at her home first thing in the morning, before the goats started grazing. "Milk will taste good only before they take a bite, so be here early to milk them," she would say. This forced us to get up and out to make sure we were there on time. We were up early, every morning, even though it was quite a way off and we were barefoot, something we just became used to. If we missed one day, there was less milk at home. On the way, there were snakes and insects, which did not please us at all. We would go around them if we heard one rattle and then continue on our way. These snakes must have been good because we never had problems with them. Even the sheep grazed around and were never bitten. Once we reached the herd, Lois would hold the goat by the hair under its chin and by its horn, while I did the milking in a can. When we brought it home, Grandmother poured some milk into a pot and boiled it on hot ashes. "It's good when you boil it really hard," she said to us. The rest of the milk we took home to my mother, who made milk-and-corn pancakes, then gave us one or two for supper. We boiled the milk and added the cornmeal to make a tasty meal. A twenty-five-pound bag of flour purchased from the trading post lasted a long time because we used mostly corn we had harvested. My paternal grandmother and her daughter supplemented our corn food with other vegetables. These people were very nice and helped us out a lot. This grandmother also taught us how to butcher a sheep as she sat and directed us where to cut and what to do; I was only four or five years old at the time, but I learned how to do it. Since my father had to care for three households, we all ate small portions of a butchered sheep as we rationed our food. We would cut up some meat, dry it, and then mix it with corn and other vegetables. The children learned to eat small amounts, not overeating as some do now.

I also learned many things from working in the cornfields and taking care of the home. We were taught how to keep house and cook. Since there were no grocery stores, we had to learn everything by using basic food supplies. The children were primarily responsible for the livestock and cornfields, while the mothers were busy with rug weaving. They would card, spin, wash, dye, and weave the wool into rugs to be sold in exchange for food. We had no such things as financial assistance programs back then. We could not depend on anybody but ourselves. Money was scarce, and we did not have free food distribution, so weaving rugs was vitally important. When our food was low, the women wove all night by the firelight.

One aunt was always weaving, which was all that she did, while my other aunt and I took care of the livestock. This aunt also cooked, carded, and spun wool for my aunt, who spent so much time at the loom that all she did was weave, weave, weave. The women then took their rugs to the trading post to buy small amounts of flour and potatoes. The store had no meat and hardly any shortening, while the coffee beans were whole, and so we had to grind them ourselves. There were several cornfields with peach trees located in the canyon near where we lived. My father owned two of these cornfields, and so my mother, Sally, and her children were assigned to work there, while Father's other two wives were in another location herding sheep. Each household of the three wives and their children was treated the same.

The boys had to look after the horses and other livestock and learned many of the same skills we did. None of us slept for as long as we wanted. We took snow baths in the winter. My parents built a huge fire in the middle of our hogan so we could melt the ice off our bodies once we came inside. My father lectured us a lot. "These baths are for the sake of the children," he would say, "to cure them of their bad habits and attitudes." We rolled in the snow and ran inside to stand by the fire, then went out and rolled in the snow again. This was done every winter. I was the oldest of the children, so I got it the worst. My mother would rub the snow all over my body including my face. It was pure torture, but I believe it has taught me respect for others as well as for myself. I learned unselfishness and not to talk back to people. My father was right about his teachings.[1]

Women's Work

Other women had similar experiences, underscoring the laborious tasks associated from start to finish with food production—a far cry from the ease of today's grocery store shopping. Sloan Haycock tells of her family experience in horticulture, the use of summer and winter camps, and following traditional teachings.

The days were long and hot. Our families planted and cultivated their cornfields using hand shovels to build the irrigation ditches to water enough corn, pumpkins, squash, and melons to last a year. I was told to get up before dawn each day and to run or take the sheep out to pasture before the weather became too hot. The children doing this were warned, "One should not be lazy; take out the carding boards and card the wool; take out the spindle and spin the yarn; weave the rug . . . learn to do these things so that you can make a living by doing it throughout your life." As young girls, our parents made us grind the corn outside the hogan at dawn, to keep us young, strong, and healthy. No one was allowed to sleep late in the morning. I also learned how to weave rugs, which in those days sold for less, but were traded for a lot of food and merchandise because of low market prices.

Susie Yazzie (right) and her sister Joanne (left) learned all of the skills necessary for traditional Navajo womanhood, which ranged from herding sheep and weaving to picking herbs and growing gardens. Life was at times harsh but their strong beliefs carried them through difficult experiences and brought peace. (Courtesy Marilyn Holiday, daughter of Susie Yazzie)

People planted fruit trees like apples and peaches, which grew well because of the rain. Each morning, until it became too hot, the children either hoed the weeds in the cornfields or irrigated the corn and melons. It was important to do a good job because it was our main source of food to last all year. Pumpkins and melons were cut into strips and wrapped around each other and dried. Later, they were boiled and used as a sweet dessert. The only means we had to move our harvest was in a wagon, and so we fetched the horses in the morning and used them to haul produce or to just ride when herding sheep. In later years, the people began growing alfalfa, which led to building a reservoir for more irrigation water. The alfalfa grew thick and tall, and when harvested, it was crushed in a hole dug in the ground, then tied in bundles with yucca fiber rope. The alfalfa sold well with the white traders who bought it for their dairy cows. The traders kept them for milk, which became a primary source of food for them.

Sometime later, the local people decided to plant their cornfields on the banks of the San Juan River at Piute Farms and so traveled there on horseback. This land was very fertile, producing a lot of food. Several people owned a field along the river and a second one in Oljato, traveling back and forth to care for both. We had a winter camp on top of the mesa and a summer camp down below. Our winter camp had several hogans that we stocked with firewood in the fall. In those days, there were plenty of trees, which we hauled in our wagons to our camps. In the spring, we moved down to the cornfields, where there was always enough vegetation for our livestock.[2]

Gladys Bitsinnie had a short respite from herding livestock when she went to school, but soon she became sick, went to recuperate with some relatives, and then returned to her family in Narrow Canyon about the time "the corn started to tassel." She continues:

Previous to returning home, my father had brought me a horse and eight sheep while I was staying with a relative in Dennehotso. When I left there for Monument Valley, my cousin and I herded the sheep all of the way to Train Rock, then reached Tsé Yaa Tóhí late in the afternoon. There were people living there under the trees as well as in five hogans. The people kept a lot of sheep together there. I was told to take care of the livestock all the time so that was what I did. I never went back to school but only herded sheep and ate milk and porridge. My job was only sheep but I did not have shoes, and in the summer, the hot sand hurt our feet. We sometimes stuck thin rocks on the bottom of our feet, attaching them with piñon pitch to the soles. Moccasins were also made for us, but these would get holes all too soon. We went about like this. Our clothes were ragged, made from flour sacks sewn together. When they got torn, we tied knots in the rips that hung at the fringe of our hems. At that time, fabrics were scarce and everything we had was hand sewn. Sometimes when we were out with the animals, we would find water, so we washed our hair and clothes where there were puddles in the rocks.

No matter what, we had to take care of the sheep and goats—and there were a lot of them. We herded sheep even if we were crying and reprimanded as we went off after them. Often, we returned to where we had been previously. In those days, whipping was a punishment if we were caught playing while herding sheep. Our mother would suddenly appear, and when we saw her, we started to run. To make matters worse, the sheep outnumbered us to a large extent and during the time when the yucca flowers blossomed, they ran wild. We cried because we could not keep them under control. When there were donkeys to ride, things got better. Two or even three of us used to get on one and head off the sheep that were straying. Sometimes we would herd the flock all the way over to Owl Spring to a planted field we had there. Our parents always directed us as to where we should go, which was usually on foot. Our father did not hold a whip upon us, only our mother. I never talked back to her like children do today. I still fear her and just visit her to cook and then I am on my way. This makes her feel good and the food she eats is delicious.

If we had a visitor, we butchered a sheep. During the night, the adults talked until it was very late. This was done in front of children who were told to sit quietly and listen; this was especially true when there was a ceremony going on. Sitting quietly and reverently was demanded. Children were raised to be shy about making noises, but now there is nothing like this. They are not shy about anything. When we had visitors, children sat still and did not bother each other. Now, children fight amongst themselves. It was not like that with us. I think about how I was back then and compare it to the children of today. They are not in any way close to the way I was.

In addition to eating sheep and goats, which were prepared in a variety of ways, there were also wild plants that we picked and brought home. Wild sunflowers grew high, and there was narrow-leaf grass, wild onions, and wild berries. Some people traveled in wagons to Comb Ridge to pick sumac berries. There they filled canvas bags, sometimes three of them at

Gender roles were clearly defined in Navajo culture and taught at an early age. Observing, attempting a task when ready, and making mistakes without criticism were some of the ways one learned. Members within an extended family shared their talents, illustrating that "it takes a community to raise a child." (Courtesy Special Collections, J. Willard Marriott Library, University of Utah)

a time, with this delicious fruit to be used in the coming months. These berries were added to porridge to give it and other things a tart flavor.[3]

Nellie Grandson remembers preparing and cooking many of these traditional foods. She particularly recalls making paper bread (tsé'ást'éí) from a thin batter of ground blue cornmeal, goat's milk, and juniper ash.

A nicely smoothed flat rock was sanded flat, then sealed with pitch and rubbed with grease after all of its roughness was removed and the small cracks sealed. The burnished slab, sanded with another flat rock, accepted the heated piñon pitch, which was then coated with grease to prevent the batter from sticking. The woman placed this new "frying pan" over a fire, then added fat when the griddle became sufficiently hot to cook the batter. The rock was nice and slick, and the thin batter was poured over it with a wave of the hand, then brushed to spread it farther as it baked and sizzled. Once cooked, the woman removed the thin sheet of corn bread, folded it, and handed it to someone to eat. Now, few people make this. Men do not plant fields of corn and women no longer use these cooking stones.

Part of this process, when making the batter or anything else that needed to be stirred, was to use greasewood stirring sticks (ádístsiin). Once the ingredients were mixed together and there was residue left on the sticks, the woman would hold them and pray that there might be rain and a huge crop of corn. These sticks are the women's weapon to fight against starvation. Once they are washed, it is said there is hunger on there that says, "Eek, she is washing her weapon." This was what was said. The brush that is used for brushing off the particles from the grinding stone can also be used as a strainer to pour liquids through, while juniper ashes were used like baking powder. This turned the corn into a nice blue color.

These kinds of foods were eaten by our grandfathers and grandmothers who survived in this manner. Horse meat, called jigóní, was a medicine used to remedy colds, while we also ate burros, rabbits, and prairie dogs. I was told that all of these foods were made for us. Now it is said there is sickness in these creatures, but if they are ill, how can these animals still be living? The sickness is probably coming from whatever the Anglos are doing.[4]

"It was not a beautiful life"—Navajo Oshley

Boys did not have it any easier than girls. Poverty and hard work also stared them in the face and there was little parental favoritism. Everyone was in it to help the family survive, with group cooperation the key. Navajo Oshley remembered:

> When I was a boy, I was called Tall Boy (Ashkii Nééz). Our names were awful back then. Eventually, my mother had six children, but my first sister died, making me the oldest one in the family. As I remember, I did not have any shoes, and my pants were a horror to see. They had holes and were too short. The fabric in my shirt was from a flour sack, and where my relatives got it, I do not know. I did not have a hat so I used a piece of rope or cloth tied together. This is how I grew up.
>
> The trading post was very far away. My mother and grandmother would take the burros there, but it was time consuming and very tedious. They brought back flour, coffee, and sugar. It took three to four days before they returned. The children would wonder when grandmother and mother would come back, so one of us would run to the hill and look for them. When grandmother returned with food, we would get milk from the goats, then butcher a sheep. Everything was used. Even the blood and intestines were fixed, and the wool removed from the hide. After cleaning the skin thoroughly, it was cut into strips, then curled around a piece of fat. We ate it like that.
>
> Life was a very hard, long struggle. Sometimes there was little food so we would have just a few mouthfuls to eat before we went to sleep. In the morning, we would drink milk and then go without food the rest of the day. We had the cornfield which we planted when it rained. If there was no moisture, we would go hungry during the summer and into the winter. Life was hard when I was growing up.
>
> When I was a child, sheep were the main source of food for survival. The sheep were separated from their lambs and the goats from their kids. They grazed while the lambs and kids stayed in the corral. One time around sundown, the sheep came home and took their lambs. I went after them, bringing a can with a spoon. After a while, my family missed me. Mother looked for my tracks and saw that I had followed the sheep far away. As she got closer, she saw me standing face to face with a coyote. I was shaking the can in my hand, causing the coyote to hesitate to charge, but it did not prevent me from wetting my pants. My mother saved me,

but my aunt scolded her for letting me wander off. When my sister came home from herding sheep and found out what had happened, she picked me up and cried, saying that I had almost been eaten by a coyote.

This is how I used to live; it was not a beautiful life. We even got water from a long distance, a mile away, carrying it in pails by hand. A person needed to get up early in the morning. When we washed, we used the same water the last person used. Since water was very scarce, if one person washed his hair, the next person also used the same water, no matter what it looked like, because that was all we had. There was no soap, either.

We ate rabbits, pack rats, and prairie dogs. They were hard to catch. When winter came, we started hunting rabbits, which we killed with sticks and stones. Sometimes there was nothing to eat. We also had a few horses, cows, and burros. During that time, people butchered horses when they were fat, wasting nothing. Sometimes it was hard to get a meal, and so we stayed hungry throughout the day. Life was not a pleasant time when I was growing up.

During the summer, things got better because we looked for plants like green yucca fruit to eat. There were also wild onions and sumac berries. Sometimes these did not grow because they only flourish when it rains. When the water did not come, life was extra hard. That is why when there are heavy snows in the winter, people are happy. My elders were right when they said they would have plenty of food in the summer. When it rains a lot, we have an abundance of all things. When it really rained in the fall, there would be piñon nuts the following year. Almost the whole family went to pick them. I picked piñon nuts in my younger days and remember how the tips of my fingers hurt, so I would use my other hand. After we had gathered lots of nuts, we went home and mixed them with toasted corn. This food was prepared by roasting the nuts and corn separately, then crushing the shells and mixing them together. This is called haza'aleeh [literally, "put into mouth"] and is often combined with meat and a sprinkle of salt. We needed any kind of edible thing to eat. There were other plants such as wolfberry, edible tubers that we dug up, green yucca fruit, and yucca stalks. We would gather these plants when they were ripe, along with spiny cactus. We also had corn, which was ground with stones and cooked with water to make mush. Leaves from the juniper trees were burnt and the ashes added to the water. Mother then filtered them through a brush, added the corn, mixed it well, then took the haza'aleeh and dipped it into the mush. We thought that tasted really great.

When we were living behind Comb Ridge, my cousins and I left our chores and played in the rocks all day long. We took big flat rocks for sleds and slid down the rock slopes, which was a lot of fun. One time we were doing this, and the rock came out from underneath me when I was halfway down. It barely missed sliding over me, but although I was badly scraped and had a nosebleed, we still laughed about it. We must have been really foolish, and now that I think about it, I could have been killed.[5]

Herding sheep was everybody's business, but the task fell primarily on the shoulders of women and children. This flock, photographed in Oljato Wash in the early 1900s, is under the care of a young girl who had the responsibility for their welfare and understood how to manage a large number of animals. (Courtesy Photo Archives, Utah State Historical Society)

Tempering the Elements—John Holiday

While the importance of the food quest has been emphasized in the early days of Monument Valley, there were events that decreased the possibility of starvation, such as the introduction of trading posts, to be discussed in a following chapter, as well as the development of technology, government assistance, and increased settlement in the area. Even so, the Navajo people maintained an intense belief in the role of the holy people who worked with them to provide what was needed in life. Prayer and ritual performance were at the center of how those things were obtained. As

Oshley and others point out, water was the key to survival and wealth in this desert environment. Monument Valley has had a number of medicine men who had the ability to control weather and bring rain during desperate times. Hastiin Tsoh, who controlled weather events during the time that John Ford filmed movies in the area, is probably the most famous one. There were others who held the same power. While this type of experience is foreign to Anglos, who often express doubt, Navajos share many stories of this miraculous event performed by those who know the ritual. John Holiday was such a man who shares his first experience as a boy learning to summon the assistance of the holy people.

One afternoon three men—Skinny Yucca Fruit [Clan] (Tsá Ászi' Áłtsózí Bineest'ą'), Blackwater's Son (Tółizhiní Biye'), and Son of the Start of the Red Streak People [Clan] (Deeshchiinii Biye') traveled to our house on horseback. "They are riding this way. I wonder what they want," I thought. There was no vegetation, so the people had to take their livestock to find food. My father's horses were down in the washes along the San Juan River where there were spots of green grass left from the river's moisture. Father also brought his horses plenty of grain to supplement their food. The three men came inside and sat down. "We need your help," they told him. "About six nights ago, a medicine man named Black Hair Who Laughs (Bitsii'łizhin Yiidlohí) began a rain ceremony that lasted for several days, but nothing happened. He had boasted that he was the best 'rainmaker' around, but there is no moisture. His ceremony did not work, we have no rain, the clouds have gone, and it has only gotten worse. Can you make it rain? We had crystal gazing done, as well as having a hand trembler perform his sacred ritual. The crystal gazer saw a 'long white streak' come down in the area of your home and the hand trembler 'pointed' toward your place. 'What is over there? Why does it [the power] see over there? Why don't you three men investigate.' That is why we came here," they said.

My father gestured by pointing his lips towards Metal Teeth. The men turned to him. "Help us. Please help us, grandfather. It hasn't rained and we are suffering and cannot take any more. Please sing for the rain. Our horses, sheep, all our livestock are starving and dying. Even the juniper trees are turning brown. We are tired of chopping down trees for them to eat." Grandfather sat and thought. The men gave him a payment of a string of turquoise beads and other valuable items. I was getting anxious because I wanted to watch him perform this ceremony and was happy about the prospect. "I will observe this and sing for rain too, like he does," I thought. Grandfather told them, "Okay. We'll be over in a couple days," and the three men left on their horses.

"Here we go, here we go," said Metal Teeth. "This is your chance, a good opportunity to do a ceremony, grandson! There is a first time for everything. Go heat up the sweat lodge; we have two days before we leave to do the rain ceremony. We shall take a sacred sweat bath and you will learn how to do what the men requested. You will learn all day and tonight, then tomorrow; we will repeat the sweat bath and rehearse the rain songs and That Which Is Taken from Underwater songs (Táłtł'ááh sin), then perform them.[6] Your 'name' is 'water' and the holy beings have already approved for you to do it. I will be there by your side while you are performing the ceremony. You already know the duties and how to do things like the sacred corn pollen ritual and the separation and offering of the ntł'iz (sacred crushed stones). You know how to do this." I did because I had assisted him with those procedures during his ceremonies, but I was only twelve years old. "You will perform the rain ceremony, my paternal grandson. The rain is not far away; it exists right here on the tips of all the bushes and trees."

Following his request, I built the fire at the sweat hogan and we took a bath. He gave me a piece of herb to chew as I performed the sweat. Before long, I began spitting up deep orange bubbles that looked like soap suds. He had me chew some of this plant several times, because it had something to do with the sacred songs and prayers that I would soon be performing. This herb was used only while learning and preparing for the ceremony. The second day and night was more of the same, then the following morning we got ready to go. We rode our horses to the Oljato Trading Post where we bought two large bags of grain, tied them to our saddles, and headed east. As we traveled, we sang the songs, passing Train Rock, going over the red sand flats to the northwest to Among the Short Junipers and Owl Spring, then Coyote Mesa Flats, and onto the southern base of Douglas Mesa where the rain ceremony was to be held. Grandfather and I continually rehearsed.

As we reached the top of the hill overlooking Mister Red House's (Hastiin Kinłichiinii) home, we saw a group of men working on the big summer shelter in which the ceremony would take place. Another large structure stood beside it where people prepared food and ate. There were many, many visitors—too many—and wagons and horses. The news had gotten around, with travelers coming from Black Mesa, Teec Nos Pos, Lukachukai, and other distant areas. Some had come in the wagon-that-runs-fast. The people had already butchered some sheep while a blanket of grill smoke came from the cooking shelter.

When we rode to the men building the large structure, we saw that one of the men was Black Hair Who Laughs, the man who had tried to sing for rain but failed. We noticed that he was putting the trees for the shelter upside down.[7] They are supposed to be with growing end toward the ground. "No, no, take them all out and set them up right. They grow upwards!" said grandfather. "We are going to sing for rain and those trees are to sit upwards to grow! Black Hair Who Laughs probably did his ceremonies like that so it is no wonder his rain song failed to work," Metal Teeth scolded him. Grandfather must have been a great man to have gotten after a medicine man who was knowledgeable. If he saw something being done incorrectly, he corrected it. He was just that way.

We brought our medicine bags inside the ceremonial place. There was a young boy and girl sitting inside, who would serve as the rain boy and rain girl. "These two will accommodate you in singing and praying for the rain," I was told. I was just as young as they were and was quite nervous. It was a critical time with all eyes upon me, especially those of the knowledgeable medicine men who had come to observe and take part in the activity. I was led to my seat against the wall of the hogan and my grandfather sat down beside me. I was scared!

The ceremony began. We performed the prayer and rituals and the next day, at dawn, everyone took a sweat bath. There were two sweat lodges—one for the women and another for the men. In the men's sweat lodge, the medicine men and the people who sat in as the patients were the first group to go inside. For this ritual, men hauled barrels of water by wagon from Water in Both Directions near Douglas Mesa. Water from Owl Spring and Salty Water Spring filled a dugout nearby. Both of these sources produced quite a bit of water.

We crawled inside the hot sweat hogan and sat down. Then out of nowhere, we heard a frog croaking. "Shine the light inside, open the blanket door. Let's see where it's coming from! These are the sounds of the female rain girl (Níłtsą at'ééd) and the male rain boy (Níłtsą ashkii). There they are, sitting side by side in the furthest corner of the hogan. Catch them and throw them in the puddle outside!" they said. The men caught the two frogs and threw them in the puddle. The poor little frogs were taking a sweat bath too, but were removed and thrown in the water with a splash! We continued our sweat while the frogs croaked in the puddle.

After the ceremony, I went to the water to wash and did the sacred wash ritual on the young boy and girl. There is actually no particular patient or client, just the two children who assisted, female rain girl and male rain boy. After the bath, everyone covered themselves with ground corn powder and spread a large blanket outside for the offerings of ntł'iz. This is the part of the ritual when the little stone offerings are selected and put together to take to a sacred spot, prayed over, and left. Before we went with these offerings, there was a request made by the men who came from faraway places. They wanted to take some of these sacred stones with them to their homes because it was not raining there, too. They also suggested, "We'll walk and take these offerings to all the water wells in different places around here." Grandfather said, "No, I don't do it like that. I place all the sacred stones in one place only." We took them to one little spot near the mesa where there was a small oasis of water. I said the prayers as we laid down the offerings, speaking to the four sacred directions of the earth. While I was doing this, there was a sound of thunder, then another, but there was not a cloud in the sky and it was very hot. Suddenly a cloud began to form above us, and just as I finished the prayers, it started to rain! The clouds poured forth buckets of water. It was a long way back to the homestead, so our homemade moccasins became soaking wet. Streams of water were everywhere, going in every direction. Once we arrived home, we did the one-night Blessingway. It rained so hard that it snowed, covering the sand dunes with a thick blanket of white moisture. Ribbons of water flowed among the sand dunes as it rained and rained for four days, proving our sacred songs and prayers a success. It was holy.[8]

A Potpourri of Traditional Practices

Every stage of life in Navajo culture—from a baby's birth to its first cry and from reaching puberty to death—has accompanying teachings, rituals, songs, prayers, and changes in status that alert people to an individual's current position. They are the core beliefs and practices that give Navajo culture its distinctive nature. The status of a family rested, in part, on the number and type of customs it enforced. If the parents were sloppy and let their youth act with abandonment, both may be considered unwise, not to be respected, and in the case of youth, less desirable for marriage and the creation of future generations. Evaluation could be based on how parents and grandparents raised children, the care a family took of its livestock, medicine practices and traditional knowledge, the clothing and jewelry within the family, and how they treated other people. At the root of it all, however, was the community's perception of traditional daily practices. Those raised appropriately understood what was expected of them and how they respected the holy people. Thus, from birth to childhood to adulthood every life stage had its instruction, resulting in proper behavior. For those interested in each of these events, see *Traditional Navajo Teachings: A Trilogy.*[9] Tully Bigman expands upon and summarizes a number of these teachings that have already been mentioned. He came from a family who took them seriously, extending an honored heritage for generations in the valley. Although not always fun or easy, he never complained about this training or felt disadvantaged but rather respected those who raised him in such an environment.

My mother was a weaver who made big rugs. My sisters carded and spun the wool, which allowed her to finish the rugs quickly. Usually, she would weave two blankets or rugs, but occasionally three, in a single month before selling them at a trading post. This was how she brought food home to us—flour, baking powder, salt, coffee, sugar, as well as the things we wore—pants, shirts, shoes, and socks. In this way our mother and father took care of us as we grew up.

They had their expectations of us as their children. In the spring we helped plant the fields of corn and other vegetables. We all worked hard while Father dug irrigation ditches for the water to enter into our garden, even before we planted so that the soil would be soft and moist. That was why we grew tall corn stalks and had good harvests.

We never slept late but got up at first light to run long distances through the desert. In the winter, sometimes we would have to plunge into ice cold water after a run before arriving home. It was unbearable. My skin felt like it was grabbed all over and it seemed like I could not make it back to the hogan. It took sheer guts to finish, but this was to make us strong through and through and to harden us against different elements that may prove a barrier in the path of life. At that time there was no saying such as "they caught a cold from the weather," no matter how frigid the weather was. As a matter of fact, the people usually took sweat baths before jumping into the ice cold water or rolled in the snow and then rubbed it on their bodies. There was not much illness going around and nothing wrong with our bodies. Even the older men washed themselves in the snow. Now, if someone begins to perspire inside a room and then goes outside, a cold enters into their body and they become sick.

Today's young children catch colds easily, but I think in the past it was not like that.

Another thing that kept sickness away was eating horsemeat in the winter. Horses were not killed any time of the year, only when it was really cold. We hunted for wild horses that we had to sneak up on and shoot. In the evening, the men brought back the meat and distributed it among the relatives. Sickness, like colds, did not bother us after eating this food. A horse's fat is not hard, melting easily. When one loses their voice because of a cold, eating horse meat brings it back. It was medicine that healed winter sicknesses. Mules and burros were also eaten as medicine, whereas cattle could be killed at any time and did not have healing power like these other animals.

There were other things that we did to maintain health and strength. Carrying heavy logs made us physically strong as did chopping wood. Hoeing weeds and digging ditches, carrying water, and hunting were all forms of exercise that built us. We became disciplined and learned to do these chores without being told. Taking care of cattle and horses was another responsibility. Every day we brought in the horses even though we were not going anywhere, and the boys roped them. The bigger boys had this as their job and so we watched to learn how it was done, as dust flew all over the place. Some rode untamed horses bareback, even when others said it was impossible. The rider would get on, helpers would let the horse go, and if the boy was not bucked off, he rode until he got tired, then dismounted. We all enjoyed this. Time went by quickly so that it soon seemed the sun was setting. It was in this way we were raised.[10]

George Tom shared other ways children learned and prepared for life. He recalled:

My paternal grandmother, Red Woman (Asdzą́ą́ Łichíí), was a great teacher. She would hold a fire poker in her hand as she lectured, gathering us children—and there were many of us—in one place to teach about our character and attitudes. She'd say, "When you herd sheep, don't look at each other, but go on either side of the flock and take care of them." All the while she would be tapping the stick or a whip in the ground in front of where we sat. "If you don't listen, I will whip you. When you use a whip on a horse, he becomes swift. It is just the same if I use it on you for a good reason. You will become swift, too. I will whip without hate, but with love, for I want you to have a decent life. Someday, if you ever find a wife, you will protect her. If you do not have good values, you will

Hair was an important concern. It not only served as an outward sign of being well kept, but also was believed to hold one's thoughts, was connected to rain, and allowed the holy people to recognize an individual as Navajo. Happy Cly uses a traditional hairbrush (bé'ézhóó) made of desert grass to comb her husband Willie's hair. (Courtesy Carolyn Davis, obtained from Goulding's Trading Post and Lodge)

run off on her, then get another woman, but she will be worse off than the first one. Pretty soon, you will be homeless, with no place to go and people will make fun of you, saying, 'He is so-and-so's son.'"

She gave other teachings about hard work. "Livestock is life. It will not change. Your hair will turn gray, but these animals will continue to support you for life." Believing her words, we did what we were told. We took care of the livestock. "Don't be lazy. Don't sit flat on your butt while you're eating. Sit up on your haunches! A woman you will marry for one time only. Do not look elsewhere, for it will kill you if you do. Hold fast to your hoe and axe. They are the tools for the cornfield and firewood. Keep your eyes on the sheep. Keep a close watch from all sides, for that is the best way. People will argue with one another. Do not take part. Leave it alone."

Red Woman continued. "The same will happen to a woman. She should hold fast to the sacred grinding stones, to weaving rugs, to spinning wool, and performing other chores and responsibilities. Whatever valuable possessions you gain, you will not destroy, if you live the right way." She predicted that in less than one hundred years people would intermarry, thus doing away with our people and causing everything to go insane. She explained, "They will be killing each other, there will be starvation and cannibalism, and parents will eat their own children." This is what my grandmother told us. She lectured like a man and was a great woman.

Traditionally, all men and women are to dress in their own respective ways. I found out that it did not matter where a person went, the teachings were all the same about clothing. It is all based on modesty and respect. It bothers me how today young people wear unusual and strange attire. For women, a velveteen blouse with silver buttons is very appropriate because it signifies her beauty and identity. Our society has now fallen short of this important tradition. Women are not to wear pants or they will develop sores on their bodies. We were not to trade clothes with the opposite sex or else we would lose our identity. You can no longer tell the difference between males and females if they are both wearing pants and walking away from you. It is confusing; someday they will realize the truth.

We were also forbidden to cut our hair because the holy people recognized us by it. If we were to cut off our protective shield of hair, they would not hesitate to hurt us. Both men and women have a right to wear their hair in a knot, which has been a sacred law since creation, but we have outgrown this law. When it is hung down, it signified death. We used to wear juniper beads around our necks to scare off hunger, thirst, sickness, and fear. This is what they believed in those days. People also used to hang their stirring sticks or a bow and arrows above the door for the same reason—to keep evil away. Our people observed many traditions back then, but time has changed all of that. I have come to realize what our forefathers meant as I look around me these days.[11]

Marriage and the family are important institutions in Navajo culture. In the past, a woman, once she had her puberty ceremony (kinaaldá), which was ideally held after her first menses, could be married to a man who might be quite her senior. Girls thirteen or fourteen years old may soon be tending a house and children at a much younger age than is expected in today's society. The intense instruction she received as a young girl was then put to use as a housemaker. This chapter concludes with a brief description of a traditional wedding ceremony that starts a new family. Jesse Black, longtime resident of Monument Valley, provides a good description.

I followed the people's way of marrying a woman, which is called Ídíkid. This was performed differently at that time. Ídíkid was done by the mother and father of the young man who was going to be married. They would travel to the home of the prospective bride, where they would ask for the woman's hand in marriage. Even though her family may not know the man's family, there may be an agreement based upon accepted terms and proper payment. In my case, we took three cows and five horses to her home on the day of the wedding. By doing this, we respected each other in this matter. These gifts are called "yigeeh." Her home became the place we lived after our marriage. It was about seven miles from where I grew up. Some of her people rode their horses to where several men and women from my family were herding the livestock. Her family members chased off the horses and cattle far and wide. This was called kii'dinoolkal, which happened when a man and woman were married for the first time, and the relatives accompany the groom.

When we reached my wife's camp, there was a hogan set aside for us. I unsaddled my horse and she took my saddle blankets, saddle, and bridle and placed them on a blanket. This was in the hogan where the wedding was to take place. The ceremony began once the sun was down and all of the participants had arrived. My party announced that we were entering. It was dark and silent outside while inside, all was quiet so that both groups could talk. Her family brought in the ceremonial basket filled with corn mush. I sat in the middle of the west side of the room with many people seated on either side of me. My wife set the corn mush down, took her seat, and then her parents and relatives came in, bringing a woven water jug coated in pitch along with a gourd made into a cup. We then poured water on each other's hands, four times, as we washed and prepared to eat. Before doing so, pollen was placed on the mush in the form of a cross, representing the four directions, first from east to west, then south to north. The bride first took mush from the east side of the basket and fed it to me, and then I drank some water. I did the same for her. This was repeated, taking mush from the south side, then water; the west side, then water; the north side, then water; then the middle. This procedure is called ihaa'it'aash. Others present were now able to eat some of the mush.

A lot of food was brought inside as well. There were also small packages, containing meat and bread, which were given to those on the groom's side who drove the horses to the camp as well as the women on his side. Following, we as a couple were lectured by members of both families, who explained the importance of marriage and how to live a good life. I was told that as a man, I was to haul water and firewood, take care of my wife and children, provide food, not let people go hungry, and raise my offspring to be good. This was what I was told. Then my wife was directed as to what her responsibilities in this marriage were and about life, in general. All the things that were taught to me when I was young were talked about again.

At the end of the ceremony, the older men said that "at the crack of dawn, people will be sleeping, but do not let the woman get up before you. Really be alert. You, as the man, should get up and go out first." This is how marrying is done. From that time forward, what the elders said, I have done.[12]

CHAPTER FIVE

Sickness, Ceremonies, and Healing

Inner Forms and the Essence of Life

To summarize Navajo religious beliefs and practices in a single chapter is challenging. There are hundreds of studies focused on various aspects of this intricate system of sacred knowledge that ranges from birth to death, from the tangible to the intangible worlds, and from the stars in the heavens to an ant on the ground. Whole books have been written about the single aspect of determining what is wrong with a patient. Here a brief introductory glimpse, provided by those specializing in healing, introduces the reader to major elements involved in diagnosing an illness, determining treatment, training a medicine person, defining different types of ceremonies, and examining the influenza epidemic of 1918. Ultimately, this overview helps an individual to understand how the entire Navajo universe is viewed through spiritual eyes.

Interacting with Inner Forms—An Illustration

At the time of the creation of the world, the holy people met in council to determine the nature, responsibilities, and powers that everything both tangible and intangible on this earth would have. All was first created spiritually, and so before becoming a physical entity, most things received a sacred name, prayers, songs, and powers unique to their role and personality. This beginning spiritual essence, known as "The Inner Form That Stands Within" (Bii'yistiin), connects with other spiritual forces that guide and direct, responds to holy words and actions, and controls sickness and healing. An animal, for instance, is said to have a spirit that, if the outer form of that creature were discarded, would look like a human being. It can think, talk, and react just as a man or woman would. In its present physical state, the inner being is limited by the role it has been given in earth life.[1]

Navajo Oshley, who spent much of his time in the Monument Valley area, told of an instance in the 1930s when he was herding sheep on the Abajo or Blue Mountain in southeastern Utah. His camp was near a cluster of berry bushes that attracted bears and encouraged them to snoop around and take freshly butchered meat that he had hung in a tree. Perturbed, Oshley

> told the bears not to eat on this side of the mountain, and they listened to what I said to them. They stayed where I told them they could. Now I am not frightened of bears. I just tell them to leave me alone, and they do. My maternal grandmother told me that if a bear blocks my way and does not move, that I should take my shoes off and throw them to the bear and that would get it to move. A couple days later this happened. I asked him, as I took off my shoe, what he was doing in my path. Then I told him that here was my shoe, and the bear took off into the bushes. . . . About two days later, when I was still quite a distance from my campsite, I saw the bear where I usually hung my food. I shot, it growled at me, but I missed him. I thought about what had happened that day before I went to sleep. In my dream, a tall man with a bushy mustache came to me. He asked why I was shooting at him, and I told him he had brought it upon himself, so he walked off without saying anything. . . . The next morning, I offered the bear corn pollen. I called him grandfather and told him I was thankful that he was talking nicely to me. I told him from then on, I would not shoot again. I had already said I would not harm them, and I kept my word, even though at times they got very close.[2]

Relationships (k'é) between people and the things of nature are real and comparable.

Oshley's experience illustrates that whether involved in daily activities or a sacred ceremony, one is interacting every hour of every day with some spiritual entity on various levels. Crossing a river, riding a horse, chopping wood, building a fire, planting crops, herding sheep, weaving a blanket, eating food—the list is endless—there is a relationship. This "two-way street" can be both beneficial but also harmful, depending on the words and actions of those involved. When something or someone becomes offended, steps need to be taken to correct the wrong. Perhaps a snake has been offended or an expected offering was not made at a particular place.

Maybe someone said certain things during the wrong season of the year or deer antlers were brought into a home. Now that person is sick but not entirely sure what caused it. Little is random in the Navajo universe; everything happens for a reason, which can be determined through divination. Just as in Western medicine, a patient starts with a general practitioner (in Navajo beliefs a diviner), who then directs that person to a specialist (medicine person who performs a particular ceremony) to be cured.[3]

The Power of Hand Trembling

There are three major types of divination—wind listening (íísts'ą́ą́'); star gazing (sǫ'nél'į́) with its subsidiaries sun and moon gazing and their affiliate crystal gazing (déést'į́į́'—literally, to see, understand); and hand trembling or motion-in-the-hand (ndishniih)—all of which are related in that they are spiritually based and serve similar functions. The origin story of hand trembling is different from star gazing and listening, while generally, women may render the former but not the latter. These practices are used to explore the unknown, to find lost people or objects, to identify a thief or witch, to locate water or other desirable resources, to prevent danger or evil, and most importantly, to diagnose the cause of an illness in order to provide a remedy.[4] Each type of divination has its own way of informing the receiver on behalf of the patient. The most common experience is sensing impressions or viewing something that serves as a key, the messages in both instances having to be interpreted. These answers are filtered through the experience of the diviner according to what the spirit is indicating.

Unlike medicine men who heal through chantway ceremonies lasting from one to nine days or nights and who have spent hundreds of hours to learn their accompanying prayers, songs, and rituals, the diagnostician spends perhaps only a few hours learning the rite, composes some of his or her own songs and prayers, and requires little ceremonial equipment. Chantways are normally performed by men who have a sacred body of lore based on complex mythology, whereas diviners may be either male or female (often after menopause) who received this gift at birth and have had its potential later revealed to them.[5] The holy people play an important part in identifying future practitioners. For instance, a holder of this power may realize his or her ability during a ceremony when its latent force is activated or they may seek assistance to determine if they have this particular spiritual ability, as in the case of Navajo Oshley, who here shares his first experience.

My mother had sisters, and one was very good at it [hand trembling]. I asked her if I could be her apprentice, but she said no because it was a very powerful thing to have. I said if it is so powerful, why am I not allowed to learn it? So later, when there was a sick man, she started teaching me. This is the only time such learning is permitted. She lightly clapped her hand over mine, urging it to move. Then it happened. My hand went out, and that is how I learned hand trembling. The man was suffering from Evilway. It felt like feathers were standing, and that has to do with Evilway. She said, "Yes, that is the one," as the hand trembling signaled the problem that ailed the man. She said, "You will lead your life this way. People will want help from you. My son, this hand trembling is not for you to get rich on. Only a few dollars are the reward for your service. Maybe from one person you might get a sheep in exchange for your service, while another man might give you very little. So, my son, through this you do not get wealthy."

When a person's hand begins to tremble, a chant is started for that person, and then another. My hand trembling comes to me when I hold out my hand. It just starts; that is all. Sometimes I hadn't even started the chant when my hand would go out at it. I used to get strong signals from hand trembling, but now they do not come as clearly. Maybe my aging has to do with the decline in receiving the signals; I do not know what is causing it. You have to have good thinking called *hóyéé'* [deep reverential respect bordering on fear] in order to get the signals. If hand trembling turns against you, it is also called *hóyéé'*. My aunt said if hand trembling turned against you, you would punish yourself by ripping yourself apart. I said I would not allow this to happen to me. I did not believe at the time, but my aunt said that was how it was. She said that when a person is hand trembling, he might poke himself in the eye or in the nose. I said a person should move his head this way or that way. My aunt asked me in a disappointed voice what I was saying. She wanted me to stop talking in this way. It took a lot of convincing to have her teach me hand trembling. She was trying to tell me that she was giving me something very holy and that it cannot be passed on just for the sake of giving it. It must be held with wisdom and respect. Holiness is sacred and comes with prayers and chants. So the main thing is to make a bridge across from daily life to the sacred and receive the signals and interpret them as *hóyéé'*.

One time I was hand trembling in Dennehotso when the power told me I was an idiot and twisted my nose. The patient was very sick with a swollen stomach due to Evilway. It was easy to interpret the signal, but I didn't. Therefore, the power told me I was a fool and asked why I had a big nose and looked like an ogre. I tried to dodge it, but it twisted my nose and almost ripped it off. I thought of a burial site, and it told me that was right. If I hadn't gotten the interpretation correct, I would probably have no nose now. One person who was watching me asked why I did that, and I replied, "My hand did it." Woman Who Owns the House said, "See what I told you. You almost ripped your nose off."

Songs accompany hand trembling. For me just a few short ones, but other individuals have long chants that go with it. When a person's hand begins to tremble, a chant is started for that person, then another. My hand trembling comes to me when I hold out my hand. It starts; that is all. Sometimes I have not even started the chant before my hand goes at it.[6]

Hands Off—Susie Yazzie

As Oshley points out, the gift of divination is accompanied by strong powers and responsibilities that reach far beyond just the desire of an individual to foresee the future or past. It is tied to the greater spiritual realm beyond a person's control. What if someone does not wish to accept this ability, even though they may have it latent within? Susie Yazzie shares her experience as a young girl growing up in Monument Valley, when she first learned of its presence but did not desire to use it.

I had some strange experiences as a child, seeing or imagining things like a vision. I used to see lights [evil powers] at night. Traditionally, if this happens to a person, they have to have a sing or ceremony performed for them. I did. It was during one of these episodes that I experienced "hand trembling" for the first time at the age of thirteen. I was asked, "How can you use this special gift to the best of your ability?" Then a medicine man did a prayer for me, and sure enough my hand began trembling. I had a vision and was told to interpret the meaning of what I saw. When I started to hand tremble, I first felt a huge stream of air, which narrowed down to a thin line as it entered my arm. This scared me. I felt it raise my body. My hand started trembling. I could hear the others telling me I had received the sacred power and urging me to concentrate on the vision I had received, to think about what I had seen. In this vision I saw my mother and me herding sheep, when out of nowhere a man appeared, riding his horse past us and on to the top of a hill, where he vanished. He had left no tracks when we went to look for them. In the meantime, this

Grandmother Cly, sitting with grandchildren outside the doorway of her hogan, is a portrait of serenity. Different forms of divination have directed her to the ceremonies she needed to remain strong and spiritually in-tune with the holy people, maintaining the goal of peace and harmony (hózhǫ́) within her surroundings. (Courtesy Special Collections, J. Willard Marriott Library, University of Utah)

strange force in me had driven my body toward where my mother sat. It literally threw me around all over the place, dragging me from the wall to the center of the hogan to the door, where she was watching. If I had been working with this gift correctly, I would have "thought for it" and controlled my thinking by seeking answers through it. The force was very strong and rough on my body, nearly making me sick—both emotionally and physically. According to what I thought, it was clear that someone was trying to kill her through a horse she was riding. At this point, my mother had been divorced from my father for some time. Feelings told me that the man in my vision was someone from my father's relative's side. I knew that as long as I guessed or got the answers to my vision, it would not happen. I continued to have these hand trembling experiences. They affected my heart in a strange way and made my mind whirl as if I was dizzy. I was too young to really understand what was happening, so it frightened me. Sometimes you will end up uncontrollably striking yourself as this stream of power passes through your body, making you feel like you are going up and down, with your heart racing, seeming to enlarge it, and moving the body about to a point where it weakens you.

Everyone encouraged me to build on these sensations and increase this strange power, but I did not want to. Sometimes when I began hand trembling, I slapped myself, or the power dragged me around. It weakened my heart and I felt numb and hollow on one side of my body. This happened off and on for two years. My mother wanted me to have a special ceremony so that I could keep the power and use it like medicine people do, but I did not want to. It made my heart hurt and scared me, especially when I was alone. Although I do not do hand trembling anymore, I still have the mental or psychic power. I seem to be able to foretell future events or figure out problems. My mind is capable of answering complicated questions. I have changed my religious beliefs to Christianity, but I still have it. Voices tell me to do this and that, to pray or act according to what I think. It still works the same way. I found out these things through my hand trembling experiences. That is how it is.

We used to hold different sings and ceremonies for our family's sicknesses. I met my husband, Fred, when I had a "crystal gazing" done for my sick son. Fred was helping another medicine man, Jack Gillis, with the ceremony. While they were doing the crystal gazing, they went outside the hogan to perform part of the ritual while I stayed inside and held my son on my lap. The men saw a bright light surround us and a black shadow in the form of a porcupine, which kept coming close to us. Still, they could not figure out what it was. They also saw lights that indicated that we should stay south of them, since all of the north side of this vision was dark. Mr. Gillis pictured a great white object sitting in the distance, which he felt meant something good awaits us in the near future. Just five months later my husband and I were involved with a movie outfit from Hollywood that really helped us. We lived on that site for six years, taking care of their equipment and things. It seemed impossible that such wonderful things would happen, but they did. These crystal gazing ceremonies helped us to see what lay ahead, and that is why people use them and hand trembling a lot.

It is said that tiny whirlwinds come down from the sun and carry "messages" to the earth, just like radio signals do. These messengers are still about on the earth and are called nílch'ih diyinii (holy wind), and they are the ones who guide the people. This same holiness is used in the hand trembling ceremony. It works for some, but not for others. The nílch'ih are here on this earth with us now. They are often given to those who are mature in their beliefs and who may be naturally gifted. It is a strange experience, one of anxiety, as if you are in fear of something and trying to run from it but cannot find a safe place. It feels like you levitate off the ground, becoming emotionally tired and strained. It is like remembering something of your childhood that you become very emotional about. Perhaps it is a song or place. Because I was afraid of this power, I told the medicine man, Mister Rock Ridge (Hastiin Tsé Dahsitání), to take the special gift away from me for good. He tapped corn pollen on the soles of my feet and the palms of my hands, the top of my head, then all over my body. That was the end of it. Hand trembling never happened to me again. Before that though, I used to get ill from it, even when I tried to throw a stick at the sheep. It automatically started, and I would get scared because I just did not want to use it. The actual hand trembling stopped, but the "questioning" or the thoughts remained with me for quite some time afterward. It did not leave right away. The meditation was still present and questioned me, or I would question things; it seemed to tell me what was good to do and what was not. The mental state of mind persisted. If I were to dwell on that feeling, it would be possible to regain my hand trembling power, but I kept myself from it, so it never came back. I sometimes think to myself, "It is probably because I gave up that special gift that I am suffering from so many health problems today."[7]

Causes for illness can range from those that are purely physical to those that are totally intangible. The sickness is a manifestation of something

Once the cause of an illness has been determined, the nature of the sickness is understood and a ceremony is prescribed that returns the patient to a state of health. There are dozens of chantways used for specific cures, some lasting up to nine days or nights. Many of them require sandpaintings that picture events, symbols, and holy people found in Navajo traditional teachings. (Courtesy Special Collections, J. Willard Marriott Library, University of Utah)

that is spiritually wrong and needs to be corrected. Even when the problem appears to be caused by something unrelated to the unseen realms, there is still a component that calls upon help from the holy people. A broken bone, medicine for fevers, or a lung disease still evokes a spiritual response in addition to the physical aid rendered by setting the fracture, selecting the correct herbs, or relieving congestion. Whereas Western medicine deals with the visible symptoms, Navajo medicine is holistic and depends on both tangible and intangible powers. They classify an illness and its cure based on its perceived cause. There are six major groupings with as few as three different ceremonies and one with as many as twenty-nine ceremonies when including variations. Each is distinct in its origin, performance, paraphernalia, songs, prayers, holy people, and cure. The major groupings are Blessingway, Holyway, Lifeway, Evilway, War Ceremonies, and Gameway—many of which are now extinct.[8] Some rituals last only one day or night, while others may require up to nine days or nights; some utilize no sandpaintings, others require many; and some enlist a group of assistants while others may only use a single medicine man. All call upon the holy people with their specialized powers to heal.

The Making of a Medicine Man and First Performance—John Holiday

John Holiday (1919–2016) lived his entire life in Monument Valley and by the end of it was the most prominent medicine man in that community. Although he had a wide range of work experiences, he spent much of his time healing people through ceremonies and was well known for his success. But it had not always been that way. As a boy he worked hard to absorb all that he could from various teachers, one of the most prominent being his grandfather, Metal Teeth. This mentor was exacting in his passing along knowledge, but he also was not averse to putting his student on the spot to see how he would rise to an occasion. John shares what it was like as a young boy to be under the stern tutelage of his grandfather and the concern he felt when Metal Teeth committed him to performing his first ceremony. From this insider perspective, one learns of the tremendous effort and personal motivation it takes to become a healer of the People.

> I was nine and a half years old when my paternal grandfather, Metal Teeth, moved to the Monument Valley area. As I grew older, he taught me his songs and prayers that I still use to this day; they have become

my means for making a living and helping others. I was seven years old when my father first wanted me to become a medicine man and asked Grandfather to be my teacher. He wanted me to learn Grandfather's sacred prayers and songs and I did. Father could not learn even one song or prayer my grandfather taught me. He tried, but could not do it! The sacred songs have a certain order that must be maintained while singing. My father tried singing just one song, but he would lose his way.

At one point, he took off his beads of coral and turquoise and gave them to Grandfather. "Here, my uncle and brother, you can have this. They are yours so that you will teach my son to learn the sacred songs and prayers. I can't seem to catch on." Father knew some songs and did some ceremonies, but he learned them from his father, Aching Stomach [Tom Holiday]. Since he had a different teacher, it was impossible to relearn them from another person for a second time. When a person gets used to singing one way, it is hard to change, and that was his problem. So Father paid for my learning with his beads and I sang the sacred songs, once, twice, three, four times. The song my father tried to sing, I finished all the way to the end. Grandfather told me, "That's very good. You will continue to sing it over and over and pretty soon it will all fall into place. It will become easier." That was many years ago, when I was only twelve. As soon as my lessons were paid for with the beads, I went to my grandfather's home every night. Metal Teeth, at times, lived near my father, so I herded the sheep in the corral for the night, then headed for his home to ask questions. "How does this song go? What about protection songs, Blessingway songs (Hózhǫ́ǫ́jí), and the sacred prayers?" We would go over and over them late into the night. I could not sleep because it was all I thought about. "I'm going to learn all these sacred songs and prayers, then become a medicine man," I promised myself. The next morning, I would take the sheep to pasture but stayed nearby so that I would have time to make it to Grandfather's home in Oljato before dark. I even made a shortcut over the mesa to get there.

When a ceremony was being performed, I put the sheep in the corral and quickly went to attend because I enjoyed singing with the medicine man and his group. I attended all of Grandfather's ceremonies, no matter where they were, and remained up all night singing. The next morning, I sang the songs as I walked home. I'm sure some of those songs were very sacred and should not have been repeated just anywhere, but I sang them anyway. Once I had gotten the sheep, it was back to herding all day long, but I would ride my horse or climb the hills singing the songs from the night before. I sang so loud, it sounded like I was performing at a Squaw

Dance. I forced out my extra energy and breath, which was a good way to build my voice and learn.

If I had to stay for five or six days to learn something I would ask my older sister or some of the boys to watch the sheep. Old Metal Teeth would ask me to prepare the sweat hogan and build the fire. "We'll spend the whole day there, while we talk," he would say. After these preparations, we spent the entire time talking about many sacred things of the world, including teachings about the mountains, their names, songs, and prayers. Their sacredness included the mountain water, darkness, dawn, sunset, night, and all there is to learn until the end of the songs and prayers. Then we would go into the heavens with its names, songs, and prayers, identifying all the stars. I asked Grandfather about all of the heavenly bodies, then we returned to the earthly "legends"—what prayers to use, what words to say for protection purposes, the events that took place among the holy beings, and what had been passed to the Diné from these events. Grandfather taught as we consumed our time in the sweat hogan. It is from these songs and prayers that I heal sick men, women, young people, and children, as well as livestock. It seems like I have done a sing or ceremony for just about everyone within the four sacred mountains.

One fall day, five of us boys left with my grandfather to do a series of ceremonies as we learned the ways of a medicine man. By spring, we had completed our special trip and were headed back home. That is how I learned—by following my grandfather around and assisting him with everything. Once home, a person came to our place, bringing news of a six-year-old boy, Willie Holiday, who had fallen off a cliff while trying to find some goats that had wandered out of a corral. Hite Chee also had his goats down there, so someone from his place found the boy lying below the ledge. He had been motionless for quite some time and people thought he might be dead, so they had covered him with a blanket and shirt and sent for Grandfather. "Please help us and do a ceremony for him, even if it seems hopeless." He accepted. We went together, but Grandfather asked me to conduct it. "As a medicine man, you will encounter such challenges, so you might as well start here with these special songs and prayers called An Aid to Cross Over (Beebideeshadeeda [ʔ])." I performed the ceremony and after I said several prayers and songs, the boy began twitching and moving around, then sat upright, threw his blanket off, and looked around. We laid him back down and carried him home in the blanket. He had a number of serious injuries and a broken jaw. When we reached home, Grandfather instructed me to dig a yucca root and perform more healing. "Make sure you do everything thoroughly," he said. There was an extra set of special prayers recited after the sacred wash. For such occasions, this was a complete healing ceremony for the patient to mend the broken bones and flesh of the body. We now had a Blessingway ceremony, which many people attended. Some knowledgeable men present who came to observe and participate were Hastiin Tsoh (Mister Big), Thin Goat (Tł'ízí Ts'ósí), Red Rock Springs (Tsélichíí'bii'tóonii), Mister Tall (Hastiin Nééz), Hoarse One (Bízhi'ádinii), and One Who Does Not Speak Up (Doo Yáłti'ii).

Thin Goat said, as he looked at me, "You mean he's performing the Blessingway?"

Grandfather countered, "Sure, he is. He's my boy."

"Impossible! How could anyone like him do a Blessingway?"

Later, when everyone was taking a break or had gone to the sweat lodge, Thin Goat returned and said, "You can't do this; you're not going to last long." His remarks were unpleasant.

"Well, I don't know. I don't even think about such unpleasant things when I do ceremonies," I said. "I'm doing this as a special request, and what you say is far from my mind."

"We'll see what happens!" he said.

"Okay, we'll see what happens," I replied. He went out the door and left for the hills, his mule's tail twisting this way and that. We continued with the ceremony and Willie Holiday is still with us today.

Grandfather taught me about the relationship between a patient with an ailment and the medicine man who performs the cure. With special offers of payment, the sick or injured person asks for help. The payment could be an earring, money, cow, horse, sheep, goat, mule, or something else of value, but it is a "special offering" to the medicine man for a particular illness, a transaction between the patient and healer from beginning to end. The exchange is treated as an important item and everything is performed accordingly. The medicine man requests the patient's "identity," asking such questions as: "Who are you? What is your name? How have your relatives identified you ever since you first fell to earth? What worthy things have you accomplished?" The name given by the patient will be used when the sacred healing prayer is said.[9] "So-and-so has this illness. He asks for help in healing his body. An offering has been made to you [holy being] and we ask for this healing."

The prayer is recited as the herbs are gathered and the corn pollen given with prayer. Every ritual is done like this. When there is a ceremony, an offering and prayers are made in a sacred place where lightning has struck.[10] For example, herbs and medicine plants are gathered with prayers for ceremonies in the Evilway. The medicine man prays to the herbs that the bad spirits of the dead will be removed from the body, piece by piece, from the soles of one's feet, to the midsection, to the chest, to the crown of the head. They are taken out of the body from the heart, to the organs, out to the tips of the fingers, feet, and head. The herbal drink removes all impurity from the body and heals the person. This is what the medicine man says in his prayers as he gathers wood from a lightning-struck tree and surrounding plants. This is how the sacred herbs are gathered for a specific person or special purpose and named in the request for healing. A medicine man needs to know how herbs are collected and if prayers are spoken when gathering them.

Ever since I can remember, I saw many wise elderly men and women serve as healers. They had knowledge of the old legends, sacred songs, and prayers, and they knew the stories of creation. They knew the stories about the underworld, the binding of life to this earth, and how the holy beings created the land and formed humans. Our ancestors had knowledge of all these teachings. They knew how to acquire livestock and care for it, how to plant corn and use it as their main source of food, and how to prepare the corn in a variety of ways. They had prayers and songs for all they did, they understood how to bless people and objects, and they knew how to become wealthy with jewelry and other riches. They knew much but hid their knowledge and died without sharing it. Some said they could not teach others and eventually died. Their life stories, from birth to old age, were never told. These elders never said much about their past so we will never know.[11]

Anatomy of a Ceremony—Perry Robinson

Perry Robinson, a current practitioner raised on Black Mesa, explains how medicine people understand ceremonial proceedings in general. While every ceremony follows a pattern that elucidates through physical actions and words the origin of the practice, powers addressed, curative elements employed, and protection from further harm, there are a wide variety of forms that all of this can take. Still there are core elements common to most. Here, Perry explains the primary pattern of a ceremony and how they open into a realm of spiritual power and healing.

As John Holiday points out, medicine men and interested individuals sometimes traveled long distances to observe and participate in different ceremonies. This group, riding through Monument Valley, is involved in the activities of an Enemyway (Anaa'jí) ceremony. (Courtesy Photo Archives, Utah State Historical Society)

One term used by medicine men to describe where a particular ceremony is located in relation to others is the word "sit," as in "it sits over there with this ceremony" but is "outside of" another. The reason for this is that a ceremony is viewed as being alive and interactive with the patient and person performing it. The ritual is put together in a spiritual way, but also has a body, with a skin or outer part, just as people have skin, but inside there is the muscle and meat, the blood stream and the nervous system. This is how it sits with the healing moment and that is how the medicine man sings about this as a whole, as a body, including mental illness such as depression and distress.

Sometimes a healer will have to bring in another ceremony to filter out competing symptoms and match the illness to the remedy. When speaking of this, one says that the additional ceremony "sits on the outside" of the main one. For instance, in the Evilway, the main focus of the primary ceremony is strengthened, not diminished, by having the secondary one added. When medicine men do this, they say, "Let's take this one and add this to it, and call it biza'a'nííł—medicine to the mouth. The sickness is one that is going to give in to medicine to the mouth." So the bowl is set on the outside of how the patient is sitting and on the outside of the sandpainting, and both will be given different herbs as part of the ritual. This is an example of how the sickness will be cured using more than one type of healing. The herbs are added on.

Take for instance, a person who has been in a very serious automobile accident. She has broken bones and fractures all over and so a ceremony is performed to deal with that aspect. But that is not all. She has also suffered traumatizing mental anguish and her fear is still there. This becomes compounded with frustration, so that even seemingly simple things become difficult and overwhelming. She just cannot let go. This is why the outside medicine sits on the outside, to add to the other ones, and in this case, to help with the mental trauma.

The image of working from the outside into the center or "heart" of the ceremony is important, because that is the way healing takes place. With the ceremony sitting there, the medicine man starts on the outside with the stories and teachings, then moves the actual ritual into the center, where the songs and prayers take him into the middle of pure holiness. By the third or fourth night, the healer enters the main, most important part of the ceremony, called in Navajo áłtséhígíí—entering the core of a ceremony. Whenever the medicine man sings that part, no one can go in or out during the performance. Everybody has to stay put until this is done and there can be no type of interference. The Holy Ones are right there participating at the core of everything. In the innermost part of that circle, all must be holy. There can be no moving about; children are not allowed—only adults; and there is no sleeping because if a person has a bad dream, it will ruin everything. This is the core of the circle, the central part of the sickness being healed, in a pattern as to how the sacredness of the medicine was set. On the outside of the illness sit the additives or tangential parts that also need to be cured like the accompanying depression. This may be done with the herbs already mentioned or with a smoke ceremony.

An example of working from the outside in is found in the Blessingway ceremony. First come songs about the hogan—The House of the Hogan Song—identifying where the ceremony is being held. That begins the sacredness of the outer layer. The doorway is blessed and then the singer sets up all the sacred mountains that sit upon the land; eventually the songs and prayers lead into the center of the ceremony with all of its holiness and magic. Once this is completed, there are other songs that return the patient to the outer edge and the everyday world. The morning dawn song may be added to make things better, and finally, the doors are opened and the ceremony ended. This is the standard form and thought for most Navajo rituals, especially the long ones.

Navajo people in general, and medicine men in particular, often provide offerings with their prayers and in ceremonies. There are four "sacred stones" (ntł'iz) composed of white shell, turquoise, abalone shell, and jet, that represent the four elements, colors, and holy people found in the four directions. These stones are crushed to a small size, mixed together, and used to bless a prayer or a place through an offering to the gods. Most prayers use ground corn and its pollen as another type of offering. In Navajo thought, almost everything in the universe is either male or female and these corn and corn pollen offerings are no exception. In a Blessingway song, when you say corn pollen, it belongs to the boy and the ground corn belongs to the girl. The word "tádídíín" (pollen) literally means "Sun shining on its son," thus recognizing the male aspect and separating it from the female yellow ground corn. White corn and white corn pollen is male, and the yellow corn with blue corn pollen (tádídíín dootł'izh) is female. They both work together but are never physically combined. The female side of the ground corn and pollen is considered the grower (aniłt'ání at'ééd) of the crop and of life in general. When saying a prayer in the morning, one uses white corn and faces the east; in the evening, one employs yellow ground corn and faces west. One might sing the song for the corn and then explain why he or she is standing there. This is a time of thanksgiving, of hope for the future, and of asking for assistance through prayer. The male part of an individual talks to White Corn Boy, who stands in the east. A second song, which identifies the individual singing, explains that he or she has half of a male person standing within who wishes to discuss their situation. The prayer is closed with white corn pollen. In the evening, when facing west, the petitioner says that there is a female part to him or her, even if it is a male person, and prays to Yellow Corn Girl, thanking her for the day, and asking to have a good night's sleep. Half of everyone comes from their mother's side, which is explained during both the morning and evening prayers. By using ground yellow corn and then blue corn pollen, the individual praying recognizes this male/female dichotomy within as he or she addresses the male and female deity. The white and blue pollen are never combined. They are two different things and are thought of as two separate individuals. You do not want to mix them up and get them fighting each other. Keep them separate because they have attitudes and want to be kept apart.[12]

The belief behind a sandpainting is that once it is completed and sprinkled with pollen, it is activated with the holy people present and the patient going back in time to the first healing event. Pictured here is the core (átsáleeh) of a ceremony as Talking God uses his power to effect a cure. (Illustration by Charles Yanito)

Symptoms, Sickness, and Shields

Traditional Navajos in the past were heavily involved in ceremonial activities, either for themselves or someone in their nuclear or extended family, or for neighbors and friends. Curing and preventing sickness was both time-consuming and expensive, but something of high importance. Teachings suggest that in the worlds beneath this one, the holy people recognized that there would be sickness that would afflict the People, and so they devised cures, assigning plants and ceremonial objects, songs and prayers, and ritual behavior to cure any malady. However, once Anglo culture became dominant, new types of sickness arose for which there was no cure—the gods had never encountered them before. The recent COVID-19 pandemic is a cogent example. Prior to this was the influenza epidemic of 1918, which was just as mysterious and destructive on the reservation. The disease and its effects became a milestone in Navajo oral tradition, people using it as a gauge or timeline for other occurrences—for instance, "two years before the great sickness struck . . ." or "five years after . . ." Historians today have measured this flu's effect on the Navajo people as best they can, although there are still a lot of questions as to the total amount of devastation.

The Spanish Influenza (Dikos ntsaa—Big Cough—pneumonia; or Sickness That Goes Around but Is Unknown [naałniih—general term for a virus]) raged across the United States and much of the world primarily during the fall of 1918 through the spring of 1919. Just in the last week of October alone, it killed over 21,000 Americans.[13] According to the statistics of the Office of Indian Affairs, 24 percent of reservation Indians caught the flu between October 1, 1918, and March 31, 1919, with a mortality rate of 9 percent, about four times as high as that in the nation's big cities.[14] For the Navajos, recently revised figures suggest that within a population of 28,802 there were 3,377 deaths or a 12 percent mortality rate, while in the United States, in general, 548,452 people died with a mortality rate of roughly 2.5 percent.[15] The disease, with an incubation period of twenty-four to seventy-two hours, attacked the respiratory system and acted as a gateway to other forms of illness, primarily pneumonia, by lowering an individual's resistance. Symptoms included severe headaches, chills, fever, leg and back pains, intense sore throat, labored breathing, and total lassitude. Once infected, a person had little desire to do anything but rest and avoid exertion. Almost half of its victims were healthy young people.

In understanding the higher mortality rates among the Navajo, one has to consider the physical and cultural circumstances found on the reservation at the time. Oral tradition has kept alive the trauma that accompanied the "Great Sickness," and though much of what was done to prevent it may appear to an outsider as ineffective, the main issue for the Navajo was a religious one. Events do not just happen, as indicated by omens appearing beforehand. On June 8, 1918, a solar eclipse occurred, presaging misfortune. Sun Bearer, an important Navajo deity, hid his light from his people because of anger, warning that a catastrophe would soon take place.[16] During the summer and fall, dawns and sunsets had pronounced reddish hues that bathed the landscape in an ominous red.[17] The tips of piñon and juniper trees started to die, a sign indicating that sickness was in the area and would be visiting humans, while some Navajos had bad dreams portending disaster. Informants indicate that the holy people sent the disease in order to make room for a growing population; still others suggested that poison gas or the smoke and fumes from artillery rounds fired in World War I somehow infected the Navajo.[18] For whatever reason, the Navajos now faced a perplexing and deadly disease.

The epidemic struck quickly. Tallis Holiday recalled that there were a lot of piñon nut pickers that September who were caught away from their homes and quickly died within a very short distance of their wagons. Seasonal rains and a cold snap added to the misery. The "Big Cough" accompanied by pneumonia seized entire families, creating a void of people to assist those who were ill. To Tallis, the disease struck the Utes and Paiutes the worst with them dying in large numbers, almost to the point of extinction. He ascribed the reason to their not having the prayers and ceremonies that the Navajo knew. They should have gone to a high hill and given offerings of pollen and ground corn to the holy people to protect their homes and families. "It seems at the time the gods were not known. Perhaps these people were naughty and so did not live long. Those who follow the holy way are protected and the spirit knows them. When people do not offer prayers and pay no attention to dreams, their children and things that they have are taken from them. When you do not pray or hold ceremonies with prayers at your home, everything just goes away. I said my well-being prayers (Ách'ą́ą́h sohodizin) and have experienced this."[19]

Fred Yazzie was another person who experienced the pandemic and gave a detailed account of how people reacted.

This happened when I was two years old when the People got really sick. At that time, I was very small and crawled among those who were ill. My paternal grandfather and grandmother died from this disease, as did a man named Gray Hair (Hastiin Tsii'libeii) but my mother and father and I did not. Lots of others, Paiutes and Navajos, suffered from it as the disease swept the land clean. Nothing was able to stop it. When people from Monument Valley talked about this, they usually mention how a lot of Paiutes/Utes living in the Navajo Mountain region became sick, then traveled to our area with many dying along the way. They moved toward Douglas Mesa, Oljato, and Owl Spring. Maybe they were the ones who caused the sickness; they certainly spread it as they traveled among our people. Where it went, people died until it finally ended. My family was aware of an entire Paiute family of six dying off. Some Navajos went to visit them and caught the disease. At that time, there were not that many people around and so people visited a lot, spreading the sickness. My grandfather said the illness changed into chicken pox or measles once it got into a body and made a person sick. When people realized what was going on and that the disease spread easily, some said it was better not to visit. My family stayed in one place. Babies did not seem to suffer from the illness the same way adults did. One baby was found sucking on its mother's breast even though she had died two days before. This is what they tell of the disease.

The sickness came out of nowhere. My father said that maybe the Anglos poisoned those who died while others said it was from poison gas used during World War I or some of the residue from all of the shells being fired. Snow on the ground during sunrise and sunset became red to match the color in the sky, a warning from the holy people of approaching calamity. Before that time, the land was new, the sky clear, and people lived healthy lives, running at dawn, eating good food, and using the sweat lodge. The earth, air, and people were in harmony. Once the sickness began, medicine men performed ceremonies to return things back to normal, but they did not cure or stop it. My father told us not to visit other people because we would spread the sickness to other family groups and so we had to cure ourselves with herbs and isolation.

Even the Anglos did not understand this sickness, but they also did not figure out Navajo medicine. Perhaps when they understand our practices, maybe the sickness can be cured. My family used herbs. Some were very bitter and taken straight, while others were mixed. These plants cured the disease. Some people drank the bitter ch'ildíchi'í and got well from it. Others boiled and drank sagebrush, while for others piñon pitch was a cure for external sores down their throat.

In addition to herbs, there are two other means to cure a sick person. One is to use a fire poker that is pressed against the body of a patient and the other is to hire a medicine man to hold a five-day ceremony. A person has to decide which of these will be most effective. Since whatever is harming that person cannot be seen, there has to be a diagnosis as to what should be done. When one has the five-day ceremony completed, they will think that what ailed them is lifted. This is real. Traditional ceremonies, if believed, help. When a group of Navajos is sick, one patient is appointed to have the ceremony performed for him or her. It may be a child or a grownup who has responsibilities over the family. The ritual might be the Blessingway or Evilway to ward off bad spirits. One brings in that which is good, while the other casts away bad spirits and protects. Both of these were performed.

The fire poker, found in every home, is another means of shielding a person from harmful influences. Navajo people consider it a protector (naayéé'ii) against disease, like a bow and arrow against an enemy. Both can ward off physical ailments. When the sickness approaches and sees these protective symbols, it moves on. Where it goes, we do not know. This is how it is explained even though it cannot be seen. When one uses the fire poker, his prayers and breath are exhaled or puffed away from him. Arrowheads perform a similar function. Both of these shield an individual against ailments that may be haunting them. The fire poker is effective against almost any harmful thing but can also be used to bless and bring good things to an individual. This is something that has been used since the beginning of time when fire was introduced. For this reason, the fire poker is powerful, strengthening prayers, guarding doorways, watching over babies, or nestling between the logs of a hogan wall or ceiling. This is called naayee'. Stirring sticks (ádístsiin) also bring blessings and protection into a home. These are used by women to stir corn mush, just as arrows are used by men to destroy enemies. These greasewood sticks fight against hunger and send off prayers to the holy people. Our ancestors prayed with the fire poker as well as stirring sticks. Before and after a meal, prayers were offered using the ádístsiin or by taking one's hand with grease left over from the meal and rubbing that grease on one's leg while praying to the holy people in thanksgiving. When the prayer is said, that person feels strong in every part of his body and is ready for what the future holds. The bow and arrow, stirring sticks, and fire poker all protect. When one prays into or on one of them, you are protected and the sickness does not want to challenge these shields.

Plain arrowheads serve a similar function in a ceremony. They belonged to the Anasazi and were used to kill animals and the enemy. Navajos collect these points and use them to kill off or protect against things that might be harmful. They ward off disease by serving as a shield. These are often placed around the sick person with prayers and chants for protection. We refer to the illness as naayéé'—something that is feared and cannot be seen. These arrowheads are placed before the ceremony starts, but also during the performance. In certain rituals, the arrowheads remain in position within the hogan for four days. If they were put outside, something might come and take them or a coyote might get near them and the holy people would not like that. It would cancel all the prayers and chants. For this reason, the arrowheads are placed within the hogan.

Once a five-day ceremony is completed, a medicine person takes the four fire pokers used during it to the east. They are placed in a tree with other plant materials utilized during the ceremony. If those things do not fall in a month of two, then it is believed the holy people have accepted the offering of prayers and chants. It will become dííyįįd. The arrowheads are gathered back after the ceremony and are kept to shield a person. That is what Navajos think, that no harm will come to them because of the arrowheads. They are protected.[20]

CHAPTER SIX

The Trading Posts of Monument Valley

Building Relationships across the Counter

B etween the 1880s and mid-1900s, trading posts became increasingly ubiquitous both on and off the Navajo Reservation. Books about them followed suit.[1] The Monument Valley story aligns with this trend featuring three primary posts—in chronological order—John and Louisa Wetherill in Oljato (1906–10), the current Oljato store (1921–2012), and Goulding's Trading Post (1925–present). A lot of materials have been gathered about these three, including self-described trader experiences (by the Wetherills and Gouldings), oral history interviews, travelers' accounts, historical studies, newspaper articles, and government documents. Indeed, Harry and Mike (Leone) Goulding were able to tell their story in its entirety, with the help of other participants, in a book called *Tall Sheep: Harry Goulding, Monument Valley Trader*. For this reason, they will be mentioned only in passing, but will be encountered elsewhere. The Oljato area is the primary focus here. Unlike most of the chapters in this book, the white traders will tell a significant part of their story, interspersed with Navajo commentary. Many of these men and women were highly integrated into the Navajo community, spoke the language, and shared the same perspective as their neighbors. This was one of the few Anglo institutions that did so.

The Wandering of the Wetherills

The name Wetherill immediately brings to the mind of most Southwest enthusiasts two important accomplishments of five brothers at the turn of the twentieth century—trading posts and Anasazi ruins. Richard Wetherill, credited as discoverer of Mesa Verde and explorer of Chaco Canyon sites, established the same pattern that John Wetherill maintained throughout his life. John left much of the trading to Louisa and Clyde Colville, his partner, in favor of discovery—Keet Seel, Betatakin, and Rainbow Bridge, along with other lesser-known Anasazi sites and geologic wonders. The post in Oljato and later Kayenta became his jumping-off sites for enthralling adventures. Louisa became the trader, a perfect match with her own interests in understanding Navajo culture. Many who knew her (including Navajos) felt that she was not just fluent in the language, but as good as any native-born speaker. She also became an expert in applying traditional teachings to everyday life to the point that many of the headmen in Monument Valley brought issues to her, then deferred to her judgment for a solution. Fortunately, Louisa understood the value of recording history, and so it is to her we turn to learn of the first trading post in Oljato.

> Into that country of drifting flocks, where the tribes had fought and the People had wrested a hard living, came three wagons. John Wetherill, his brother-in-law, John Wade, and Clyde Colville, a business partner, came with their goods to the place later known as Moonlight Water [Ooljéé'tó—Oljato]. The way had been beset with difficulties. Working into the new country by way of their old home at Mancos, they ran into snow near Farmington. Between Mancos and Cortez, they encountered mud, and outside of Cortez they pulled through muck up to the wagon axles, taking a whole day to make five miles. Near the San Juan River their wagon broke down. "Someone's got to stay here," they decided. It could not be John Wetherill, for of the three, he was the only one who had been to Oljato before. The other two drew straws; Colville stayed at Moses Rock with part of the load.
>
> John Wetherill and John Wade continued into Navajo country. Between the great buttes of Monument Valley and into the land where he had come as a prospector, John Wetherill appeared now as a trader interested in settling. On March 17, 1906, he and his brother-in-law arrived at the place of Moonlight Water with its cottonwoods and high red mesas.

A tall, thin man, with a face already lined and gray hair, met them. As the son of Chief Hoskinini [Hashkéneiniihii], and a man respected in his own right, he had authority. He always rode with an escort of four armed men and was accustomed to obedience. Quietly, firmly, Hoskinini-begay [Hashkéneiniihii Biye'] told John Wetherill and John Wade to leave. John Wetherill stood his ground. "We will talk about this," he said to Hoskinini-begay, and to John Wade, he said, "You can go back now for Colville."

While John Wade returned for Colville waiting at Moses Rock, John Wetherill stayed alone at Oljato. He suggested to the Navajos that they have a rabbit hunt and a feast.

"You get the rabbits, and I'll furnish flour, sugar, and coffee," he told them. They accepted the invitation of this quiet man, coming back in three days for a feast of rabbits. In front of Wetherill's tent, the fire burned, ready to cook the rabbits, while he made bread from white flour. The coffee and sugar were his gifts to the People. Together the men, with their velvet shirts, silver belts, and bracelets, sat down to eat the feast. From sunrise to sunset, John Wetherill talked his way into the new country, encouraging the Navajos to counsel with each other. He pointed out the advantages of having a trading post at Oljato, where they could buy flour and sugar and coffee when they needed and sell or pawn their silver and turquoise. "It is far to Round Rock—90 miles to take your wool and skins," he reminded them, "and 70 miles to Red Lake and 80 miles to Bluff—a long way to ride for flour to cook bread like this." They agreed. "But we have lived all of this time without white men here," they said gravely. "This is our country and we want no white men here."

In the silence that followed, an old man spoke. "There were hard days long ago. Days when the People gathered piñon nuts and built platforms of sticks in the trees to protect themselves from the wolves; days when they dug roots for food and made clothes of cedar bark; days when the rains did not come and the grass failed so we had no food. You have heard of those days." They were silent, waiting for him to continue. "The white men brought us sheep so we had meat and wool for our clothing. It is not hard now as it once was. I had to tell my grandchildren this only a few days ago. It will be better still if this white man comes among us. Then we will not have so far to go to sell our skins, wool, blankets, and cattle. We can get food when we need it. It is good to have the white man here."

John Wetherill through that day listened to them talking, heard the quiet voices of the old men as they sat before his tent, looking over the far sand and rocks of their country, as they came and went. There were rabbits cooking for them; white bread, hot, and crusty from the fire; coffee boiling and ready. They rode away, then returned. The old men and young men, with long hair knotted at the back and tied with bright headbands, wore calico trousers slit to the knees, moccasins decorated with silver buttons, velvet blouses, silver and turquoise bright under the winter sun. With the dignity of men who had lived far from towns, who had not adopted the ways of an alien race, these men deliberated. At sunset, Hoskinini and Hoskinini Begay told John Wetherill that he could stay at Moonlight Water.

When Wade at last returned with Colville, Wetherill set out on horseback for Pueblo Bonito. He told the two men that he would be back in ten days or two weeks (late in March), knowing that he could get supplies on the way so took only a box of crackers and a can of corned beef with him. He started over the long miles to the post where Slim Woman [Asdzą́ą́ Ts'ósí—Louisa Wetherill] was waiting. It was 90 miles from Oljato to Round Rock, 35 miles farther to Chinle, 45 miles to Fort Defiance, 50 miles to Togay, and 35 miles more to Pueblo Bonito. He expected to get supplies at Pueblo Bonito and return to Oljato alone, but Slim Woman, who had dreamed since childhood of this new land into which they were going, refused to be left behind. "We're ready to start," she said and would not listen to the Navajos who came to the trading post and told her, "Don't go. There are bad people at Oljato. They will kill you." She also did not listen to her mother, who warned, "You'll be lonesome. You'll never see anyone, and all your life you've had people around you." But Slim Woman had met and conquered loneliness and fear, knew what it was to nurse a dying brother with no one near to help, and she had already learned the language of the People. Slim Woman did not fear the "bad people" at Oljato.

They started at once, Slim Woman driving the buggy, John the wagon. At'ééd Yázhí [Little Girl—Georgia, a.k.a. Sister, age seven] and Ashkii Yázhí [Little Boy—Ben, age nine] rode horses and drove the cows, while young Orson Eager drove another wagon, who with Lillian Scurlock and Maude Wade comprised the rest of the party. At the last moment, the children insisted on taking two rabbits to add to the 14 horses, 3 cows, chickens, buggy, and 2 wagons of the cavalcade. It took them three days to get to Gallup. The trip had its problems: a horse ran off and had to be found, two mules next disappeared and had to be retrieved, one of the horses dropped dead, while mud mired the wagons, making travel difficult. Through melting snow and hub-deep mud, they struggled over the mountains and down into the desert. One day they made two miles, the next two more, then five the next day. Finally, they reached Chinle—a trading post and priest's house—and the last settlement before vast stretches of desert and mesa. For days they traveled until they spotted the height of El Capitan, called by the People "Agathla, the Place of the Scraping of Hides," then traveled a number of days before reaching it to make camp.

John Wetherill, who had gone ahead to Oljato for fresh horses, returned. He had been received with rejoicing by Wade and Colville, who, when a month had gone by, had given up hope of his return, and with all their goods sold, had been ready to pullout for Gallup. Before nightfall and 20 days after leaving Pueblo Bonito, the travelers reached Oljato. That night, from the tents which were to be their living quarters and store until they were ready to build, they looked out over this country. High red mesas stood on three sides, touched with ruddy light as the sun sank. To the north the Henry Mountains turned rose at dusk, deepening to purple and black as night fell. Over the low plains of light, the sheep drifted in as the children herded them out of the wind into the warm light of their hogan fires.

Back across their long travel route, the Wetherills sent a freight team to Gallup for supplies. Those who stayed pitched their tents nearer water, laid a board across two coffee boxes, and readied to trade. A little girl made an early, friendly overture to Louisa when she ran up to her on her way to the spring, took the woman's hand, and walked back with her to camp. All that summer she spent her days playing with the Wetherills' two adopted Navajo children, Little Girl (At'ééd Yázhí) and Little Boy (Ashkii Yázhí). Each night her people came for her and took her home to bed; each morning she was back again. Gradually her elders also learned that they could trust the new traders at Moonlight Water. In from the desert they rode, bringing wool and goatskins and blankets to sell along with silver and turquoise to pawn, buying leather, velveteen, calico, sugar, and coffee. They were not interested in the white man's clothes, and the one man in the country who owned a white man's shirt was famous for it. Sometimes they bought flour, but preferred their own corn, ground to a fine powder between their manos and metates. A case of matches, these traders discovered, lasted them for a year, since the People saved their fire.

The days following the Wetherills' arrival were busy with settling in their new home. Realizing that the tents in the shade of the cottonwood trees would not do when the cold winter winds swept over the desert and red ridges, the traders began to cut timbers for a house and store. They

Louisa Wetherill became famous for her ability with the Navajo language and sincere desire to preserve many aspects of the culture. The People appreciated her solid judgment based on their value system and turned to her to solve issues that would have confounded most Anglos. She conducted affairs at the trading post while her husband John led tours and expeditions exploring Anasazi ruins and the geographic wonders of the region. (Courtesy Harvey Leake, Wetherill Family Archives)

hired Navajos who worked at a slow, unhurried pace. One by one their faces and their names became familiar to Louisa: Hoskinini, straight and keen-eyed, the last chief of the Navajos; Hoskinini-begay, his son, riding on a white mule with an escort made up of four armed men—his two sons and two sons-in-law; the young men who gambled away their silver and turquoise, sometimes even their horses and their saddles; the Paiutes to whom they always lost; the two gambling women; the old men who disapproved; the quiet man who never joined in the gambling, who never joined in the arguments, to whom all the others seemed to defer, named Wolfkiller. These were her neighbors.

Unhurried days went by and the freight team from Gallup had not returned. For 20 days no word of it came to this isolated post as its dwindling food supply ran low. Finally, there was only corn, which they ground in their coffee mill. They heard that Hoskinini-begay had set out for Round Rock, 90 miles away, to get food for himself and his family. Ninety miles of rock and sand on the little white mule. Four days later, the chief's son rode up to the tents under the cottonwoods, returning from the Round Rock trading post with supplies on the way to his hogan. He stopped at the white settlers' camp to share his coffee, sugar, and flour. As he rode away, they knew that the gift had been a gesture of friendship and welcome. Less than two months before, he and his father had given permission to John Wetherill to establish his post, but now that the white settlers were in need, the chief and his son kept their pledge of friendship.

Still, the new traders faced challenges with the People. Soon after they arrived, a Navajo came to them with some Mexican silver, which he intended to make into buttons and ornaments. At his request, they promised to keep it for him and put it in the cash box until he returned. The next day, he retrieved it and counted carefully. "Give me four pieces," he said. "I own four pieces more." The Navajo bystanders listened with interest. The Wetherills knew that any course they took could lead them into trouble. If they paid the Navajo the four pieces of silver which he claimed, the others would be sure that they had stolen it. If they refused to pay him, he would work up feelings against them. Louisa knew that the issue had to be settled then and there in the presence of Navajo witnesses. She sailed into the Indian with a tongue-lashing that left him frightened and humbled. When she was through, the other Navajos laughed at him, sure that he had been trying to bluff and lie.

When the summer rains held off, there was more trouble with 40 armed Paiutes who attempted to water their horses at Wetherill's water-hole. Ordered away, they refused to go.

"I am not afraid of Americans," said one scornfully. "Your horse may be afraid of Americans," said John Wetherill, and dropped a stone under the nose of a drinking horse, causing it to start back. The Paiutes were angry while the few Navajos around the post looked on with interest but took no part in the argument. Louisa, facing the very Indians whom she feared in the past, used the same method which had proven successful before. She hotly laid down the law to them, ordering them away from the waterhole. They withdrew. Navajos and Paiutes learned that they could trust Slim Woman. The Navajo women who could not count up their bills were afraid of being cheated, but they came with confidence to her because of her ability to speak their tongue.

Soon it became known that the chief was calling her his granddaughter.

The years passed before her. She had come to the country of the People, and built her hearth fire at Moonlight Water. It had been a pattern woven as if with design on the loom of years. In the heat of summer, the People came frequently at night, riding in from the country beyond El Capitan, beyond Laguna Wash, even from the Sleeping Ute Mountain, to the trading post under the cottonwoods. One evening in the post, she heard a faint thread of sound far off. As it gradually came nearer, she realized that it was a song so went to look out of the door.

"You must not watch these people come," said her friend Wolfkiller. She turned back to him in surprise. "When I was a boy, I heard a song, first faintly, then louder as it came nearer. I started to climb a high knoll to see who it was but my mother called to me and said, 'My son, have you no courtesy? Can you not hear them singing the hogan song? They are friends or they would not give us any warning. You must sit quietly and wait for them. If they saw you watching, they would not be pleased. It would be as if you were spying on them and we do not spy on our friends.'" Louisa turned away from the door and went back to her chair. They listened to the hogan song, clearer now, coming closer through the night. To the trading post at Moonlight Water came friends.[2]

Random Navajo Glimpses of the Wetherills

More than a century ago, the Wetherills moved as traders from Oljato to Kayenta, Arizona, due to easier winters and increased commerce, remaining there for the rest of their lives. But they were not forgotten. Even as late as the 1990s, there were a handful of Navajos who remembered the old post in Utah and the couple who lived there long enough to give the area its name. Nedra Tódích'íi'nii recalls its founding.

> Winter came and went and as spring came near, a white man moved to the place called Oljato. He was called Bilagáanaa Nééz [Tall White Man—Clyde Colville]. Another young man called John Sání [Old John—John Wetherill] and a woman called Asdzáá Ts'ósí [Slim Woman] moved in. The white man said, "The Navajo people will work for me. They will build some buildings for me. They will work for me." Some Navajo people were passing his words around, saying these things. My grandfather, who was called Hastiin Tsé'naa'í, my older brother, who was called Hastiin Na'niłkaadí [The Man Who Herds], and Hastiin Woshnee [?] [Clyde Colville] were just young men. This man was called Woshnee because whenever Navajos came to the store or came to help him, he would tell them to hurry. Anyway, there were a lot of boys who made a house for the white man. They were hauling wood and rocks by Navajo wagons. They made a very nice house for them, but there were few things in it and so a big wagon train pulled by large horses went to Gallup to bring back supplies. They always ran out quickly. It would not take more than three weeks before they were gone. The white man used to go over there all the time to get more and so he was called Hastiin Na'ałbąąsí [The Man Who Drives Around]. These white people settled here. Other posts developed in the area and by the time seven years had passed, more whites came into the area and sank their roots there—they never went back.[3]

Sloan Haycock, who was a young girl at the time, remembered the two Wetherill children.

> I do not know how or where these traders came from. They had two children, Little Boy and Little Girl, who they raised with great love and care. They used to help around the trading post with chores and were very helpful toward each other. The traders were extra kind and used to bring food out to the people's homes, sometimes giving ready-made

The Wetherills established the Oljato Trading Post in 1906. By 1908, when this photo was taken, this rock and adobe structure served as their home (left side) and store (right side). A livestock corral on the far left, wooden frames to protect planted trees, and wagons tell a story of industrious people carving a home out of a desert environment. Oljato Wash and spring, their sources of water, are located twenty yards to the front of this site. Nothing of the post remains today. (Courtesy Harvey Leake, Wetherill Family Archives)

yeast dough. We had Dutch oven pots in which we baked the bread by putting red hot ashes around and under the pot and on top of the lid. It was good. These traders later moved but I don't know why. Their two children acted just like Navajo children. They went to different Navajo homes to play with the children and ride horses. I remember how they used to stay out late in the evening to play while their parents waited for them at home. These two children never turned up their noses toward anything or were never picky—they were just like the rest of the kids and were very well received.[4]

Ada Black tells how the word Oljato became a place name.

One of the good things that came to Oljato and Monument Valley was the trading posts. John and Louisa Wetherill operated the first one, a couple of miles south of the post that stands in the community today. This was built at the place where the water comes out of the ground. Nearby was a rectangular house made of wood with logs that stood straight up with juniper bark stuffed in the cracks between the logs. Now, there are only rocks scattered around here and there. One of the main things sold at this post was coffee, one of the first items these traders brought with them in their wagon. The coffee beans at that time were not roasted or ground, and the sugar was a dark color, as was the salt. Soon other items like flour, lard, and basic foodstuffs moved across the counters of this one-room store. The Oljato (Ooljéé'tó—Moonlight Water) spring nearby had a small basin dug to collect water. One night under a full moon, an Anglo [John Wetherill] and Navajo man went to fetch some water and saw the reflection of the moon in the pool. The Anglo said that it had come to draw its own water, giving the site its name. This is what the people living around there said.

I was still a young girl when my family moved to that area. A man called Hastiin Béésh Íí'áhí (Mister Windmill), who married my aunt, wanted to live there, so we went to shear sheep; the wool was taken in a wagon all the way back to our home near Shonto. The road was not as difficult as it would later become. A man called Tsé'anaa'í (Enemy Rock) was going to do this for us. Because of him, we moved down from the mesa and sheared the sheep in the foothills. During this time, we went to the second Oljato trading post, the one that is there now.[5]

Some of the local Navajos also helped with John's wanderlust for exploration. A number served as wranglers, caring for the horses and mules, saddling them and cinching down the packs, and bringing them to grass and water when John ran archaeological field trips or parties of exploration. Fred Yazzie remembers the excavating. "They uncovered the Anasazi. That's how the Navajos got to know them. My father helped him at Poncho House ruin, to dig up the Anasazi. They moved all over the place looking for ruins in sites like Narrow Canyon, Shonto, and Betatakin. Then they moved back to Kayenta and established a place there. They made lots of Navajo friends again. That's how that Kayenta Trading Post was established."[6]

Heffernan Establishes the Second Oljato Post

Soon after the Wetherills left for Kayenta, the weather, wash, and water began to gobble up the remaining structures and cause rapid deterioration. In a decade, a new Oljato post sprang up, roughly a mile and a half north of the first site. Joseph A. Heffernan (Dibé Yázhí—Little Sheep), a veteran trader who had previously operated posts in Aneth, the Four Corners, and

McElmo Canyon, followed the usual pattern for establishing a new store when he set up a tent and then set to work building a single room trading post that would soon see additions. The money he had to put into this last project came from a sale of land on Cahone Mesa; his draw to this area was not just trading with the Navajo, but also the possibility of discovering other forms of wealth. He certainly was not averse to excavating, his daughter, Anna, claiming that everywhere he went he dug a well—his last was in Oljato. Born in 1867, those who knew him by the time he reached Oljato refer to him as an old man. From 1921 to 1925, he ran this new post until he had serious heart complications and died at the age of fifty-four. This was the same year that Harry Goulding and Mike established their trading venture—beginning with a tent and herding some livestock. As a newcomer, Harry wanted to meet this veteran trader, and arrived, fortunately, at a critical moment for Joseph's wife and daughter, both named Anna, who were manning the post.

Goulding begins:

When this old fella moved in, he built a new store at Oljato. But there was another old man who had a little farm down below Oljato. Everybody called him Bidághaa' Nééz (Long Whiskers), because he had a mustache like the old saloon keepers, coming out to here then twisted. He lived down there among the Indians, farming and not afraid of anything! "There's fine gold down on the San Juan River, lots of it, big heaps of gravel that is loaded with this fine gold." There had been quite a few people who had come in there earlier, and tried but could do nothing with it because it was so fine. I wanted to see if I couldn't get to the river to learn for myself, so I stopped at his place and asked if he'd like to go along with me. He agreed and so after our trip, I let him off where he lived on the other side of Oljato Wash then went to shake hands with Mr. Heffernan.

His girl came to the door. She was 20 years old and very capable, always hauling in the merchandise for the old fella. I said, "I been wanting to come and meet Mr. Heffernan and get acquainted." "Oh, he's awful sick," she said; I could see she was worried. I told her, "I haven't had anything to eat. I'll go to the back of the trading post and cook a bite to eat, and if he gets worse, you just call me." When I returned she was crying and said, "I'm afraid my father is going to die. I'm awful glad you came." We went into his room and I could see a deathly pain was getting him and he was about to roll off the bed. I went over and took hold of him, and about that time, something inside of him broke and came out of his nose as he threw up all over me. The whole room smelled of it as he died, right there, in my arms. It was just me and his daughter. I do not know where his wife was, but suddenly other people started to arrive—a total of eleven. One blessing was that a man and his wife came in, and she had been a nurse and knew exactly what to do when a person died. It was all pretty rough but she directed us and cared for the body. I wouldn't want to tell you what we had to do.

Bidághaa' Nééz could see from his place the cars coming in and knew something was wrong and so joined us. I was glad he was there. We had already driven down with the old truck to the river, but now we went to Kayenta for boards to build a wood box to get Heffernan out to a coffin. We got it fixed up with a cover and brought it back to Oljato. We got him in the box and into the truck, with all 11 people helping or standing around. His daughter said, "This is the biggest crowd of people that ever hit this trading post! We've never had over three or four. God has certainly done something for me." Then Bidághaa' Nééz and I started driving to Cortez with the body. When we came by our place, Mike came out, looked at the coffin crossways close behind the cab for less jolting, and said, "Harry, you ain't never going to be able to take that coffin up there that way! It'll tear off on them rocks in Snake Canyon as you pass through them!" So we turned it around and got it back up.

That was about the longest day's drive I ever had! I had no way to clean up, had not eaten (although I had no appetite), and I was so tired that Bidághaa' Nééz had to keep waking me up. I did all the driving, since he did not know how, trying to avoid the bumps. "You just keep me awake. We've got to get this man in or it will be hard for them to work with him." So he kept shaking me until we reached a little cold stream near Monticello, then took a bucket and splashed me with cold water to keep me alive. We finally got to Cortez and an undertaker, after a day and way into the night. In fact, it was close to morning. I slept for a solid day and a night before I started back home. We kept quiet about a person dying in the trading post. The Navajos would not have come back to trade if they knew. I could have gotten rid of my competition if I'd let them know. The girl told them that he went out with me to do some business, had become sick and died out there.[7]

Problems for Heffernan's wife and daughter did not cease after his death. Shortly before selling the post in 1926, Anna, his wife, asked a visitor at the Oljato post to show her how to shoot a small automatic pistol. The man instructing her removed the clip but forgot that a round remained

The second Oljato Trading Post began in 1921 and continues to exist today. The first traders to occupy this spot started with a tent, then a small stone building that over the years expanded into a multiroom store-and-family-dwelling. There are a number of outlying structures, among which is a guest hogan for visiting Navajos. (Courtesy Kay Shumway)

in the chamber. As she talked to him saying, "And I guess this is where you pull the trigger," she shot herself in the leg. The daughter, who had ridden to Kayenta miles away to get the mail, returned home to find her mother in bed, making no mention of the incident. The next day when Anna went to make the bed they shared, she saw a bloody mess, which forced her mother to explain what happened. Fortunately, the bullet had missed the bone. The man who had been teaching her how to use the pistol encouraged her to put chewed tobacco on the wound, which must have worked "because she got alright, but she finally had to tell me about it."[8] Heffernan's wife lived for three more years, dying in 1929.

The post remained vacant for a few months before John Taylor (Chį́į́h Nahíí'áhí; also called The One with a Big Nose) and his wife, Jane, took up the trade. Mike Goulding gives a brief description:

We went down to Oljato to see the Taylors when they moved in there. Johnny and his wife, Jane, didn't move in until sometime in January 1926. We had real nice times together. They were a lovely family and so we frequently visited back and forth. They had a house, such as it was, because they had to do a lot to repair it. There were only two rooms and a little tiny store which is today the same as it was then, but they added onto it a whole new room and fixed their living room.[9]

Sloan Haycock recalls that the Navajo called Jane "Freckled Body Woman" (Asdząą́ Bizhiinii). Elizabeth Hegemann, a trader at Shonto and wealthy adventurer, recorded her visit the year the Taylors moved in.

> They had not been out for several weeks so we took along their mail [from the Wetherills' trading post in Kayenta], and found for the last miles down Moonlight Wash that we had to make our own tracks as a rain had washed out all vestige of Johnny's route. Finally, we caught a glimpse of Oljato to the right of the wash near some cottonwoods under the landmark of a red sandstone butte. We felt its charm of location as we stopped alongside the trading post where Janey Taylor insisted upon our having the hot noon meal with them even though we had practically materialized from nowhere as far as they were concerned. . . . With her youngest boy only five and the oldest twelve, she did not have the time to get very far away from that isolated trading post.[10]

The Taylors stayed for about eight years and were followed by Jim Pierson, who remained for only a couple of years (1935–37) before selling to O. J. (Orange Jay) "Stokes" Carson (The Poor One—Baahojooba'í), who sold it to his daughter, Mildred, and her husband, Reuben Heflin (Big Whiteman—Bilagáana Tsoh), who bought the store for $6,000, the inventory for $3,000, and the necessary federal license and bond for $5,000 in 1938.[11]

One new attraction that the couple brought was that of a radio. On Saturday mornings the Bureau of Indian Affairs Agency at Shiprock broadcast a local program that attracted people to the post and was a featured event, especially during the World War II years. Other modern conveniences followed: a windmill to pump water from a raised tank in the backyard; this led to indoor plumbing after Reuben made a bathtub and sink out of concrete. Into this concrete and around the fireplaces, Mildred set chips of fossilized wood. Still, the underground water was strong with alkali. In 1944, a generator began providing electricity on a dependable basis, but nothing was more consistent than the outhouse, which remained a permanent fixture.

Mildred had lived her entire life in and out of different trading posts that her father and mother had operated. She had many close friends in the Navajo communities in which she lived and spoke the language well.

From this came a deep respect for the People and their customs, something that every trader sought to develop. Mildred, speaking of her family experience, both when growing up and at Oljato, testifies of these respectful bonds. Speaking of medicine men, she believed

they truly performed miraculous cures—psychologically or otherwise, they were great. I grew up with it and my parents always had the same attitude. The medicine man was really great, and we were taught to have high respect for his ceremonies. A lot of people had the attitude, "Oh, this is just foolishness, just heathen stuff." Oh, no, that's not right. My parents never felt that way. They strongly believed that the Navajo had a right to his viewpoint and that the Indian was correct more often than wrong.

My mother was always going out to anybody sick and trying to do something for them if they asked her. She never went unless she was invited. You don't interfere with other people's lives, but she'd go out and take them special food or try to help them with medicine, anything that might be effective. I can remember both of my parents going out often, especially when there was a death. The Navajos have a terrible fear of death and feel that the evil spirit that caused a person's death can attach itself to anyone in the family or those closely associated with the deceased. If they thought a person was going to die, they isolated him, by taking him out of the hogan and putting him in a little hut all by himself. Often, my mother went out and stayed with these people. If they didn't come for her before the person died, then they might come for her or my father after the individual had passed. My parents would then go out and help prepare the body for burial, dig the grave, and assist with funeral arrangements. It was very serious when a baby died, much more so than when an older person did. I don't think they do that so much anymore because people are taken to the hospital when it is thought that they are going to die.

If there was going to be a ceremony, Navajos always came in and said, "Now, look, we're going to have a sing. We need some flour. We need some coffee. How much can you give us?" My parents always donated and gave it to them free. This was all part of community life, but everything else was conducted on credit for six months, one year, or pawn because there was no money. In the wintertime a lot of the people came in and put their jewelry and other important items in pawn and we gave them credit. They bought merchandise in exchange. We had to build a cement vault to keep the pawn in. They would return in the springtime when they sheared their sheep, pay it off, and take it out. Sometimes they would leave it all year-round because they said it was safer there. They did not have any secure place to put it in their hogan, so they would leave it there until they wanted it for a ceremony and then, if they were reliable customers, we would let them borrow then return it when through.

The weavers in Oljato were not very good like the ones in Shonto where we moved later. The rugs were very poor quality, but I think they have improved lately. My favorite memory from Oljato is the people coming in from Navajo Mountain whom we did a lot of trade with. Their donkeys were laden with bags of wool—the poor little things were practically hidden. The owners would drive them in and we always had a hogan out there where they could spend the night. So they would unload their donkeys, bring in their wool, and my husband would weigh it. They would buy a few groceries that night, and then the next day come in and spend the whole day trading, in some cases, getting a year's supply to take home.[12]

Many Navajos who did business with the Heflins and earlier owners had similar, positive recollections. Tully Bigman remembers,

At Oljato, a white man called Dibé Yázhí traded with the Diné'. He bought handmade rugs, sheepskins, wool, and silver products like bracelets and concho belts the Navajos made. These were much heavier then and were pawned to get things like coffee, flour, and clothing. Sometimes the traders helped for free or were paid back in the spring when the wool came in. In the early days, no meat was sold in the store, except for that which came in square-shaped cans. This was pig meat with lots of salt on it. A person would ask for a certain amount and have it cut for them. It cost quite a bit, and a lot of it was fat that was fried in a pan and eaten with bread. I found it too salty and bitter. There was only one kind of candy, round in diameter, that people brought home and broke into pieces to eat. Now there are many varieties with a lot of different tastes, but then that was the only thing we had. Flour did not cost a lot; one dollar and fifty cents bought 25 pounds and two dollars 50 pounds. Thirty or forty dollars bought a lot. It was pretty good. Saddles that now sell for $1,000 at that time only cost $30. Men's blankets used to cost only $8 but are now over $100.

Shoes made at this time were good with two rows of nails going around the soles. These bottoms were thick, lasted for a long time, and cost between $10 and $12, later going up to $18. This was all during

Freighting to trading posts could be a difficult task, depending on the weather, size and type of wagon, number of horses available, and skill of the drivers. Many Navajos did this for employment. The wagon is making its way past El Capitan en route to the Oljato Trading Post. (Courtesy Harvey Leake, Wetherill Family Archives)

World War II. Those times were hard. Little coffee, even less sugar—maybe the size of an aspirin for a cup. We used burned corn as a replacement, which the older men and women drank, but the children were unaware. The elders got used to this and suffered for two or three years, until they were able to return to a normal diet, obtain good clothes, and buy gasoline once again.

In the old days, as winter approached, we used four or five burros to carry flour and coffee back home. At the trading post those people who came from far away, especially during the cold months when they had no place to stay if it was raining or snowing, stayed at the guest hogan. It was close to the trading post. We would get an arm load of firewood from the trading post before sundown. The trader piled it there for that purpose as a friendly gesture but we also gathered some of our own fuel. We used it to cook our meals and warm our home before going to sleep.

The traders used wagons pulled by teams of four or six horses or mules to bring in their supplies, sometimes from Winslow or Flagstaff or Gallup. There would be several of these wagons filled with food and goods covered by tightly drawn canvas. The trader filled out a form that he gave to the driver, ordering his supplies. Even though the roads were rough, poorly maintained, wound around sandy places, had steep inclines, were filled with dips, and looked impassable, the traders were the first in our community to get cars and trucks to haul merchandise and bring in the mail. They wrote letters and ordered things for the People. Many of us did not know how to write and did not understand the English language and so did not follow what was going on. The Navajo would just glue the paper shut and send the letter, telling the trader, "Send this off for me."[13]

In 1945, Reuben and Mildred sought greener pastures after eight years in Oljato, moving to the Shonto Trading Post, where they remained for ten years before taking up residence in Kayenta. A cousin, Fred Carson, leased Oljato for two years until Stokes bought it back and managed it for another ten years, employing the help of his daughter, Virginia, and her husband, Edward, until they bought it in 1958. Of all the owners who had passed through Oljato's doors, Ed and Virginia (a.k.a. Chin) were the proprietors who lasted the longest, until 1986. Their daughter, Wynona, and her husband, Al Townsend, took over the post, remaining only until 1991, when Evelyn Jensen, the last trader, leased the property until 2010.

While each owner made contributions to the community and the business, the Smiths and Evelyn Jensen will serve as examples of the changing trade environment. Virginia, representing a long line of traders in her family, describes a typical day in 1959. Nothing dramatic, nothing noteworthy, just daily life on the reservation.

Opened the store at 8. 1. One car waiting for gas. Bought $2.00 worth and went to uranium mine to work. 2. No one in store until 8:30. Small boy brought in two goatskins. Paid him 25 cents. He bought Cracker Jacks and gum. Asked for mail for his mother. 3. Man came in car to get gas, $3.50, and wanted to borrow hose (lending hose for that purpose) to fill water barrel at missionary's well. 4. Man and wife came in wagon. Had letter from daughter in school in Oregon. Wanted letter read to them, and also a letter written to her. Pawned a hatband for $8.00 to buy a basket and cloth for a ceremony. The lady's mother is very sick. Everything quiet; no one around for about a half an hour. Boy brought in saddle blanket, paid $3.00 for it. He wanted to buy a large sack of flour which cost $3.75. Bought coffee and sugar, salt and baking powder

instead. Took all of his groceries and left. Came back later to pawn bracelet for flour. Told him he could go to school in two days, if he wanted to,
but did not wish to go to school. A dozen small purchases followed. 16.
Another man came in to see if his father had a relief check. Wanted me
to write to Tuba City Hospital to see how his brother-in-law was getting
along. Broke his leg at a squaw dance when he fell from his horse. Now
about 12:30 so closed for lunch. Opened about 1:15. 17. One old man
from Monument Valley waiting to get in. Didn't think much of idea of
being closed. Pawned a bracelet several months ago. Paid $5.00 on it.
Wanted to buy a hat that cost $12.00. Only had $10.00, so charged the
other $2.00 on the bracelet.[14]

At 6 p.m. the door closed, the biggest sales of the day being a $30 leather
purse, payment of $20 on an account, and $15 worth of groceries—all by
a man employed at one of the uranium mines. That was a typical day at
the post.

Virginia worked behind the counters while Ed enjoyed the airstrip
(first bladed in 1949 by Stokes but eventually paved for light aircraft
around 1960), which was on the east side, adjacent to the post. He also
assisted with the heavier chores. Honed by years of buying and selling over
trading post counters, she offered fair prices and evaluated Navajo hand-
icrafts based on extensive experience. Speaking of her business at Oljato,
she said:

We have quite a few Navajos come in and buy rugs. A lot of them will
buy them on credit and then take them to Blanding or some other town
and sell them for cash or trade them for horses. A lot of the traders
have really worked with the Navajos, particularly in weaving rugs, to
help them improve by making designs more pleasing, using colors that
attract, and obtaining a tighter spun wool. In the earlier days, they were
purchased by the pound, especially saddle blankets. They were easy to
make and always sold. I think many people have heard that rugs are
getting very scarce so they are responding to that warning. With cars
available, Navajos are traveling around so much more that they don't
stay home and weave which creates another problem. We used to just
give strictly trade for rugs, but now I'm paying cash for everything. I had
a very nice rug brought in yesterday—a Yé'ii Bicheii with seven figures
in it, not too large, and not that well-made, so offered her $150 cash.
She took it somewhere else, thinking she could get $200 for it. Many of
these women take a lot of pride in their work, while others just throw

something together. We used to have an outline rug called a Holiday rug, which was very popular, and sold a lot of them, but the family does not make them anymore. The old grandmother who used to do all of the carding and spinning for those rugs died, followed by a couple of her daughters. I have been trying for years and years to get one of them to weave one, but no success.

Many trading posts sell pre-spun yarn, but we do not handle it because it is quite expensive. Unless you have a very, very good weaver, it does not pay to use it. I heard that the lanolin has been removed and so rugs made out of that type of yarn will not wear nearly as long as the others. That's what one rug buyer who has been buying rugs for 30 or 35 years told me.

When we bought our wool in the spring, we just stored it outside. Now, there is no price for wool which is absolutely worthless this year. We used to buy sheep and goat hides, but they are not worth much either. When we found that there was no market for wool, we tried to encourage everyone to keep their wool and make rugs, but I do not think anybody did. They could have gotten so much more out of it. For instance, at Inscription House, a lady brought in a rug. The trader figured how much she would get for it compared to the price of raw wool, and it worked out to $35 a pound if she had kept all her wool and put it into rugs.[15]

Relationships

Human interaction was at the core of everything that happened at the Oljato Trading Post. Taking part in community events, holding a large Christmas party each year, and a host of services sometimes were forgotten when business ruled in the bullpen. Virginia recalled:

One fellow came in the other day who owed me quite a large bill, over $500. He wanted to borrow $200 to buy a new car. I told him, "No. You owe too much, and you won't be able to pay it back." He has been mad at me ever since and he has not been back. They usually trade where they can get the most credit. I know many, many of them started trading with us and then when their bill got high and I would not extend credit, they went somewhere else and ran their tab up there. I know some of them have traded at three different places until their bill got too high. One side of our pawn vault used to be full of concho belts, but now we do not have even a quarter as many as we used to have.[16]

These Navajos, standing in the "bullpen" of the Oljato Trading Post, bring a lively interaction with the trader behind the counter. Traditional dresses on the ladies and homemade moccasins on both men and women speak to the values of the people and their connection to the past. (Courtesy Special Collections, J. Willard Marriott Library, University of Utah)

Ada Black had her own complaint against Virginia, even though she said that she generally approved of all of the traders. Speaking of "Chin," Ada said,

> She really understood the Navajo language and used to call me "My Sister." The very first time she saw a belt I owned that was a family heirloom, she liked it. There was a place called Bééshłichíí'ii Haagééd (Copper Mine), where they were hiring people to work. There was lots of digging involved to clean up this place, and so they sent a big truck over here to obtain workers. My husband, Harvey, wanted to earn money there but had no food to take with him, so I pawned this concho belt for fifty dollars, even though its silver was from the old times and valuable. I think I loaned it for twenty-five days and went back within twenty. I did not want to do that at all, but I felt like I had to. Because this was in the springtime, we were shearing sheep and planting crops. This meant that money could be obtained by selling the wool, and so I saved the fifty

dollars I owed. When I went to pay the money and redeem the belt, she said it would be sixty dollars due to interest. I returned with that amount in the late afternoon, but she said no and gave me another belt to take its place. I told her that the one she gave me might not be made of real silver and that I would not accept it. She refused to give it back to me.

During this time people were mining copper in this area and had a piece of equipment that detects it. The belt she gave me read very high on this machine, buzzing away when it was close to it. By now, the sun was going down, and so I told her I would return in the morning and that I wanted my belt back. We were not living very far away, and since my children were close by, I wanted to know what they thought of this whole incident; I showed them the belt she had given me. I do not know why I did that and think now that I should have left it. In the morning, because of some things going on at home, I did not get to the post until around ten o'clock, although I had told her I would be there earlier. She had already left for Flagstaff to conduct trading business. Once she re-turned to Oljato, I confronted her about taking my belt and treating me this way. I said I was not going to let go of it because it had been passed from generation to generation in my family. Every time I went there, I reminded her that she needed to give it back, but she never did. Shortly after this, she drove off a cliff, and even though I voiced my concern for the belt, nothing came of it. I still have the other belt. [See endnote 18.]

Many of the traders were kind to their customers. When people arrived at their post after a long journey in the wintertime, the trader would pour a hot cup of coffee and give a slice of folded bread or crackers with something on it. All of the men and women who ran trading posts did these kinds of things, were very generous, and good-natured. Money was scarce, and so they extended credit on flour and other necessities. The traders knew everyone back then, and so even though you had nothing, they would allow you to pay in the future for anything you wanted on the counter, like coffee, flour, salt, sugar, or shortening. Payback came twice a year—in the spring with the shearing of the sheep for wool or in the fall with the sale of lambs. During other seasons, a person might work for a trader or someone else for money to pay him back. We never went into debt that could not be paid off, and we are still like that. It is good to pay every month so you don't owe people.

The traders also helped with big family events like ceremonies, pro-viding food and candy for free. When they gave it, they would call us by kinship terms such as my sister, brother, grandfather, grandmother, mother—whatever term they were comfortable with, since they really understood the Navajo language. They expressed their relationship by saying, "My sister, I will help you with whatever you wish," and then pack it for you. They also attended the event and may have had a Navajo ceremony performed for them. One might say, "I had a bad dream," then have a medicine man provide a cure or else say, "I am traveling a long distance to go and purchase food, and so I want a blessing for the journey," then get one. He would have a good trip and upon his return, express appreciation for the blessing.[17]

In fairness to the Smith family, mention must be made of Ed, one of those colorful characters, set in his opinions and memorably bombastic. Les Wilson, owner and trader at Two Grey Hills, New Mexico, shared some thoughts on Ed when Les visited and did some trading at Oljato. He said,

> Uncle Ed was not the trader at Oljato, Virginia was. I remember him constantly complaining about most everything, politics and otherwise, in his high-pitched voice. His speech was constantly profane. Sometimes every other word was a cuss, but Virginia ignored it. Ed always dressed in khaki work clothes, I think even at the funeral for his wife and Jo Drolet.[18] Ed kept his plane, and a mint-condition old jeep in the garage behind the store. My friend Ray Drolet said that it was in readiness for Uncle Ed's fear that 50,000 Communist Chinese might invade the United States, coming up through Mexico. The Oljato Trading Post would have presumably been one of its prime targets.
>
> They kept a goat in the house as a pet. It may have been their daughter Wynona's. Uncle Ed once said in front of everybody, "I hope one day I'll drive around the edge of the Oljato rock formation and there'll be nothing left of the store but an inch-high pile of charcoal." That, of course, was a culturally wrong thing to say for someone living in Navajo land. Ed used to invite the LDS Elders [Mormons] into his living room, in order to argue with them. He would say, "Well, let's see what Smitty (Joseph Smith) had to say about that" as he thumbed through his Book of Mormon. The Carsons were Episcopalians.[19]

The Smiths witnessed substantial changes in the trading industry. Beginning in the post–World War II era of the 1940s and continuing to their time, there was steady innovation in the Oljato post and what it could offer.[20] As mentioned previously, gasoline pumps, an airstrip, refrigeration, electric generators, and increased vehicular traffic gave a modern upgrade to its services—something that Navajo customers appreciated. The uranium industry encouraged the paving of some major road networks while also creating a spiderweb of plowed dirt roads throughout the region. All of the fenced corrals at the post were gone; a bread truck, milk truck, and fresh groceries came in once a week; a ware room had been added by Fred Carson; Ed and Virginia improved the pawn vault; the Seventh Day Adventist Hospital in Monument Valley proper relieved the traders of handling burials; and Ed did not bother learning the Navajo language, feeling it unnecessary. They even cemented the traditional guest hogan in the 1960s to preserve its use and stop deterioration. There was still one more significant change to come.

Wynona and Al Townsend took over the post after Virginia and Ed passed away but remained for only five years before moving on. The void this created left the door open for Evelyn Yazzie Jensen, a full-blooded Navajo from the Bit'ąhnii and Tó Áhání Clans, to lease the facility. Born on Black Mesa in 1954 as her mother collected wood, Evelyn was old enough to remember her mother weaving rugs, then riding a horse twelve miles to exchange her craft for groceries. She also recalled going to a post for the first time, standing in the bullpen, and staring at all of the wonderful products; the friendliness and chatter of the traders; and the assistance they provided for bereaved families, or those lacking letter-writing skills or in handling legal issues. She did not start to learn English until the age of nine, when she began school. After she graduated, there followed a short stint at a bank with her eventually rising to the position of manager. This was when Wynona approached her about taking over Oljato. She agreed because "I thought it was romantic to have a trading post in some remote area, with a potbelly stove and a blue coffee pot, having people come in and visit to share a cup of coffee. That was my dream." In 1991, it came true.

Even as a Navajo with many Bit'ąhnii Clan relatives in the area, Evelyn had some of the same issues that previous traders faced.

> When I started, I was really doing a booming business because I offered credit, which when I went before the chapter house, the local people, especially the most traditional ones, wanted me to do. If I had known what I know now, I would not have done it, but we had a very successful business and I was doing very well with the community people. Two or three years down the line, however, they started to drift off and did not come back to settle their credit. This really hurt me.[21]

She tried to diversify by offering "Navajo Country Guided Trail Rides"—ranging from an hourly fee to a two-day overnight experience, but it just was not enough to keep the store competitive with corporate chain stores. Gasoline sales had dropped off for similar reasons and now the old underground tanks had to be removed for environmental reasons. Evelyn did not have that kind of money and so sometime in the first few years of the twenty-first century the store and its museum of local Navajo arts and crafts closed. In 2001, the Navajo Environmental Protection Agency removed the gasoline storage tanks and the tribe voided the lease agreement in 2012, long after the post had ceased to function.

The building, like the people and much of the traditional culture, were now relegated to the past. Evelyn paid a fitting tribute to what she recognized as disappearing in 1998, when she said:

> The grandmothers and grandfathers, the grassroots people—this is the last of them. I think that is why I consider myself lucky to be amongst them, because once they are gone, that is it. It is so sad, maybe to see a grandmother out there with her grandkids not treating her very nicely, being rude. It makes you want to cry. Sometimes you see some older men, maybe in their late seventies, come in to the trading post and exchange jokes. You know how they grab each other. I just feel like crying, because you do not see that anymore. I think I learned to value that. These people are the last of it and you won't see any more. I think this is the only place, too, that you will see Grandpa or Grandma riding a horse and hitching it to a post outside, or maybe chasing their sheep across the valley floor. You don't see that very much anywhere else. It's an era that is fast going, and I am just glad to be a part of it—even a very small part.[22]

CHAPTER SEVEN

Livestock Reduction

Slaughter on the Sand, Killing in the Canyons

Wealth on the hoof—sheep, goats, horses, and cattle—dominated the economy and cultural traditions of the Navajo into the late 1920s. With livestock reduction starting at this time and ending with a few vestigial remains in 1946, the People had weathered one of the two most dramatic and traumatic events in their history, the other being the Long Walk era. By the 1950s, the old way of life was fading, wage labor became the ticket to prosperity or at least survival, and the dominant society made inroads into the reservation as never before, bringing with it a different way of life. Following a brief explanation of why it happened, three lengthy oral histories provide different perspectives from those involved. Nedra Tódích'íi'nii presents emotional observations of what she and a number of livestock owners encountered in the Monument Valley area; Ed Smith, introduced last chapter as a trader at the Oljato post, worked as a range rider, part of the enforcement arm to reduce the herds; and Mildred Heflin provides the perspective of the traders, who generally disapproved of the government's actions but felt helpless to foment change. Together, these individuals paint a picture of devastation and turmoil that began to uproot many past practices.

Although there have been a number of studies that look at the roles the government, Commissioner of Indian Affairs John Collier, and Navajo spokesmen played in this drama, relatively little has been written explaining what the Navajo herders thought about their circumstances.[1] The most prominent works—Donald Parman's *The Navajos and the New Deal* and Lawrence Kelly's *The Navajo Indians and Federal Indian Policy* rely on government sources to evaluate the livestock reduction program, providing an eagle eye view of its effects.[2] The perspective of the Monument Valley Navajo is presented here. The events that set livestock reduction in motion were rooted in the past, long before the slaughter started. Although the Navajo Reservation expanded at a sporadic but significant rate during the late nineteenth and early twentieth century, land acquisition did not keep pace with the growing number of Navajos.

Little did the Northern Navajo agent, B. P. Six, understand the role of livestock in Navajo culture when he wrote, "These Indians will be willing to dispose of all of their range stock in exchange for a farm of adequate size to support their families."[3] He did, however, watch the herds expand. During 1930 in the Montezuma Creek and Aneth area, 19,514 sheep and goats passed through dip vats filled with medicine to prevent scabies. The Oljato and Shonto areas produced 43,623 more animals, while some Utah Navajos undoubtedly went to vats located at Kayenta, Shiprock, Dennehotso, and Teec Nos Pos. Still others probably skipped the process entirely, but if the totals from the Aneth and Oljato areas are combined, at least 63,137 sheep and goats ranged over the reservation lands of southeastern Utah.[4]

By 1934, the entire Northern Navajo Agency reported that government officials had killed or sold 70,000 animals, and that the Utah Navajos' herds were now down to an estimated 36,000.[5] Because the nation's economy wallowed in the depths of the Great Depression, the agent could price a sheep at only two dollars and a goat at one. The annual report went on to say that "an excessive number of goats and sheep were slaughtered for food. There is every reason to believe that the next dipping record will show even a greater reduction than indicated by the number sold."[6] Horses and cattle suffered a similar fate.

The cold, hard statistics of livestock loss matched the scientific logic of trying to save the range. Depleted vegetation, soil erosion, silt accumulation at Hoover Dam, expanding herds, restrictions on off-reservation grazing, poor animal quality, and the faltering national economy were all part of the motivation to reduce livestock and modernize the Navajos' livelihood and management of resources.[7] In Utah, as in other parts of the reservation, scientific logic proved to be an economic and emotional disaster for the Navajos, who depended on their herds for survival.

Starting in 1933, the goat herds were the first to be selected, gathered, and then killed. A year later, the sheep came under the knife, followed by horses and cattle. Although in some areas this pattern might take a different form, the end results were the same. The reduction that had started out as voluntary and just one more incomprehensible government program soon became a major threat to the Navajos' subsistence economy. Richer Navajos were more powerful and harder to coerce, so often the poorer people, those who could least afford the losses and still maintain self-sufficiency, were the first to suffer. Impoverishment and dependency on the government became an increasing part of reservation life.

Tribal policemen, Soil Conservation officers, range riders, and local BIA officials administered the program. Many of these public servants did not fare well and often faced the possibility of physical confrontation. The BIA cultivated informants who reported names of people hiding sheep or not cooperating with the government's program. Arrests soon followed. Jealousy between those who lost livestock and those hiding them arose, feeding the cycle of spy and counterspy. It seemed like people were "crawling among themselves."[8] Out of all this turmoil emerged a lone figure, the lightning rod and focus of all the fear, hate, blame, and tension in the hearts of the Navajos—John Collier, Commissioner of Indian Affairs, who directed the BIA as a driving force behind the livestock reduction program in cooperation with the Soil Conservation Service. In spite of the fact that Collier wanted to foster Native American self-determination through his Indian Reorganization Act and other programs, to the Navajo, he stood for one thing—the man who destroyed their flocks.

Nedra Tódích'íí'nii Experiences Livestock Reduction

When I was sixteen, I married a man who I found out later had a lot of livestock—herds of cattle and flocks of sheep. Two years later, we learned that vaccine shots were being given to horses who had become victims of a disease called *dich'id* [?] caused by small worms crawling through a horse's stomach. Navajos, who did not know this, continued to eat horse meat, became ill, and slowly died. People from Gallup traveled over the reservation, telling about these things and saying that the horses had to be given shots. They gathered them into a small canyon with a huge corral filled with horses then gave them shots. We took three from our own herd but never got them back or received pay. One was a beautiful jet-black stud with a white streak across its eyes that belonged to my brother who lives near Oljato. After the people from Gallup herded the horses into the corral, they selected then removed the best ones, which we never saw again.

One year later, a man who owned many horses, rounded up those grazing over the area and herded them into a corral and branded them. This went on for about a year and then we learned that they had bad blood. One day, I was busy tending our flock of sheep when one of my fathers, Joe Fisher, came riding towards me, saying, "Your horse, which you are using to herd sheep, has bad blood, they say, my daughter, so I have come for it." I thought to myself, "What will I do with the saddle?" so I told him to take the horse back to the house and remove the saddle. He did that but also took another horse, too, a tame, red one. Later that day, while I was herding the sheep back, my little sister asked me, "Did somebody pull your horse out from under you?" I said, "Yes," then gazing about, I saw my saddle, bit, and bridle, and looked in the direction he had gone with our horses and almost cried. My horse was a beautiful four-year-old. That is how two of them vanished.

The next year, these people returned and again took the best ones. They came to our homes saying they wanted the branded animals, including the mares, colts, and fillies—seventeen total—leaving only the old ones. Some of the horses became frightened and tried to escape, and at one point, a pregnant donkey got swept in with them, but got away. Some of the Navajos knew about this and chased it into the mountain to hide. I think the government only paid $5 for each horse, and when they took 17 of them from us, the price came out to about $70 total. One of the men handing out the money told our family members to buy a wagon, but somebody said, "Who is going to pull it? You took all of my horses! They usually pull the wagon for me!" My husband tried to beg for the horses, but he became sick and was unable to. People refer to this time as "When the Goats Vanished," or "When the Horses Were Being Chased Away."

The following year, the talk was about reducing the sheep and goats. The first call was for rounding up the goats and taking seven of them. They never considered that I had nine children and my younger sister eight. So we stood and watched them drive our goats away in a cloud of dust. I thought, "I guess it was just like this when we had enemies stealing our flocks." Some people were saying that they were going to hide their herds in small, concealed spots in tiny groups. Charley Ashcroft and some other officials called *Akałii Nééz* and *Akałii Chíí'* were range riders, always scouting for livestock and shouting after them when they found them. If they did not catch the animals, they just shot them, even doing it to the sheep and goats as they herded them. Some of them, like the goats, were killed in the corrals, with men coming constantly. The goats would be crying as they were shot down by the guns then just fell down. That is how they were killed. This whole thing threw us into poverty. Some of the Navajo women who had their horses taken cried for them. As for the burros, I heard they were rounded up, soaked with kerosene, and burned, which was frightening. The more conservative Navajos fought with the police when they came around, saying, "We heard that you're stingy with your sheep. For that, we'll just take them from you."

At this time, a man named Imitator (Hastóí Ádíl'íní) and John Chee almost choked a white policeman to death. (Imitator received this name because as a small boy and into adulthood, he imitated people.) When the police started to chase Chee's sheep away, he blocked them. The policemen rode up to him as he explained that he did not want his sheep taken and that they should stop. The Navajo policemen dismounted, grabbed him, and a fight started. There was a law officer there named Sharp Edged Policeman (Siláo Adigishí), who received that name during the fight when he pulled a knife and cut one of the men. Sharp Edged Policeman pushed John Chee over, but he scrambled to his feet and continued to resist. Some people stood staring at them while they fought. Eventually some men pulled the combatants apart and took the protestors to jail where they stayed for months.

These policemen did the same thing to The One Who Acts Like a Man (Hastóí Ádíl'íní), but at night. I bet if it had been daylight so that he could see, he would have really whipped them. The One Who Acts Like a Man used to say, "I was almost killed while in jail because of my horses." The officials were fighting with him all year because of this. People really worked to get him out of jail, but he remained there throughout the year until the following winter when all of the religious ceremonies were over. He returned with John Chee. When the police took these two men away, they also removed their livestock from the corrals and killed all of their sheep.

Another incident that happened to one of my children's in-laws occurred in Teec Nos Pos, Arizona. This woman had her sheep in her corral when the officials told her that they had to be divided in half to be taken away. She forbid it. A man named Harry attacked one of the policemen, tied him up, and a woman leaped on the range rider and tied him with his own bandana. I heard that she climbed on top of him so that when he got tired, his urine came out. This is what some of our people did during stock reduction. If anybody ever tried to do this again, the fight would be so great that the white men would choke from the dust. If they did this now, they would be killed because today our boys are not afraid of anything. A long time after all the sheep and goats had been chased away, a man came into our house and said, "Your livestock has again increased.

Now maybe we'll have to take them away." He said that he had heard it talked about, but I told him, "No."

Some of the sheep were placed in corrals and others were just driven down in a canyon and chased against cliffs or in the corners of rocks and killed. The white men who did this were stockmen who counted the sheep, as well as the policemen who came from Kayenta, Gallup, and other areas. I think some of the policemen were there in case somebody spoke against the killing of the animals. In some places, the sheep were dipped and as they came up from the vat and into the corral, the animals to be killed were separated from the rest. This killing was such a big waste. At that time, there were a lot of coyotes that came in and ate some of these sheep, as did some of our dogs. You can still see their bones lying around. Some of the castrated sheep were killed even though they were still good. The men in charge of this slaughter said to us, "You who have no livestock left, kill some here and take the meat with you" but we said, "Why do you take these away from us, kill them, then tell us to take them back? It is too late to do anything. You take them. You're the ones who were longing to have them! Why don't you eat them yourselves?" My family did not eat any of our sheep. We all said, "Why should we do this, trying to get the last piece when they make us suffer so much?" That is why we did not eat any of the slaughtered sheep. There were some people who took a lot of meat from the dead animals. They skinned them after they were shot. The men in charge said, "Cut their throats right from here, leave their hooves, tail, and wool on but take the rest. Skin them like you would a buffalo and take the insides for yourselves." So some of the people skinned their sheep right there. It is said that your grandfather skinned one over at Tségiizh [near Gouldings] but then decided not to and so he and others took off on their horses, saying, "We don't like the way you have to skin them. It is frightening."

The men from here used to go over there to see what was happening. My grandfather, The Man Who Came Across (Hastiin Tsé'naa'í) and two other men, used to go over to the shooting to see what was taking place. The goats were bedraggled, some of them blind, and acted lost wherever they went. I heard that many of them were dying from gunshot wounds. "What if their [white men's] livestock and possessions were treated the same way as they treated ours? How would they feel?" When this happened, I used to think that they almost wiped us out for good. At one point, there was talk about the children. Fine girls and boys were to be picked and sent away to the enemy's territory (school). They also told

One of the two most traumatic events etched into the tribal memory, second only to the Long Walk era, was livestock reduction. A warm relationship exists between herders and their flocks, many older Navajos recognizing personality traits, characteristics, and values assigned to each animal. The phrase "sheep is life" was not an overstatement for many traditionalists. (Courtesy San Juan County Historical Commission)

us they would ship us off somewhere. They said land was bought somewhere for people called the Navajo.

I don't know where John Collier came from, but he came upon us. There was a Navajo named Dan Phillips (Hastiin Bi'éé' Łikizh—The Man Whose Clothes Are Spotted) who traveled around the reservation talking against these things. He recruited three lawyers, two of whom came from our area and shared his views and concerns. They went around speaking about these problems to the people and later went to Washington. I always wondered how much more damage the white men's minds would have done to us if Dan Phillips and a group of men had not gone to Washington. Maybe all of our stock would have been taken, leaving only our homes to live in. Dan Phillips, John Chee, Little Fat One (Neesk'ahii Yázhí), and others went there and things started to slow down, but by then the situation had become pretty bad, to the point where very little livestock was left. Still, range riders continued to come around to those who had few animals and tried to take them. They said, "Try very hard to take all the stock away." This is what some of our own people who worked for those reducing the stock said. These were our own people who lived among us.

The elders used to say that the earth was getting tired and could not give anything more. In the Navajo way of thinking, it is believed that the sheep, horses, and everything around us are what you live by. It is said that they have a holy being. When the sheep are thirsty, they pray to him, saying that the livestock needs something to drink. Then the rain comes and waters the sheep, the grass will grow, and the earth is well. It is like that on some of our enemy's land where there is abundant grass when it rains. The Navajos live in a bad situation, in a place where trouble is always nearby. I heard that there was going to be a ceremony held especially for this problem, but it never happened. I think that at times, because we do not practice our religion as we used to, we do not receive very much happiness. A long time ago it was not like that. There were a lot of sheep with plenty of sunflowers, big fields of hay, mountain rice, and grass. All around, it was dark with vegetation. When you walked over the land, it was difficult because of the grass and weeds in your path. Now, it looks different. The land has turned white because of the lack of vegetation. Our enemy's land is very good. Yesterday, I went past Bluff. I saw a lot of black greasewood, sand sage, grasses, weeds, and mountain rice and thought to myself, "I wish our land was like that."[9]

Nedra's comments reflect the experience and feelings of many of the Navajos living in Monument Valley and throughout the reservation. A number of themes emerge from this and other testimonies that challenge the Anglo perspective as to why it was done. For instance, the main motivation driving the Soil Conservation Service of the federal government was to preserve the land from the ruinous effects of overgrazing and erosion by wind and water. Scientific studies showed that there were parts of the reservation that had lost up to 90 percent of the topsoil, gullying had increased, and there were just too many animals for the desert lands to support. Some of this information was later refuted, but at the time and with the great dustbowl experience in the Midwest, reduction seemed the correct course of action.

The Navajos viewed it differently. For instance, the government told Guy Cly that the animals had eaten all of the vegetation. "This was what we were told. It wasn't happening like that. I told of the plentiful vegetation at that time. The sunflowers were this big and the cattle walked among them. There is only food available for the animals if there is livestock. It is through them the land is alive. There was lots of vegetation and it rained often. The sheep and the horses were happy about the rain. That is how life was back then."[10] The animals knew the songs and prayers that ensured the rain and snow.

Another theme that emerges strongly is comparing livestock reduction to "Navajo reduction" of the 1860s. Hite Chee, from Monument Valley, clearly linked livestock reduction to this past.[11] He told of how during the 1860s, Navajos had their sheep "gunned down," creating starvation for the people. Both the Navajos who stayed behind and those who went to Fort Sumner decreased in number because after soldiers killed the animals, "There got to be much hunger around here and it was even killing the children. . . . I guess they thought we would eventually be exterminated as a people."[12] Chee went on to say:

There were no sheep left. Before that, there were quite a few sheep running around. The bones of the horses that were laying around were boiled; it was not enough for a stew. Hunger killed some of them [Navajos], but the people were strong. . . . [Finally, the leaders of the two opposing groups] spoke to each other. They said: "From here on we will not do any harm to each other again. . . . Here are your sheep, the ones we have done away with. . . ." This was what the Navajo people were given. . . . There were many [sheep] later. After so many years there came people called "horse rangers." The talk of sheep and goats came about, "They were a nuisance and so much trouble around," and they [whites] started planning again. That is how it came about. . . . Then they shot all of them [livestock].[13]

Fred Yazzie agreed that the past was linked to the present:

At that time, men knew how to pray. These prayers were answered. That's how they got rich and with those prayers, the corn fields flourished. Because of Fort Sumner, we couldn't progress. The Anglos controlled us too much. When we wanted something or did something, they said we were not responsible to freely do things. Back in the later 1930s, Navajos had lots of sheep, cattle, and horses. The government didn't want Navajos to flourish too much. They came up with permits. The permits put limits on the number of sheep, cattle, and horses. They threatened us if we did not comply. They would kill our livestock. John Collier and the government did this.[14]

Kayo Holiday felt the same way.

Across from here [west of Promise Rock], there was a picketed corral. They herded the sheep and goats in there, killed them immediately, and left all of the bones. Behind the Oljato Trading Post was a horse corral in the hollow of a rock where some were also killed. That is what the people were saying. It was from Washington, a person named John Collier, he was the one trying to wipe out the Navajos, but he did not succeed in gathering us all up.[15]

Another prevalent theme was the violent nature and personal shock to many witnessing the slaughter. Although some people owned large herds of sheep, goats, and horses, there was still a bond of friendship and cooperation that existed between owner and owned. These animals were not just wealth on the hoof, but assisted their caretakers when treated with respect. But respect for life was far from the carnage of livestock reduction. To Guy Cly, "There was chaos. People felt terrible putting the livestock to waste, many referring to them as the poor creatures when the animals were taken. The older women felt bad about the whole thing. In the Goulding area where the airport is now, the goats and sheep were butchered, with the horses being taken away. I think there were fourteen taken from us along with their colts."[16] Cecil Parrish remembers the cremation. "Just a little way from here [Oljato] where the old store stands, it is said that many of the sheep were burned. Many, many sheep were piled up and set on fire. All of these were just burnt."[17]

Ada Black catches the emotional trauma and empathy she felt for her animals as they suffered in the killing corrals.

I remember the killing of the goats near our home. The officials hauled our goats to two sheep corrals by the mesa. They told the people to butcher the animals and that the government would only take the skins. The meat was for the people who slaughtered the goats. The Anglos sent out messages to people to gather there and help kill and prepare the animals for food. Navajos came to help. When my husband and I arrived, there was meat strung along the corral fence and hides piled in the midst of all of this. As soon as someone stripped off the skin, it was added to the pile. There were small, young, beautiful goats there, causing one person to exclaim, "What great sacrifice! I wish we could put them back in our corral." The People were concerned about the waste of meat and how it could have been used if the slaughter had been handled properly. Instead of spreading it out over a period of time, this mass killing ensured that much of the meat went to waste. Angry words flew about, but the butchering continued until there were only two or three animals left. Other corrals and similar scenes in the Oljato, Goulding's, and Kayenta areas fanned the flames of resentment.

At one point, the officials ordered my husband to kill goats, but he refused, telling them to do it themselves, before he started home on foot. I had come with some friends and sat in their automobile watching events unfold. An official told them to go into one of the corrals and start killing animals, but they refused. He threatened to take the Navajo man off of the rolls of the CCC project in which he was employed unless he did what he was told, to which he replied, "The heck with all of this. I am going home." I agreed and asked them to take me also, which they did. I got to ride, my husband ended up walking, arriving home at sunset.

A second time we received word that there was going to be another slaughter, but this time at Goulding's. There were many women now living in the Monument Valley area who were invited. An automobile came for us, and since my husband was around, the officials wanted him to be there, too. He was working in the CCC Program at the time, so he and his fellow workers were needed and expected. Harvey initially refused but the next day relented, and we went to the site. When we arrived, meat was again hanging on the corral fence as before. Women were scattered all over the place butchering. The goats' throats were slashed, placed by a woman, and allowed to bleed out as the animals churned about in the dust of the corral. Some were old goats, which displeased many of the people. Men hauled the remaining ones away, then shot them with rifles. Workers stacked the dead goats, creating a tall pile of bones that would be there for years.

In Oljato the same thing happened, but there they drove them into a box canyon before shooting the animals. Right next to the rock where this happened, there remained another large pile of bones. The Navajo people involved remembered for a long time how they had been wronged. There was one man named Tódích'íiniidííl who fled to Blanding and lived in that area for about three years. When everything quieted down, he moved back to Monument Valley but never surrendered his livestock to reduction. The range riders never counted his animals or got any of them, but he also did not receive a grazing permit. Those who stayed behind and lost livestock did get one.[18]

There is no way of knowing how many animals were actually killed. One way to determine the net effect is to refer to the results of one stock holder as a representative for many. LaMar Bedoni's experience will serve

The killing and butchering of livestock was performed with reverence and followed an exact procedure that showed the sacrificed animal the respect with which it was viewed. The mass slaughter during livestock reduction was the antithesis of how things should be done. (Courtesy Photo Archives, Utah State Historical Society)

as an example of the impact these events had on the people of Monument Valley.

Sixty-three years ago, when I was 24 years old, the talk of goats came about. I still remember the events from the time when it began. About 160 of our goats were driven into a canyon corner and killed. During the shooting, one man was wounded in the leg. I still remember it beautifully. The goats were taken from us for only 50 cents a head, but even then, we were not paid right away, but had to wait for six months. Some of us did not receive any money for three years, and when we did, it was not very much. For the 160 goats taken, we were compensated only $20. All of them were killed, causing the people to suffer and beg for things. From that time on, we herded only a very small number of sheep and horses.

Then they did the same thing again. During this time, we fought with some range riders. I was the one who roped the gate of the corral open so that all of the captive horses in the pen could escape. Navajo men went in with their horses and chased them out. That was why the range riders were after us and some of the men were taken away for their actions. The government sent White Hat, Shorty Yazzie, Charley, and a crippled named Hastiin Luke, to jail in Fort Defiance for six months.

From that time on, the range riders took 78 cows that they cornered in a canyon and shot to death right in front of us. Their bones remain where they fell. This time, they paid us nothing and just did it. I heard that the men who were in jail got out in return for the killing of the cows as a payment. Officials told us not to replace the missing horses, sheep, and cows. This was the law. We felt like we were all tied up and could not do anything. At this same time, I used to have 68 goats and all of them were taken from me. As for horses, I used to have 33 of them, but they even took the studs. I also had 28 cows that were chased away as well as taking my grandparents' and relatives' livestock and there was a lot.[19]

Bedoni echoes the feelings of other livestock owners, pointing out the unfairness, psychological harm, and uncertainty that these actions created.

Range Rider with a Heart—Ed Smith

At this point, most readers are probably ready to lynch the nearest range rider that can be found. Yet as so often in life, there is another view, a second side to the story. Ed Smith provides such a perspective. Born in New Jersey in 1915 and later transplanted to the West, where he held a multiplicity of jobs, he eventually ended up as a range rider working for the Bureau of Indian Affairs (BIA) in the Shonto–Navajo Mountain area, close to Monument Valley. He later married Virginia Carson, then lived and worked at the Oljato Trading Post. He provided a lengthy interview in 1972 that gives a very different perspective than the one told by Navajo people of range rider Charley Ashcroft, who covered the neighboring district of Black Mesa and Monument Valley. Ed shared his reasoned, balanced position as an insider to the government program, which, at least philosophically, was enacted for the "benefit" of the Navajo people. As we have seen, often these good intentions went astray in the hands of those enforcing the rules and achieving desired outcomes. Ed begins:

After the BIA found out I was a cowpuncher, they put me to work, desiring cowpunchers handling stock reduction rather than sheep men, who would have done a better job because they understood the situation. I went into the field as a range rider, but they had made a mistake, because I had been trained as a stockman rather than a cattleman. I had just as much love for a sheep as I did for a cow and was not at all sympathetic to the policy of destroying them. There was no doubt we had to reduce the sheep, but some people in the government service had the idea that

Indians were something below them, and so for years, that was the way the Indian Service looked at it.

When you get in the field, you learn that a Navajo has so many head of sheep, how many animals he eats a year, and where he hides many of them. Navajos do not dock the tails of the sheep that they are going to eat and just leave them long. They dock the tails of the ones that they are going to sell or breed, but on the wethered lambs—those castrated bucks—the tails are left long. So when you count the sheep, as you ride around these different canyons like Rainbow Bridge and others, you look across and see all these "stones" on the far hill that are hidden, except that they are moving. If these stones have long tails, the stockmen did not count them, because if you did, then the government would want to confiscate them. The Navajos would be forced to sell them, then they would not have enough sheep to eat in winter, and by summer they would be starving. So a good range rider had to be enough of an outdoorsman to be reasonable rather than going strictly by the book. That did not go over well with John Collier and some of the men that were trying to put their finger down on the Navajos.

Stock reduction fostered a lot of hard feelings against some of the old range riders who were very cruel because they were cattlemen. Of course, the sheep men and others got along fine with the Navajos. When the government ran out of funds and could not bring the bucks in, then we brought them in at our own expense, paying for them out of our own pockets and selling them to the Navajos. That was our word. The government told us what to say to the Navajos, but if one does not go through with what they say, then they are liars. We cannot be liars to the Indians because they have heard from too many of those over the years. We felt a responsibility. And even though a Navajo could not pay for it at the time, in those days his promise to pay held true, whether they could do it in one year or ten, they would do it.

There were those who never went to Fort Sumner and declared that they had never signed the peace treaty with the United States and so anything the government said had nothing to do with them. Reduction became a case of negotiation whereas force was unreasonable. If you hurt me, then I will hurt you, which is common sense. If no one had physical power over the other, then we sat down and talked about it and agreed that if they would allow us to cull their sheep that were not very good and the horses that could not be broken because they were knock-kneed and deformed, then we would bring them in and see that they had studs and bucks. That is why we personally felt obligated to keep our word.

As range riders there was another policy that the government did not approve and did not know about. If an Indian turned in so many of their horses to be sold, we would theoretically keep them in the corral, but if another man had a worse horse that he did not have to sell, then we let him exchange it for the better one, as long as every morning we had the same number of horses in the corral. Nobody was supposed to know what happened to the horse because it might have changed color. It could have been a dust storm that changed a gray horse to a brown. So that is one thing we did. If any stock was going to be sold at butcher-market prices and the condition made no difference, then if somebody wanted to make an exchange without our knowing it, they would be perfectly welcome to. This was also true with the sheep. Someone could come in at night and exchange an old sheep for a good one because we actually did not start branding animals until after the reduction. Of course, the government did not approve of these exchanges because it felt that we were not being strict enough. It has nothing to do with helping another human. Still, the herds had to be reduced; they were tremendous. A Navajo's wealth was determined by the number of horses he owned, even though a man might have hundreds of animals that were crippled, knock-kneed, and unusable, but number determined wealth. When he married a woman, he gave so many horses for her and sometimes might take three or four girls at one time to marry.

I volunteered to be a range rider and understood what I was getting into. I thought that somebody who liked stock ought to be out there to help the Navajos. There were enough men running around trying to boss them without having anybody that the Navajos could depend on. I thought that if I got out there, maybe I could help them understand why reduction had to take place. All over the United States on federal land, everything was overstocked because the government had never controlled units per acre. Even a white man was allowed to run as many sheep as he wanted to pay for, and so the land became overgrazed and the entire country needed the conservation movement. It was a good deal if it was handled right because the ranges were just terrible. The government tried to explain the entire problem because of overgrazing. But, when it rained, the grass grew! We fenced off sections of ground to show people that the area that wasn't grazed was better than the one that was, but the sad truth was that when it did not rain, the fenced area did not grow grass any better than the other one. When it rained, both areas grew grass! So we were unable to convince many people that grass grew when it didn't rain whether you had sheep or not. There was a long drought at that time and stock reduction came about at the end of a long series of them. I think that was what forced the federal government into this kind of conservation act on overgrazing. Had it been raining all the time and we had had ample moisture, nobody would have thought of it any more than they did before. Still, it was a good thing. By the end of reduction, through the Taylor Grazing Act, livestock owners were set up so that each man had so many sheep units in relation to the number of animals he had. Some of the clever Navajos, like Chee Dodge and others with big families and wealthy, scattered their sheep among their relatives so that the family controlled a lot of sheep units. No matter how they did it, as children, grandchildren, and great grandchildren appeared, there would not be enough land to provide adequate sheep units. There would not be sufficient sheep for everyone to make a living.

Those appointed to carry out the program varied in how they approached it. Some police officers and range riders got their job done without any friction, while others only did it by bullying. Those who bullied got their head bashed in and a lot of them disappeared, never to be seen again. Others had no problem. It was up to the individual. This was a fair thing because we were only counting heads. We weren't counting conditions. There wasn't any idea of selling them for any value other than just butcher value, which was in pounds. So all in all, if they were smart, they got along just fine. We would set a time, then I would ride around to check and see if the herd contained as many sheep as they said or if they had hidden some. That's when you had to use a little discretion as to what type of "stones" you saw moving around. When they understood that you were on the level, then they were on the level, but if you tried pulling authority, that was a good way to get yourself shot. After all, those animals were their personal property as well as their food.

This is not to say that there were no bad feelings, especially about John Collier because he would say one thing then do just the opposite. He talked out of both sides of his mouth all the time. The Anglos were used to it, calling it "political speeching," but the Navajos did not believe him. For instance, we would not say, "We will meet you to dip your sheep on such-and-such day," then expect the herders to be there before we arrived. No. We would camp there the night before and they would come to see if we had kept our word. If we were there, then they would come. If we planned to come rushing right up like big bosses and have everybody waiting for us, they would never have shown up. There was no expectation that the white man would keep his word. If you were there, then you had kept it. In other words, our theory was that you were expected to keep your word to them whether they kept theirs to you or not. It wasn't wrong for them to break their word, but it was wrong for you to break yours.

It was important to sit down, talk, and understand what we were trying to accomplish, what they had to do, and listen to the reasons they did not want to do it. When you get the reasons for and against and put the two together, you probably would find very, very little reason why they did not want to. It might be because they would not have enough sheep to live on and so you cannot blame them for hiding those wethered sheep for them to eat; if they hid them, then you do not have to count them. What you can't see, you can't count, but, of course, you know by your range riders just who's got what hidden where. When they have a ceremony or some other get together, they might have to butcher 25 sheep to feed the people that attend. If a man is keeping out one hundred sheep and explains that he is going to hold a squaw dance or some other ritual in the fall, you can count on it. They will not lie to you and you understand his thinking. All you are trying to do is reduce the overall number of breeding sheep that he's going to have during the year and he will not have any complaint because you understand what his thinking is when he objects. I have been riding on the range and had an old Navajo come up and tell me he needs some money. I would reach into my pocket and give him $20, which in those days was a lot. I didn't know him, but he knew me. Maybe a year later a boy appeared on horseback and handed me a bunch of coins amounting to $20. I would ask, "Well, what's this for?" and he would say, "My father borrowed it." Then I thought way back, "Well, I guess that's right. I remember now." That's the way they were.

The government, on the other hand, was all about estimating and keeping track of numbers. The Bureau of Indian Affairs compiled all of the figures, but they didn't mean anything and were ridiculous. But that is what they wanted, accompanied by a lot of paperwork. They used to call me the "paper cowboy" because of the branding. I would have all these branding slips and things in the corral, and be trying to keep track of everything while branding a cow. Then the animal would start kicking and running around, spilling my papers, and there I'd sit in the middle of corral with a branding iron here and papers all over there. That's how I got the name. Oh, I had a lot of fun.

I did not go to the Oljato Trading Post until I married Virginia, after livestock reduction was over. Even then, I was still attached to animals. Of course, when I got married I had to change everything. I couldn't bring my horse in the house anymore. It was terrible because before, all you had for your company was your horse. You'd get out in the corral and eat with him, and when you'd eat in the house, he'd come walking in. But when you get married, women do not understand this type of thing. They think you do not have to spend more time with your horse than you do with them. That's a bad thing when you try to explain, "I can't let my horse down." It's kind of like one fellow who was here. I asked him if he was still married, and he said, "No. My wife had this little poodle. Do you remember?" and I told him that I did. He said, "Well, she made such a fuss out of it you'd think it was a child, so finally, I just put my foot down and said, 'Honey, either you choose between that dog or me!' She got the divorce about a year ago."[20]

A Trader's Perspective—Mildred Heflin

While livestock reduction had a huge impact on the Navajo, it also caused a significant change in the economy of the trading posts. Dependent on wool, lambs, woven products, and a credit system tied to all three, these stores suddenly saw their financial base pulled out from beneath them. The spring and fall payment plans now were greatly curtailed, while Navajo men and later women increasingly moved into an off-reservation economy. It became more and more difficult for men to remain home, maintain certain cultural practices, and avoid the impact of the dominant society in everything from employment, school for their children, the necessity of learning English, and increased technological sophistication. Not all of this was necessarily negative and grazing pressure on the ranges was diminished, but the old ways went into decline.

Mildred Heflin at the Oljato Trading Post recorded her reaction to the loss of livestock.

> The Navajos were quite upset with stock reduction. Of course, we couldn't quite see the overall picture, either, but were in sympathy with the Indians because this program was forced on them. I suppose it was a necessary thing, but like all government projects, there were a lot of people involved and some things were unjust. A lot of Navajos hid their livestock, mostly sheep and a lot of old horses that were not worth a darn; the government never did find them. In one sense, the program was a very good thing because it got rid of a lot of worthless livestock. There was a lot of unproductive animals and the owners did not know ways to improve them and yet a herd of sheep was a Navajo's investment, his

total capital. This might be everything a person had other than jewelry. It was very upsetting to have someone come in and force a family to sell its property, but it was especially bad because for Navajos, since individuals did not have other resources and no training to find different work.

As traders at this post from 1937 to 1945, we felt helpless. The Navajos told us of their problems, but we could not do anything about them except let them have some money to go to Washington to protest. We listened and sympathized, but we were at the mercy of the Indian agent at Window Rock. Our post was on reservation land and we could lose our lease and be kicked off at any time. As far as we were concerned, we carried on as usual, and even though reduction loomed large for a few years, when World War II started, everything was forgotten and the Indians either joined the service or went to work on the railroads. We took a lot of people to little towns around the borders where they joined crews to work on the railroads. As for our business, we did not have the same amount of sheep or wool as before, and so they did not buy as much until the whole economic situation changed with the availability of outside work, which in turn, changed the whole economic setup on the reservation. The traders in this area were affected because now there was work on the railroads for all the Indian males who wanted it, while employers started hiring here for farm labor and all sorts of other workers. Before stock reduction, we were dependent primarily on the Indian economy, credit, and pawn. The government did, however, come and put in lots of dams and other Civilian Conservation Corps (CCC) projects to give people work. This greatly relieved economic pressure, as far as stock reduction was concerned.

At that time, I was really mad at John Collier just like the Navajos. I thought he was pretty bad, but as I grew a little more mature and looked back over the situation, I thought what he did was probably for the best, but very poorly handled. Whenever you tell anyone that they have got to do something, there are going to be problems and resistance. If the government had offered a good price, events would have worked better. The Indians on the reservation were not allowed to sell livestock prior to reduction. They should have opened up the reservation and said, "Look, we're going to let you sell all the livestock you want." The government could have just let the traders or some livestock buyers come in and pay the Navajos a good price for their animals. There would have been no problem or stirred-up mess like they got. The big stock owners kept most of their animals while the little guy got hit the hardest. It wasn't really fair.

My experience with the few range riders I had anything to do with, left me feeling they had done the best they could. They were as fair as anybody when working under such difficult circumstances. The Indians were upset about these problems and most of the range riders did not speak Navajo and had no interpreters, so just guessed about certain things and could not really do a great deal. The few I knew were really sympathetic with the Indian and tried to understand his problem, but the government stood on the opposite side going in a different direction. Washington did not always understand the problems out here and so I thought the Navajo reaction was justified. I would have felt the same way if people had told me for years and years that I must build up my flocks and save my sheep and that this was the way to conduct my life, and then, all of a sudden come in and told me that I had to sell half of my flock. Any individual would have reacted the same way. Their thought: "The problem is not caused by overgrazing, but because the white man is here and we do not have any rain."[21]

Shine Smith and the Washington Delegation

A cause needs an activist, and for the Kayenta–Monument Valley region, that man was Shine Smith, a Presbyterian minister, who befriended both John and Louisa Wetherill along with Reuben and Mildred Heflin to the point that he became a fairly permanent fixture at their establishments. We turn here to Willow Roberts, who in her study of Stokes Carson, paints a picture of this man-of-the-cloth—his personality and the role he played with the local Navajos during livestock reduction.

A missionary named Shine Smith (Doojiishdódí), who had been with the Presbyterian mission at Ganado in the 1920s, arrived at the Wetherills' in Kayenta during the mid-1930s, then at Oljato around 1937, where he "sort of came and stayed." Not everyone felt warm toward him. One trader said that he liked Shine Smith because it made him feel good when the man left. Shine had a habit of cooking a large pot of stew from ingredients he gathered from the trading post shelves, but did not volunteer to pay for it, feeding all the customers in the store, which not every trader appreciated. However, the Navajos in the area liked and appreciated him taking them to the hospital, driving them about the reservation, and helping when he could.

Shine Smith was an easygoing individual who often drew an admiring crowd of friends. During the livestock era, he became a spokesman with his Navajo neighbors, visiting Washington, D.C., to fight on their behalf. While many traders agreed with their customers that what was forced upon them was wrong, few advocated for their customers, or else the government would revoke their trading license. (Courtesy Special Collections, J. Willard Marriott Library, University of Utah)

At Christmas, parcels of food, clothing, and gifts were sent to Shine by friends and charity groups with whom he kept in contact, and he always gave a party, wherever he was, a tradition shared by many trading posts as an annual event. Oljato furnished food and coffee prepared on an open fire. Shine presided over the distribution of gifts, a tall figure in the black cloth of the missionary with a laugh and a smile for everyone. He rarely pressured the Navajo on religion and attended ceremonies often avoided by other missionaries. Laughter was constantly with him, pulling jokes out of every situation. His sense of humor was wonderful and infectious, hence his nickname "Shine" because he made everyone feel brighter.

There was also a serious side to Shine. Once, while he sat at the Oljato post with Mildred, Freddie, and another frequent visitor, C. E. Purviance, an academic doing a study on Navajo child development, a discussion arose about religion. Purviance announced that he doubted not Christ's goodness but his divinity. Shine became apoplectic. Scarlet in the face, he began to slap the table, crying, "Purviance, you're going to hell." Purviance, a man who never raised his voice, was more concerned that Shine would have a heart attack than for his own life in the hereafter. But the incident gave a glimpse of the religious concerns, intensity, perhaps even anger, that lay behind Shine's sense of fun and laughter.

Shine became a frequent visitor, if not an almost permanent fixture, at Oljato. He had his own room, and when he was there, he followed the routines of the house. He sometimes helped in the store, doing odd jobs, keeping the family in good humor. At the end of a busy day, when the customers had gone and the evening had come with its customary solitude, his cheerful presence was welcomed by the Heflins, especially by Mildred when Reuben, trailing the fall lambs to Farmington for sale, was gone for weeks. In October 1940, Mildred's first baby, Edie Jo, was born. Jessie Carson became a grandmother and Shine Smith a babysitter. Like Jessie, Mildred went to Farmington to have the baby. There was no telephone at Oljato, and the nearest doctors were at the small hospital at Tuba City (the sanitarium in Kayenta had by this time closed down).

As stock reduction became an increasingly inflamed issue, Oljato took the path of political action, sending a small delegation to Washington in May 1941. Members of the community came to the post to pawn bracelets and bead necklaces in order to collect enough money to pay the fares of six people to visit with President Roosevelt: John Chee and his senior wife, from Oljato, John Fat and Little Fat One from Navajo Mountain, Old Man Salt from Kayenta, and Shine Smith. Reuben lent them his truck, so that they could drive to Durango through Utah, because rumor had it they would be stopped if they went through Shiprock. In Durango, they met up with Stokes and Jessie, who brought the truck back to Farmington for Reuben, while the delegation left by train for Cortez, where there was an airport.

Once in Washington, Shine managed to get them an interview with Eleanor Roosevelt, though not with the president. The wife of John Chee told her, through an interpreter, "Our sheep are our children, our life, and our food. The rain gods would send no rain," she said, as there were no animals to eat the grass. Mrs. Roosevelt was sympathetic, but it was beyond her power to help. This little group returned home. To raise everyone's spirits, Shine did an imitation of John Fat in line in a busy Washington cafeteria, carefully unwrapping his money. First, John unrolled a piece of calico, then a piece of buckskin, as impatient heads waved in line, but

John slowly counted out the correct change and slowly rewrapped the money, returning the package to his shirt bosom. With imperturbable patience (and perhaps a private resistance, a thumb-of-the-nose to the haste and impatience of Easterners) John repeated this performance each time he paid for his meal. Shine's mimicry made Mildred and the Navajos laugh, a little piece of comparative ethnography they all could appreciate.

The trip to Washington gained them nothing. Rational action had proved ineffective, but the demonstration of Navajo opinion caused trouble, at least for Shine. The Agency superintendent, E. R. Fryer, was not happy when he learned about the trip. An outspoken man, a good and conscientious administrator, and the superintendent of the Navajo Service from 1936 to 1942 throughout the difficult and touchy situation of the stock-reduction program, he worked hard to achieve the results that Collier saw as crucial to Navajo welfare. Upset by this expression of disagreement led by a missionary, a somewhat unofficial one at that, he drove 250 miles of dirt road from Window Rock to find Shine Smith and threatened to "expel" him from the reservation. BIA officials once again complained that neither missionaries nor traders gave the government much support for its programs for the Navajo.[22]

Mildred Heflin agreed. In her words, "We could have gotten in very serious trouble over our involvement because here we were going against what the United States government was telling them to do. The Indian agent was quite upset, of course. Fortunately, he blamed the missionary more than he did us. But the Navajos that went, wanted Shine to go because they had never been off the reservation in their lives. He became their spokesman."[23] Although nothing concrete came from this visit and the World War II economy increased jobs, it was not until 1946 that reduction had run its full course and the Taylor Grazing Act was fully implemented. By this time, tribal figures indicate that dependence on agriculture and livestock had decreased by 57 percent in a little more than a decade, though this figure varied by region, by outfit, and by individual, depending on the number of losses.[24]

CHAPTER EIGHT
Stars of Sage and Screen
Moviemaking in Monument Valley

I n 2001, I published a chapter entitled "Indians Playing Indians: Navajos and the Film Industry in Monument Valley, 1938–1964" in *Navajo Land, Navajo Culture: The Utah Experience*.[1] In it, I discussed much of the "how" of that industry during those years—recruitment of Navajo actors, role selection and payment, logistical support, interracial relations, acquisition of props, and the leadership of John Ford and John Wayne. There was also a fair amount of oral history provided by Navajo participants recalling those days of adventure, hard work, and friendship, which was not to gloss over some of the issues that arose. Many of those actors and extras provided recollections of performing in specific movies and some of the fun things that happened. Indeed, there was a great deal of material that I did not use due to space limitations and the more academic theme of the chapter. Since that time, a number of people have commented that they particularly enjoyed those parts provided by the Navajos, learning how traditional beliefs were an important aspect of the experience, as well as illustrating differing perspectives between cultures. Their *Stories of the Land*, as they relate to the film industry, are the topic of this chapter. For a more scholarly discussion of those years, read "Indians Playing Indians." In keeping with the chapters of this book, oral history illuminates the Navajo experience.

Fred Yazzie (1915–2002) lived in the heart of Monument Valley his entire life, near what is today called the "Crossroads." Raised in the traditional Navajo world and a permanent resident of the valley, he is an excellent person to share his experiences of how the land and its people have changed and what the forces were that changed them. The movie industry and the "discovery" of the scenic value of this area is one of those important stories. Certainly, Harry Goulding's promotion of both is an important part and well-told from his and Mike's perspective in Samuel Moon's *Tall Sheep: Harry Goulding, Monument Valley Trader*.[2] Their views as entrepreneurs differed from that of the Diné who frequented their post, acted in the movies, and worked in the uranium mines—the topics of this and the next two chapters. He and Mike were skilled promoters of business endeavors that brought prosperity to many people, but as a number of men involved in the movie industry note, there was often a significant difference as to how the Navajo viewed these activities. Fred, who was involved from beginning to end and even the denouement of the John Wayne–John Ford years, begins our narrative.

From Bows 'n Arrows to Proprietor—Fred Yazzie

Fred Yazzie remembers:

> Harry Goulding moved this way to the small box canyon where his store is now. Anglos who came from the hot places began planning and as time progressed, more and more came. This was in 1925 when I was first put into school. Time progressed and with the coming of the movies I returned from school, when there was talk of another one being made. I just wondered what this movie was. Then in about 1930, it was clear to me what this moviemaking was and what the Anglos were doing. When I was nineteen years old, a man called John Stanley and his brothers, who were young and in good physical shape, started selecting other Navajos for parts. The movie they were in was about Anglos capturing Navajos and it was to be filmed in Monument Valley. They talked me into going over there and I was picked with others but did not know what was going on. During this time, there was plenty of vegetation in the valley, rain came often, and the horses were fat and gentle to handle because they were used to herding sheep, so they were selected to be in the movies. But there were also expensive horses transported in on big trucks. These were well-trained and had been flown in on airplanes from Hollywood.
>
> The movie people had tents in the valley, close to where they were filming. We were told that we were to live in those tents that had everything we needed: food for breakfast, lunch, and supper as well as clothing to be worn when acting. The Anglos who were performing were grouped separately. They ate only the finest food with no spoil in it. We were

also taken care of and given good food. This was how they would come among us each time they made a movie.

This film was about the soldiers coming into this area to capture the Navajos and bring them to Fort Sumner. One scene included burning hogans that were not real, women wearing traditional wool dresses (biil), and men dressed in pants that were too big and armed with bows and arrows. It looked funny because some people did not look right in the dresses and baggy pants, but others appeared very distinguished in this clothing. The people laughed at this, especially when they were pretending to fight in their poorly fitting clothes. We would jump on our horses as the Anglo soldiers invaded our land. The director told us to chase them down a ridge leading into the valley where they would gather in the rocks. They were very good, racing on their horses and darting between objects. They probably had practiced a long time, but we did not really know what was going on and so just did what we were told.

We would make the movie for about fifteen minutes, then just sit around until it was time to again do something. This lasted for about two weeks. When the hero went riding away on his horse, the camera equipment followed, but finally the hero died among the standing rock buttes, where he was buried. It felt very real. The Navajo men at that time said that this was ugly, was foretelling tragedy, and did not like what was going on. Others just laughed at this thinking. They said that they had killed an Anglo. Another movie used a stagecoach. This was filmed where the ranger station is located. The crew took about a month to make the movie here. Then winter went by and spring came again, and there was word going around of another moviemaking. We were involved this time in almost the same way as the one about going to Fort Sumner and were paid six dollars each day. That was a lot of money. We did not know about the green [paper] money until this time. We received five, ten, and twenty-dollar bills for pay. When you had only five dollars, it felt like a lot, but when it was twenty, you felt rich like it was a thousand, since during that time, things did not cost as much. With a twenty-dollar bill, one could buy flour, coffee, sugar, salt, and a whole pile of goods for that amount. When you were finished buying, you would have a lot of things like shoes and clothing, too. You can buy an entire outfit for less than twenty dollars. For instance, what we call ké tsósí (boots of some sort) were two dollars, a pair of pants a dollar and a half, and the same for a shirt. Money was worth a lot. Nowadays, twenty dollars buys a very small amount. The price of food is too high. Money is not worth much. It is like that today. This is what you will think about now. It was through the making of movies that we got to know what money was as the film people brought money among us.

During that time, Kayenta was the first stop because there were offices there. It was like an agency where the moviemakers were tied up first. This was the headquarters where we received instructions as to how everything was going to run. The money that the movie outfit brought remained in Kayenta. The film company had Window Rock's approval as to what would take place, so we did not really count. It is in this way they stole Monument Valley from us and it is the same to this day. Once the word went out that they were there, people came in to be selected. There was a man named Lee Bradley and also Harry Goulding, who intercepted the movie people as they arrived, to coordinate things. By 1940–41, filming movies became bigger with each effort. Some people did not like this because it was being done in sacred places. The Anglo would tell us to get up in those sacred places and roll rocks down. We pushed down imitation boulders onto the wagons passing by. The horses and wagons rolled under us and into the crevices of the rocks, as the rocks fell on top of them. These imitations looked real, as if the Anglos were really being killed.

Some medicine men did not like this. They would say that we were not supposed to do that, it was crazy, and it was the money that pulled people into the business. My father was one of them who protested, along with Mister Blackrock (Hastiin Tsézhinii) and Dághaałbei and Hastiin Ntł'ahí; they did not like it. At first, there were Navajos who said "No" to what was going on and tried to stop it. For instance, my father and Mister Blackrock rode in front of the moviemakers where the road goes down into the valley. As the film crew was shooting the movie one morning, my father rode up and told them to stop. The next day, they packed up and went back with the wagons and teams they had brought in, following what the people wanted. Leon and his brother Frank were upset over the incident, probably because that was how they got their money. Frank said in despair, "What have you done? We could have received some money and you messed it up for others." Harry Goulding was also upset. The movie crew was told only once not to do it and they stopped because they cared what the people said, so the filming ended. This scene was probably refilmed another time. Navajo attitudes changed, however, when the director offered money. A twenty-dollar bill handed out to individuals stopped the complaining. This was how the Anglos got people to do their bidding. One time they wanted my father to paint his face but he did not want to. There was friction even over things like this.

Once he agreed, other Navajos would say, "You said not to do this, yet you are painted." The saying was that money did it. He received twenty dollars and so agreed to it. He did some of his acting at the ranger station where pictures were taken. Sometimes I now see him in a movie when he was still young and in good shape.

In 1946, Harry Goulding arranged with the Hollywood people to bring wagons, stagecoaches, and a variety of horses. The stagecoach had to have animals to pull it. The Navajos dressed in the old way and chased the mail carriers. This was how the movie was made. There were soldiers in it who fought against the Indians. Lee Bradley and his brother Frank had first choice in selecting actors. They both helped with this and got a lot of money, while we received only a little bit. This same year, the film-makers made a big set of houses and buildings in the flat area near where the high school stands today. For this movie, *My Darling Clementine*, the staged area represented Tombstone, but we called it Ghost Town. It took them about a month to construct it, and it looked like a real town with well-made saloons and houses. The insides were beautiful and the bar looked like the real thing. When the actors were drinking, they acted like they were drunk. It was during this time that there was another movie being made, which started in the spring and continued into midsummer, that was also filmed there. The movie started in the Monument Valley area near El Capitan, moved up to the town, then went all the way to the San Juan River. The people rode their horses and chased the Anglos into the water. Kee Stanley's horse started bucking under a tree, which left his wig hanging in the branches above. People laughed at the dangling hair and his getting bucked off.

My main job was to guard a lot of the equipment and animals at night. There were many horses, maybe two hundred head, that were kept in dugout stables. There was also a water trough and a garage that was also dug out. Some of it was cemented in where one can still see the handprints of some of the actors who had been there. My father's hand and name still show. I worked as a night watchman and so was familiar with where all of the filming took place and heard what happened each day. I mostly took care of the horses along with the many saddles and equipment that went along with them. Walking around each night, I made sure that everything was secure, so I was paid around two hundred dollars for a month's work, a part of which I received each week. Lee and Frank Bradley probably were paid more. When the movie people gathered their things and left, I was told to take care of the houses and buildings on the movie set. As a newlywed, I took my wife and stayed

Fred Yazzie was one of the first Navajos to record his impressions of photography and moviemaking in Monument Valley. His work with John Ford and interaction with various stars and crew members on different sets kept him occupied and happy. As one of the caretakers of the movie set of Tombstone, he had hoped to turn it into a business featuring tourism. Unfortunately, it was not to be. (Courtesy Special Collections, J. Willard Marriott Library, University of Utah)

there for several years. The movie people appeared each filming season and used this Wild West town. They just touched up the place and got to work but they also filmed scenes all over the valley.

When they stopped coming, I received one hundred dollars a month and took care of Ghost Town for about six years. John Ford and several other men flew in occasionally to check on it. One time they brought ten Mexicans to fix up the place because the moviemakers were going to return. I suggested that in the future, he let me maintain the structures and asked if this was possible. He agreed to let me repair the buildings saying, "You will take care of this and be in charge." I thought that if it was well-repaired, I could keep my horses there and have a horse-back guided tour for Anglos into the valley. I went to Window Rock to see what they had to say about it. These were my plans based on what was happening in Hollywood since John Ford had agreed to my suggestion. He said he would help me with one thousand dollars if I was really serious and the houses were kept well-repaired. He told me that this could be my start—a guided tour business on horseback for sightseers. This is what I planned on.

Things did not work out that way. At the time there was no ranger station or tribal park. The Navajo Nation put a man named Keith from Fort Defiance in charge of a different scheme, said that he was the one who came up with the idea, and pushed my plan aside. Several years later, it was said there would be buildings constructed for the ranger station. I asked if this was my plan that was being used and was told that I had no part in it, that it was Keith's idea. He is the one who thought of it and implemented the whole thing about tours in the valley. I asked why I was not given credit for thinking this up and providing the plan. Then the people opposed me and I came out alone with no one to speak on my behalf. It is good when there is someone else backing you up, but without this, I gave the idea up.

I still was in charge of repairing the houses and thought that I could run my own tours from there. Then I learned that they were thinking of tearing them down and Keith told me the property had been given to him and that I could take care of it for $25 a month. Yet John Ford had been paying $100. I told him that will amount to nothing and that he should pay me $100. We disagreed, so I went to argue my case and had no pay for fifteen months. Eventually, I received $800 but was never given the rest I was owed. Lee Bradley received all of the houses that I had been told were going to be mine. Keith and Lee probably met about this and agreed to what would happen. They just took it and gave it to someone else. I asked if I could have only one house, but that did not happen either. Lee said he had bought all of it for $1,000 and that I should step aside so I did. My involvement with the houses just barely paid for my bills, which had piled up. I was, however, able to pay them off, such as my debt at Goulding's, where I owed about $500. This was paid back, but the rest was on me. Men came in and tore the houses apart, leaving nothing. I told Lee that I thought he and Keith were greedy but there was nothing else I could do. Even to this day, I am told that I do not have any say about what is happening.[3]

Filling in Some Details—Seth Clitso

Seth Clitso, like Fred Yazzie, was one of the keepers of the massive amounts of equipment, props, production gear, and other logistical items that had to be maintained and emplaced on a daily basis to ensure a smooth flowing operation. This gave Seth an opportunity to be heavily involved in much of what transpired at the filming locations. He also served as one of the actors, sharing much of his experience in an interview that covered a wide range of activities.

In the movie, you are always conquered, the Anglos being the only ones who win. The producers hired Navajos to fall off their horses when shot. They were told, "If you are willing to fall you will be paid $50." Everyone wanted to be the one who got shot. People would ask if they could be the one to fall from the horse.

Movies were made in the summertime and so the people slept any place in the Goulding area or went home and returned in the morning. There were also tents to live in. People were brought back to this place and the next morning went out with the horses and maybe some cows to the site of the filming. At noon, we received lunches. There were three of us who managed the props and equipment—me, my father, and a man named Leon Bradley, who understood and conversed with the Anglos. I worked mostly as a home sitter, but sometimes participated in the movies. The film crews would leave their things in the valley, so I stayed with the equipment wherever it might be. There was often a collecting place where they gathered the wagons and the crew's trucks that carried gear. This is where I worked along with Fred Yazzie.

Brothers Frank and Lee Bradley had Navajo and Hopi blood and did much of the organizing and cast selection of the Indian actors. They were tall and well-built, owned livestock used in the movies, and were not hesitant about things. This was why they were picked.

They chose the Stanley brothers—John, Jack, and Johnnie—because they too had long hair, were tall, and had strong facial features. Kee John Stanley, Johnnie's son, was also selected. He was good at falling off his horse when shot. I was a son-in-law to the Stanley brothers. Lee Bradley did much of the organizing before the filming started and picked the people who would be in the movie. What he was looking for were men who were tall with long hair. John and Johnnie fit this description. They were often killed in the movie, either being thrown off a horse or falling off a cliff. The prop men used rubber images to represent them when they were shot and fell from a height a long way down.

From Black Mesa came a man called Bijaanééz Háłóonii. All of these people chosen were from the Towering House (Kinyaa'áanii) Clan, born for the Salt (Ashįįhi) Clan and so this was how they were known and therefore picked. Others came from Oljato as well as distant places like Tuba City, but it was the relationship that helped with the hiring. Others were selected just for their looks or if they said they had participated in moviemaking. Occasionally I was picked to play a role. Some of us did not have long hair, so we received wigs. Even if a man had a shaved head, he could use fake hair that was fitted tightly. Sometimes there was a great need for long-haired people. One movie made in Page, Arizona, wanted people with beards. They also used camels, long-haired sheep that came from overseas, and long-robed Catholic priests. Many of the Navajo people in this movie were given beards to wear. This movie had to do with the long-clothed people in the olden times and the one who was on the cross. There were houses built for this on the edge of the water in Page. We spent two weeks filming there.

The clothing we used in the movies in Monument Valley was very shabby, but that is what they brought and wanted us to dress in. A person did not use his own good clothes. The people on the other side wore dark military clothing. A number of the Navajos understood the English language, which helped. If we had our own horses we would use them and if we had cattle, we were told to bring them in. Spotted horses were really desired. Everything helped to get the job. All of these things were considered ahead of time, before starting to film.

John Ford was the main director. The Navajos gave him the name of One Eye or Patched Eye because he wore an eye patch on one side. John Wayne was just known by his Anglo name. Ford was in charge of making the movies and so told us what to do. A person was told how to act by the moviemaker and then had to do it just right. Filming was very strict and serious business. If a person made mistakes, they were told to do it again in a certain way and say it just right because it was all being recorded. If we were told it was a sad occasion that is how we acted as they took the pictures. But there was always a crowd of onlookers who would see it as funny and laugh. For instance, a man might fall off his horse when shot. People would joke about this with each other. The ones who are making the movie also made fun of each other, telling and describing what happened when someone was thrown from a horse. Navajos love to joke, so they would make fun of each other. There was happiness in this. Afterward, the people laughed about someone's acting and had fun.

There were funny things that just came out naturally while filming. Navajo language appears in movies but is being spoken by Navajos playing another Indian tribe. The Anglos talked in their own language and so we did, too. We followed orders from the Hollywood directors, who

asked us to speak in our own language. Johnnie Stanley did and kept
saying, "We are starving," which had nothing to do with what we were
acting out. You can still see him in the movie saying this, which makes
Navajos laugh. I have not seen all of the movies that I was in. One time
we filmed in St. George, where we were asked to ride through a camp of
burning tents with both sides of the main encampment on fire. We had
to dart between these burning structures. One of the men got scared so
he hid behind some cover. When he was caught, the movie men asked
why he was still over there with his horse and not preparing for the
charge. He confessed to being afraid and so the Anglos told him to go
home. This happened when anyone did not follow instructions. If people
hesitated like that, they were usually sent away.

We rode our horses bareback with some having bridles and others
only a rope tied around their lower jaw. In this scene with the fire, they
put something flammable on the tent, like kerosene. The horses were
very nervous and jumpy at everything around them and were fat. As we
readied to ride through, the horses felt very slippery with no secure way
to hold on. When they started to run, it felt like there was no hope. In
the race through there, some of the Navajos fell off their mounts, which
was funny, but there were those who ended up in the burning tents. Their
clothing got singed as they crawled out. Others fell off where we were
supposed to stop after the charge; I know I almost did. There is fear in
doing these things. If you get scared easily, it is not good. It is like you
are going in there to die when you are part of moviemaking. Next, we
were told that we would ride down a canyon and into the water. Others
were sent across in a rowboat. We rode into the mucky water that covered
us with mud. Some people ended up floating in the river while only the
horses made it across to the far shore. They were good swimmers.

Many of the movies had a similar plot with soldiers fighting Indians.
We were armed with bows and arrow and at first would be winning.
Soldiers died, men rode into dangerous places, wagons burned, and they
were about to lose. Then everything changed and we were the ones who
always lost. Now these moviemakers are missed and only Anglos are the
ones employed. Navajos think of this as stealing, using the land but not
paying the people to work. These Anglos come to the Holiday Inn, drive
around in buses, and take pictures of the rocks, and no one is there to
stop them. This is what is happening now.

A long time ago the Anasazi lived in Monument Valley. Their pottery and houses were left behind, and many of their sites were places

that became desirable for making movies. Navajos believe that when a person dies, part of their spiritual essence remains in that place. If it is a Navajo who passes away and is buried there, it is called tohachoi. As the movies were filmed in these sites, no one ever bothered to stop the effects of this tohachoi place. Park rangers now have a boundary around these places that runs along Mitchell Butte and Mesa, over to where El Capitan sits, then close to Kayenta and up to the place called Kisiibiito. This is where Anasazi pottery lies about, and yet moviemakers filmed in these areas. Right on top of Comb Ridge the boundary continues, then onto the road from the other side of the ridge, over and along where the rocks are standing, then it runs into the highway and in between the rocks and back to Mitchell Butte. Now the rangers are told to take care of this place, but back then there were no such instructions. There was no talk of getting bodies out of this area because people came mostly for the buttes that stood there. Still many people used to live there and have since passed on. The moviemakers did not recognize there is tohachoi in these places, so they just made movies with no one to talk to them about it. The films were about people killing people, which invites death to stalk the living. What they did was taboo. The people pretended to die when shot, fall off their horses, and lie there. They might have an arrow sticking in them with oozing fake blood.

Some Navajos got to travel about to different locations where the filming occurred. This included places like Ahooteel, St. George, and Moab. They even went in an airplane to Mexico on the edge of the ocean. Some were scared to go to these places and felt like those pretending to die were witching themselves. They did not like seeing a person getting shot and then a bloody rubber doll falling from a cliff. This was truly witching because the dolls are like the people pretending to die. They did crazy things. Maybe this is why there is no more moviemaking.

During the time the main people were picked, others who were not in the movie were envious and there was conflict. When Navajos were at Ahooteel, people came together from all over Tuba City, so there was envy and competition to see who would get hired. The people did witching against each other, it was said. I, too, was in the moviemaking and it was just like that; this is probably why there were those who did not reach old age. At least this is my thought. Somewhere out there, their images were caught and are still shown among the Anglo. It is like that with John Ford, who also died. There are ceremonies to counter this problem that act like a shield and serve as different forms of protection.

It all depends upon the individual, but I would hear the songs being sung at night. They would also build fires, heat rocks, and have a sweat bath. Once in the sweat lodge, they would sing for protection. The people made these sweat huts near the filming sites and visit them. I do not know what songs they would sing while in the sweat hut, but people said they were songs about being shielded from harm. With this protection they went to make the movie.

Another thing that caused conflict was the many materials and buildings left behind when the movie people finished and left an area. The Navajos wanted these things for their homes. They began claiming parts of the building, then conflicts erupted. The moviemakers came, knowing that these things would either be destroyed or else taken back to Hollywood. Some people tried to distribute the good things, but without having someone to definitely say who an object belonged to, different people would claim it saying, "It is on my land" or give some other reason. Individuals took boards from the buildings for their personal use. Those living in the midst of Monument Valley got them but I do not know what they did with them. People ran off in all directions with these good materials. Nobody says now that this was from the time of the moviemaking. I do not know what they made out of these materials. Maybe they used it for a sheep corral, while some of the boards that were really good were probably used to make a house, but no one claims that is what happened.

If they were to have moviemaking again, there is a great need for the people to work. During the previous era, even women were in the movies. If it was said there was going to be a film, they probably would like that because the children were in rags and that is how they appeared in the movies. If a film crew came in, who is going to lean away from this work? The people would crawl in front of each other to be in the movie. A person thinks, "I will be the main person in the film and will provide livestock for it." This is what some people said and it happened.[4]

A Potpourri of Experiences

Many Navajos shared similar experiences as Fred Yazzie and Seth Clitso. Yet each person brought additional insight that further explained what filming in Monument Valley during the John Ford–John Wayne years meant to them. Here, short excerpts from a number of participants are shared to round out that experience. Starting with Bud Haycock, his

From left to right, John Wayne, John Ford, Harry Goulding, Ward Bond, and Harry Brendon (standing). The director and cast members discuss with one of the crew the shooting of the next scene. While Ford may have used white actors to play major roles as Indians, he also had Navajo performers that he used over and over again in many of his films. (Courtesy Carolyn Davis, obtained from Goulding's Trading Post and Lodge)

moviemaking took him into the films entitled *Stagecoach, She Wore a Yellow Ribbon, Son of Cochise,* and others.

The movie director usually instructed us as to what to do for each scene. The trained stuntmen were separate from us, doing their own thing when it came time. The movie outfit had a variety of fake props and equipment like rubber knives and guns, as well as horse and human dummies. When they gave us the cue, "Action!" we started in motion. Sometimes fake knives were already tied or attached to our bodies, so that when someone stabbed us, we would fall down with the knife protruding as we pretended to die. It looked real when you later watched it on film. The person in charge of sound-making followed us around, but otherwise, it was quiet while we went through these motions. It was funny to watch Navajo men rehearse their parts. Many of them were afraid to play "dead," especially the older men who did not want to be shot, although the younger men did not mind. This type of acting is forbidden and so should be treated with respect by our people. It is scary (yiiyá—Leave it alone!). They have always held the belief that it is wrong to pretend to die or kill someone. Even today, some of our people do not attend a funeral because they respect the sacredness of it. Those who took part in the movies back then are now trying to "erase" or "undo" this curse by having ceremonies performed because they are having health problems. They believe that since they acted out death scenes and talked about it, these actions become like suicide, dooming them with a curse that might come true. Just as there are ceremonies and prayers for people who have bad dreams, the same is true for those who acted in a make-believe way this killing and dying. The rituals seek forgiveness by emplacing the "sacred stones or pebbles" as an offering in a sacred place.

Our people got along well with the moviemakers. John Ford was nice. He used to check out all the trading posts' money in Oljato, Goulding's, and Kayenta, then pass it out to the people, even the little children. The posts often ran out of cash. The movie company provided more than enough food for its workers and jobs for anyone who wanted to earn money. Every department of the film group had a Navajo "supervisor"— the cafeteria, the actors' section, equipment, personnel. This made it convenient and safe for everyone. The Anglo and Navajo workers respected each other and had a good time together. In the evenings, the people would gather around the workers' camp and do all sorts of fun things like singing songs in both English and Navajo and having the stuntmen do some of their unusual tricks. I believe the Hollywood people wanted us to be happy and have a good time, and we sure did.[5]

Gambling was a prominent pastime shared by both cultures. The men demonstrated prowess in feats of strength and skill, which were always a welcomed addition to stir excitement as each group chose their champion. John Holiday recalls three such incidents.[6] The first was when he volunteered to Navajo wrestle one of the white men with bets amounting to $200 for the triumphant. In this type of contest, the winner was the one left standing. Holiday sized up his burly opponent and noticed that he had a thin waist. As the men started to grapple, the Navajo grabbed the narrow waist bobbing before him and gave a terrific bear hug. The man went limp and did not revive until water splashed over his face. Another bet derived over hauling firewood. One day Navajos and whites were scouring the desert floor for wood when they came upon a log so large that none of them could encircle it with their arms. Many men tried to lift the ponderous load, but to no avail. Billy Katso rose to the occasion, collected a sizable sum, put a horse harness strap around the log, set it on end, padded his shoulder, hoisted the beam, and staggered to the truck several yards away. He won the bet. Perhaps one of the most amusing wagers focused on a small sweat lodge when Mr. Ocean Water's Son led a group of movie employees on a guided tour of the monuments. The eighteen white men seated on the sightseeing bus gaped in awe as their guide explained there were eleven men crammed into the small conical-shaped hut dug in the side of the hill. The various sets of clothes arranged outside testified of the number. No one believed it. Each man offered twenty-five dollars if there were that many. There just couldn't be. As the disgruntled participants interrupted their sweat and crawled into the blinding sunlight, those outside started the count. All eleven emerged, much to the chagrin of the losers, and even after the whites inspected the interior of the lodge, they still could not comprehend how so many utilized such a small space.

Cecil Parrish also got along well with those filming, but was asked to do some dangerous things. At least one time, he was part of the "burning equipment" scenario mentioned previously. He explains:

I used to ride around in a wagon pulled by four horses. The film crew poured on water fire (kerosene?) then told me to ignite it when they fired the cannon. I had flames behind me while I drove the burning wagon around. You really have to watch yourself and carry life very carefully, ever so carefully. This is the only way it is good. Indians on horseback and on foot carried imitation guns. They shot at and killed each other. They would be riding fast on horses near the rocks of Monument Valley. It was mainly for the rocks that these moviemakers came. When they finished filming, they gave to the Navajos who participated a lot of the props that were not going back to Hollywood. They told them that it was theirs and they could do whatever they wanted to.[7]

Bud recalled that the movie outfit once left a train and some buildings down in the valley, where they decided it would remain, but someone tore it down and all of the materials vanished. "It happened each time something was left behind and so it lasted for only a short time."[8]

Billy Yellow, who lived by Eagle Rock, worked in a half dozen movies and was always "on the list."

I carried a gun, even though sometimes my horse bucked when I fired that 30–30 rifle. This was a real rifle but I just fired blank cartridges that made smoke come out of the barrel. Sometimes the horses got scared and ran away; I rode after them and gathered them back together. I was raised on horseback and so I felt like I was glued to my saddle. A long time ago we were filming in the Mountain with No Name (Dził Bízhi' Ádinii; Henry Mountains). There was a rim that we were directed to ride to and stop. They took pictures constantly of us doing this. I was often in the lead, riding ahead of everyone before reaching the rim. Another time we filmed behind the La Sal Mountains, where we rode our horses into the swiftly flowing water. A man named Seth Bigman got swept away in the river when the current took the legs of his horse. He fell into the water as the rest of us charged across and reached the other side. White men went into the river and brought him back out, preventing him from drowning. We did this same kind of scene of charging across the river below Mexican Hat Rock. Before filming, we floated our things across on wood poles. The elders told us that the powers inhabiting the ridge next to it should not be disturbed but we filmed there anyway. In Monument Valley, there is a place where lightning and wind do not permit people to walk about. The wind stakes out its own territory. Respect has to be shown to these entities so that the holy people are not angered. This can be done by putting corn pollen in that place as an offering. These sites have power and are connected to the forces of nature. For five years it did not rain. Two years ago, I left an offering at one of these sites and it rained. Last year it really rained throughout the year. These ceremonies are powerful if the land is respected. It is said that these powers are very dangerous things to handle. The elders have warned about this. They also warned about not cutting our hair and so I kept mine tied up. If this happened, there would be no rain; it would stop watering the land. This is why you do not do this. We were told not to be like the enemy and wear our hair like him. This was how we were raised. Now, it is only like that and women wear pants, which was also forbidden. Some people still observe the sacred ways, but at that time, we began not to follow the teachings of the elders.[9]

The medicine men of this time were powerful spokesmen for traditional culture. Maintaining the values found in the sacred narratives and understanding from those stories why things are done or not done, has always been part of their role in sustaining cultural values. One person in particular whose name was associated with the film industry of this time was Hastiin Tsoh (Mister Big). Stories abound of his control of natural phenomena—not just with the Navajos but also among the filming crews and John Ford. He was particularly noted for controlling the weather. While this may be met with skepticism from the Anglo perspective, there were many who joined Navajo observers to witness these powers. Bud Haycock tells of Hastiin Tsoh, his maternal grandfather.

I have known him ever since I can remember. He was an excellent horseman and used to travel around a lot in his wagon, going to faraway places like Gallup or Flagstaff. He was like a "truck driver," hauling in food and merchandise for the traders around here. He had a huge gray wagon, the kind issued by the government, to haul in loads of flour, sugar, coffee, and other supplies. He was a medicine man who sang the Blessingway (Hózhǫ́ǫ́jí), the Evilway (Hóchxǫ̨'íjí), "charcoal healing way," (At'eeshjí), Windway (Nííłch'iji), Enemyway (Anaa'jí), and the "sacred stones offering bearer way." He knew quite a lot and performed many ceremonies and prayers for the people.

I am not sure how he controlled the weather when working with the movie companies, but he was often present on location and John Ford paid him for his services. It cost the filmmakers a lot of money if they were delayed by the wind or an overcast sky, so they used to have Hastiin Tsoh stand by to perform rituals to clear the weather—and amazingly, it worked. They made sure he was always available from the beginning of a movie to completion. Who knows, he might have cleared the rain for good, then died without correcting it because we have no rain now.[10]

Hastiin Tsoh was a powerful medicine man whom John Ford maintained on the payroll until his last film event in Monument Valley in 1964. Stories abound about how Hastiin Tsoh controlled the weather and delivered what the director requested. (Courtesy Photo Archives, Utah State Historical Society)

Cecil Parrish remembers Hastiin Tsoh as an in-law.

He was a medicine man who knew some of the most sacred ceremonies. The Anglos would be making a movie and the clouds would start to gather. This was during a time when there was plenty of rain and it was often overcast with clouds all the time. He told the movie people that he would talk to them and change the weather into what they wanted. He would do this and the clouds would part. I do not know how, but they did. He really had sacred powers through the prayers that he had and did this before my eyes. His prayers were very powerful. I used to work with him in his planting field and at other times and saw this type of thing happen. According to his prayers and what he asked, it happened accordingly. One time we were hunting, and he said, "We will have snow. Is that okay?" The men in the group agreed that it would be helpful for tracking. He said, "We will see what will happen." He went to a cedar tree and took a hold of it, then touched it as he went around it. He said, "Now it will snow" and by sunset it had arrived and soon became very deep. I think that the elements really minded him. I wonder what he said. He told it to drift apart and it did. I marveled at what great powers he had for the weather to do what he asked. He must have had great knowledge that had been passed on from many previous generations. I had a maternal great uncle whose name was Chaa di niih [?] who had this type of understanding passed down to him as his son. It is probably from there. There was another man named Hastiin Tsii'názt'i' who also had these same powerful prayers and songs. It is from these men that Hastiin Tsoh and Hastiin Tsii'názt'i' got these teachings. He performed several ceremonies such as Diyin K'eh but it was through the Windway that I believe he controlled the weather. He asks for a change such as for it to rain or for the clouds to depart. I have seen him perform it and heard him talk about it.

I used to go hunting with him, and on several occasions, he would talk to the animals. Even though deer are easily frightened, he would talk to them and they would remain calm and not scared away, but would just walk around our camp. We would kill them. It was like that, and I don't know how. I asked him how he did it and the sacred name that he used to address them. He said he did it through Talking God (Haashch'ééłti'í) because these were his creatures. He said that he asked him for the deer and that he gave them to him. What words he used I do not know, but this was what he did in front of me. I asked for some deer and he gave them to me. Sometimes they would corral deer and herd them into an enclosure and shoot them with bows and arrows. They were able to do this by asking for them. The elderly men used to do this a long time ago. They would ask the owner of the deer and they received them. This is just like when we ask for things and know the right words and prayers, the holy people bless us. The rest I do not know.[11]

A medicine man who has this type of power must be very careful as to how it is used and when to use it. For those interested in the moviemakers' view of Hastiin Tsoh and his powers, Harry Goulding in *Tall Sheep* shares a number of instances showing that even outsiders believed and witnessed his powers. One of Tsoh's sons, Tallis Holiday, provides a sobering look at the old man's demise—one that is very characteristic of the Navajo view of handling sacred powers. Tallis begins with an incident.

One time when the movies were here, they [film crew] were all ready to go, but day after day there were thick clouds that just settled and stayed there. The movie director gave him [Hastiin Tsoh] a hundred dollars and asked him to make the clouds go away.

But I think he made a mistake. That kind of ceremony is danger-ous, because you can't control nature. Year after year after that, when there was drought, the people blamed him. "You are the one!" they said. I told him as soon as the movie was over he should have done another ceremony to bring the clouds back, but he did not. He did not know the other part of the ceremony. That is what killed him. The first big rain we had after a long dry spell killed him. He could not bring the rain back, but when other people's prayers and songs brought rain, the moisture affected him and he died. I told him that if he did not know how to bring the rain back, he never should have done it in the first place.[12]

By now, it should be obvious that women played a much lesser role in these action-packed westerns than did the men performing as warriors. Most women were relegated to camp scenes as contextual background as opposed to the men exhibiting horsemanship, fighting, or aspects of tradi-tional life. There were a few exceptions such as in *Cheyenne Autumn*. While many women willingly discussed the film industry during the Ford years, their experience was fairly lackluster. Two women—Ada Black and Betty Canyon share their thoughts about making movies. Ada had her most in-tense experience in Moab, after John Ford retired and close to the time of his death in 1973. Speaking of Monument Valley as one of its residents, she said:

This area is famous for moviemaking; the only one I was in was filmed in Moab. For two days of work, we were paid twenty dollars, and for five it was eighty-nine dollars. We did not receive that much money because part of our pay was in food and the gas it took for a bus to pick us up in Monument Valley and bring us to Moab. While filming, we lived in big tents that were pointed at the top with floorboards on the bottom. Some of the people stayed out in the open or in their pickups, while others had campers on their trucks and brought their own food and bedding. We stayed within our own group, and one woman gave birth to her child. In the evenings, there was bathing close by. As for the work, I did not have a very exciting part, just standing around in a crowd. In another scene, what they had us do was ugly. Supposedly, a person had died and was being buried. That was ugly, even though the body was covered when it was carried around. We were told to stand in line at this funeral. I did not like what was going on, so I remained in camp.[13]

Betty Canyon, on the other hand, did not have much to say about the film industry until she was asked how the movie companies affected sacred places. She left no doubt.

> They do a lot of damage. The movie outfits do outlandish things; it is no wonder most of our Navajo actors are dead today. In the first place, our people were forbidden to take part in such things but money has made them blind. One such incident was when Mister Hite Chee, a medicine man, was asked to make a sandpainting inside a hogan while a coyote stood atop watching him through the smoke hole. The coyote was taking part in the movie. [All of] this was absolutely forbidden in our Navajo beliefs. It caused his death. Many of our people complain about his dying, but it still happened. The white men have taken our sacred sandpaintings with them to do what they wish with them.[14]

Today, filming crews continue to roam Monument Valley looking for just the right location while often bringing their own actors instead of utilizing local talent. Never will they match those early years when John Ford, John Wayne, and others turned the landscape, relatively new to the viewing public, into the iconic West. The string of feature films they turned out year after year did not lose their viewing audience, but continued to successfully draw crowds to watch the red man face off against the white man in stereotypical fashion. Starting in 1939, *Stagecoach* became the first, followed by *Kit Carson* (1940), *Billy the Kid* (1941), *The Harvey Girls* (1944), *My Darling Clementine* (1946), *Fort Apache* (1948), *She Wore a Yellow Ribbon* (1949), *Wagon Master* (1950), *The Searchers* (1956), *Sergeant Rutledge* (1960), and *Cheyenne Autumn* (1964). Central to these movies were Navajo actors who knew the land, worked hard, were skilled in the talents needed to make a good western, and were willing to work for men they admired—John Ford and John Wayne. While the money was greatly appreciated, the acting and interacting enjoyable, side benefits such as building materials valued, and pride in work welcomed, there was an underlying cultural view that looked at the tasks in a different light. Those making the movies were usually sensitive to these things they did not understand in deference to the Navajo. Yet there were really two worlds at work—that which was visible and could be filmed, and that which was spiritual and cultural and not within purview of the Anglo filmmakers. For those who followed Hollywood, these Navajos were stars of sage and screen.

CHAPTER NINE

Americanizing Traditional Culture

Beginning the Process

T he Navajo people are proud of their culture and belong to one of the largest tribes in the continental United States, one that consistently works to maintain its traditional identity. Throughout the twentieth century, there have been both intentional and unintentional inroads that have challenged holding on to that culture. At times, foreign elements have been adopted, adapted, and utilized—take for instance the truck, paved roads, and building structures—to the Navajos' benefit. At other times, there have been forced issues such as livestock reduction, boarding schools, and language loss with the intention of helping the Navajo while at the same time contributing to cultural degradation. In some respects, the People came late to their arena of change for a number of reasons. The place that they chose to live was far less desirable to westering Anglo populations looking for well-watered agricultural and grass lands. While the mountain ranges with their mineral wealth, adequate rainfall, and natural resources such as wood, water, and grass beckoned some intruders to their heights, those resources on the Navajo Reservation were protected by treaty rights and government control. The military, under the watchful eye of the Navajo agent, often escorted interlopers invading Indian lands off of the reservation. Not only was this territory protected, but it was added upon by expanding boundaries. Between 1868 and 1958, there were twenty-three additions to the original treaty reservation (1868). The federal government permanently added Monument Valley in 1933. Isolation from the dominant society was quite possible, allowing the

Navajo to maintain their traditional way of life, free from outside influence deemed undesirable. However, culture has and is always changing and adapting to various influences, good and bad. The question soon becomes the rate and direction it will take.

This chapter examines elements that accelerated a shift from the lifestyle of those born during the first quarter of the twentieth century. At that time, life centered around livestock and agriculture, ceremonial practices were at their height, trading posts allowed Navajos to remain on the reservation while obtaining desired supplies and equipment, and the elders—especially medicine men—held strong spiritual powers and traditional knowledge that guided the people. Strange things may have occurred beyond the bounds of the Four Sacred Mountains, but within, it was safe and predictable. Inroads began to create fissures in that accepted world. While there were any number of elements that encouraged cultural shifts, we will briefly look at four that became prominent change agents, any one of which could easily have its own chapter. They do not follow a neat chronological sequence since many of them not only operated simultaneously but also fed off of each other, expanding the impact. Here we will look at the effects of (1) technology with an emphasis on cars; (2) the development of roads; (3) boarding schools and the educational experience; and (4) work in the Civilian Conservation Corps (CCC). Their interconnectedness becomes obvious as we see the introduction of the automobile call forth the expansion of road networks that went to trading posts and serviced the movie industry (not to mention the huge impact of uranium mining discussed later), the development of schools, and the CCC program. The larger question here is how traditional Navajos viewed all of this.

Technology—A Horse of a Different Color

Many anthropologists have noted that the Navajo people are quick to adopt and adapt to those things that are beneficial. Technology is among the easiest to evaluate, then accept or reject, while other concerns like educational and religious beliefs take more time and experience to determine their helpful or harmful effects. There are new landscapes that may beckon without a clear view over the horizon. The presence of a different people and new ways of thinking can be challenging. Perhaps no form of technology has had a greater impact on the Navajo during the twentieth century than the automobile. What follows is a lengthy discussion of traditional views about this object. Similar thinking was and is applied to any number

of devices or products, ranging from glass and Alka-Seltzer to the first
airplanes, harnessed electricity, telephones, computers, and credit cards.[1]
Here, Navajo elders recall their reaction when they encountered their first
white man and then his technology. John Holiday remembers how it affected him as these strangers entered Monument Valley, an experience
similar to those expressed by many others of his generation.

> I was six when I first encountered a white man. I don't know where they
> were coming from, but they came to us. They had great beards that were
> probably a foot long. They shaved only around their mouth. When they
> talked you could see the red part of the mouth moving. This took place
> near what is now the ranger station. It was there they came. Their mules
> were all packed with ropes all over the packaged things covered with
> canvas. They moved there for only a little while. There were five of them,
> four men and a woman.
>
> Me and my father left very early in the morning to go to their camp.
> At that time, I had no idea what white man's food was like. Once in a
> great while we might get some potatoes, which were tasty, but not much
> more. This time, however, when we arrived in the morning, they were
> frying their breakfast of pig meat floating in fat and eggs boiling in water.
> They made a meal for us of fried pig meat, potatoes, bread, and eggs
> which we enjoyed. My father understood the white man's language and
> so he talked with the Anglos while I walked around still fearful of these
> strange people. They were short and wide, looked weird with their hairy
> faces, but seemed kind. When we were ready to leave, they gave us apples.
> When I bit into this fruit, it was really good, but at that time, I did not
> know what it was. This is when I first really became aware of what was
> going on. I liked the taste of the apple so much, I only took small bites
> then put the rest back into my pocket, to make it last a long time. It got
> smaller and smaller until I finished it at sunset. That was how I was as a
> little boy.[2]

If John thought that seeing white men for the first time was strange,
he was in for even greater surprises with the things they brought with
them. Most people, when introduced to something new, expand their understanding by comparing the familiar to the unfamiliar. To move from a
horse-drawn wagon to an automobile may seem like quite a stretch in our
world of automation, but imagine how Navajos would feel about this new
invention when it first appeared around 1908 at the Wetherill Trading

Post in Oljato. Later, John, at the age of six, saw his first automobile and remembers clearly his impression.

We were living by a totem pole–shaped rock at a place called Logs or Objects that Floated Ashore (T'ábąąh níʼéél) which is located on the way to Lake Powell about six miles above Piute Farms. There is a wash in the direction of the lake that when it rains hard, fills with water, carrying large tree stumps and debris to a big curve in the wash bed where they are deposited on the banks. It was late afternoon, when a few family members and I spotted some objects slowly moving along the rocky streambed. There used to be a camp further down, where white men panned for gold or other valuable minerals. We named that camp Group of Tents (Níbaal Nidaaznil), and this was where the objects were heading.

These cars looked very fragile with spoke wheels similar to those of a wagon. The people called these first automobiles The One that Sniffs Around, Nose to the Ground, or Smoky Butt. Later they were called "chidí," then "chogí," the name changing several different times.[3] People made songs for them: "The sniffer, the sniffer—I have made you a part of my mind; the sniffer, the sniffer, I am riding you." My father was familiar with automobiles because he had taken some white men down to the mining camp before and had seen autos elsewhere. They used to send the panned gold by wagon to the old trading post that sat on a hill above the Oljato reservoir. The traders, Old John [Wetherill] and Slim Woman [Louisa] used to ship the gold for the miner Old Charles by wagon to Flagstaff, Farmington, and Gallup. It is from these bigger towns that the automobiles came, ending up on the wagon trails to the tent camp. One day father came home saying, "A thing called 'chidí' came to our area today. It runs on its own." I do not recall anyone being afraid of these automobiles. Father rode in them and told us how fast they went on smooth surfaces. My grandfather, Metal Teeth, was one of the first Navajos in this area to own an automobile. The next person was Long Hill (Hoolkʼidnii) from Dennehotso, a man from Kayenta named Man's Car (Hastiin Bichidí), and then Lee Bradley's father Red Mustache (Dághaałchíʼí)—a white man from Kayenta. He brought many automobiles back to sell. Our local traders from Oljato, John and his wife, also introduced automobiles into our area. Many others with cars followed after that.

The first type of car was like a wagon covered with a tent. Grandfather used to bring it here on his visits and it was pretty fast. Two years later, he brought a truck. They called it Big Little Car because they said it was big but without much room compared to a wagon. He would pack the back with his belongings then crank in the front to start it. The gas tank was by the front window and a tall pipe stuck up in the front so that water could be poured in. It had other odds and ends all over. My older brother drove it around and grandfather would yell after him not to ruin it. There were only two or three electrical lines attached to it, which seems like nothing compared to today's cars. But it sure had power to run!

We had no highways, only dirt roads. I am not sure where people got gas, but it was probably from Gallup, because I have heard stories from others regarding this. Navajos used to say it was quite dangerous to travel through Chinle, because some of the residents were bandits who chased a driver down on their horses and turned the car over. My grandfather and Long Hill went on a trip to Gallup where they bought a small barrel full of gasoline from Big Mexican's store, but accidentally lost it on the return trip. Long Hill had purchased some whiskey, buying two small barrels and four one-gallon jugs. In those days, people used to haul liquor from there to sell here. When grandfather and Long Hill were passing through Chinle, they were attacked just as they were about to run out of gas. The bandits were coming closer and closer, when grandfather remembered the whiskey. He quickly grabbed the bottles and poured the whiskey into the gas tank, and sure enough, they were able to escape, making it home to Dennehotso. They learned that whiskey works just as well as gasoline. So I suppose if one knew how to make whiskey, he would also know how to make gasoline.

There are Navajo teachings about how a car works. This vehicle is very much like a horse, operating on the same principles. The automobile is considered more "intelligent" and we think of it in such terms. The automobile is made of iron and steel taken from the earth. This iron is the earth's spirit which has been made into the "body" of the car. The trees, as vegetation, were also taken from the earth and made into rubber for the tires. The air or spirit is the same as that of a horse's "breath of life," instilled in its body. The arms and legs of the auto make it move. Then there are the dark storm clouds and heavenly bodies like lightning, which are found inside the vehicle to give it power. This is exactly the same power the horse has. Water, which comes from the earth, is put into the cooling system. Oil from the earth is similar to the fat from the earth a horse receives. Just as gasoline comes from the ground as fuel, plants are in a horse's body, to make it operate. Therefore, horses and cars are the same in every way. Even the battery fluid comes from the heavens as an electricity-maker. Humans possess that same lightning or electricity in their hearts to keep them alive.

When one buys a new automobile, it is treated like a horse. The sacred "Horse's Song" (Łį́į́' Biyiin) is sung while one sprinkles corn pollen on it. We pray for its safety and for its productive use. We also pray that "envious" people will not do harm to it in any way. Every human is born with ugly envy or jealousy. Some people are worse than others and want to bring harm through these feelings. For all these reasons, one should do a sacred ritual for a vehicle; never leave it undone. At the end of the ceremony, the mirage or "heat wave" is applied to the automobile. This is for its endurance and protection for as long as it is driven. This song or ritual can be used for other things with the same results.

The feathers that hang from the rearview mirror are for speed and endurance on long trips. Some people will have "sacred miniature bundles" tied inside their autos. These will contain "shake-offs" from various sacred birds and creatures. These are made from the horse's body dust and saliva; "shake-offs" from the rainbow; "shake-offs" from humming birds and small swallows that swoop down above the water; "shake-offs" from the gray bird that sits on the sheep's back or are found around homes; and "shake-offs" from the horned toad. They are all in the miniature bundle. Some people carefully fix these, but others do it any old way. In the past, people used to tie these bundles and feathers to their horses' tail. We do not know these things unless we ask about them.[4]

George Tom agrees with John's thoughts when comparing a horse to a car.

An automobile is more than a horse. It can hear, make noises, and run. If it weren't alive, then why does it move? It is alive. It's perfect to look at, is similar to a horse as far as its usefulness, and is blessed just the same. We pray for the horse, "In beauty we will travel without trouble and hunger. Be my good horse always. May our journeys begin with a rainbow. May the holy people be with us wherever we go." This same prayer is spoken to the automobile. I have become familiar with some mechanical functions of an automobile. Everything inside it, including the smallest objects, has a part in making it run. When it comes time to fixing a troubled spot, I'd lie awake at nights trying to figure out the problem. Sure enough, I'd see the "flickering blue flame" [divination] on the spot. It certainly has life all right.[5]

The automobile was a new invention that Navajos initially understood by comparing its functions to a horse, something they knew. Many of the elders now laugh at their first impressions and how they treated this strange machine, but today cars and trucks are truly the "workhorse" for this highly mobile people. (Courtesy San Juan County Historical Commission)

Cecil Parrish remembers his first experience concerning an automobile.

I was six years old, herding sheep. During this time, many of the people talked about how it gathered children and took them off to school. This was a frightening thing for the young ones. As I followed the sheep, I heard a strange sound and wondered what was making it. I looked everywhere but saw nothing. I realize now that it was an airplane, but I was trying to hide from what I thought was an automobile instead of the plane overhead. I climbed up a tree and sat there while the sheep wandered off, hiding until dark before starting for home. When I arrived there was an automobile, which I learned belonged to my maternal uncle. It had wheels right on top. They looked kind of weird. That was my first time. Their designs are getting more beautiful each time there is a new type. There is this thinking when you start looking at them. Now I know it is a strong working tool and so I am glad they invented it and am happy.[6]

A final memory about the introduction of the car to Monument Valley is shared by Fred Yazzie. He recalls:

When I was a boy, probably about nine years old, there were no automobiles running among us, only wagon roads first plowed to Kayenta. Near Narrow Canyon, there was a second night Enemy Way ceremony that I attended. After sunset, there were lights moving toward us where the wagons had driven. As boys we were wrestling and playing a little way off, when there appeared these bright shining eyes coming toward us. The boys said it was Big Snake (Tł'iish Tsoh) and started to scatter and hide, while the men remained unaware. Then it went to where the people were singing and stopped. It was black and looked like a spider with its wagon wheel spokes and so that is what we called it. People were looking it over before us boys started to move in cautiously. Soon we were touching it and told it was called chidí. It stayed there and soon we got used to it, ran around it, and were happy when its shining eyes turned on. In the morning, an Anglo came out, cranked the handle in front, and finally started it. Putt-putt-putt it sounded, then drove on its way. That was when I first became aware of an automobile.

Later I learned that its gasoline was like a refined food. As cars became more common, gasoline became a bigger business for the trading posts, especially Goulding's. Beginning in the 1940s, they started hauling it here in drums. There was a horse-drawn vehicle called Big Wagon that used to bring it in. Another fluid that came in around 1925 was called "liquid fire" [kerosene], while grease, like we used on our wagons, oiled the moving parts. Automobiles need these things to run, but the driver has to do the thinking for them. If you go to sleep while driving, it will run off the road because it does not know when to quit like a horse does. The horse knows what is going on around it while the automobile just keeps on running. Feathers from the flyers of the heavens are tied to it to help. In this way, it is your horse. One feather called iiná bits'os is tied inside it to help think and direct the car. With this, harm is avoided so the vehicle will not run off a cliff. If it did, the driver will not be harmed seriously and the feather will be blown out with him. It is by your thoughts that you are protected.[7]

Roads—The Black Snake in the Desert

Monument Valley is deceptively flat, giving an impression that it would be easy to traverse. Many of the first motorists approached the task with confidence until they began bogging down in endless windblown sand pits stacked at the base of hills, in previous ruts, and within a sea of sage, while storms obliterated tracks within minutes. The Wetherills were among the first to have this adventure when going to their post in 1908, but the Curtis Zahn family, composed of five brothers and uncles, wanted to be the first to forge 250 miles of new road from Kayenta to Los Angeles. Their starting point was the southern end of Monument Valley. They packed 4,600 pounds of gear including dynamite, winches, cables, and shovels for "road" work; hard tack and jerked beef for food; and a compass for navigation. The Franklin Camel, which got its name because it did not require as much water as other vehicles, sagged under its load, especially after the men deflated the tires to minimum pressure to traverse the sand. Rarely clipping along at its maximum twenty-eight miles per hour, the four-cylinder auto traveled in low gear and carried its own spare drum of gasoline for use until the party could reach prepositioned supplies.[8] Such were the necessary preparations for desert vehicular traffic in those days. On October 26, 1915, the group camped on the San Juan River, twenty miles from its confluence with the Colorado River at the base of Navajo Mountain. Further adventures lay ahead.

Even before the automobile appeared on the scene, some Navajo elders had premonitions of what was to come. Jesse Black remembers their dialogue.

> During this time when only horses were used to travel, there were several men who talked with each other about future events. One man said, "Way on the far side of us, there is a small mountain ridge, where on the other side there is now a highway that goes to Tuba City. Eighty years ago, there was nothing but it was foretold that there would be something black with things running back and forth over it and that these moving parts would be called 'One Who Will Run on Fire' (Kǫ'na'ałbąąsii)." This was what he said, that it will run back and forth over there. This was when there was no thought about these things and only horses were used to go about; horse trails, not even those for wagons, were all that existed.[9]

Today's main artery through Monument Valley, State Highway 163, follows a foot trail, then later wagon road, that has existed for millennia. Fred Yazzie recalls what it was like when it first came under substantial improvement.

> A man called Dibétsétah made the very first road that went from the south side of Mexican Hat. It went through these standing rocks [Eagle Pass] then on to the ranger station as well as straight south to

Kayenta. The bulldozer called The Object That Turns Over Sand (Leezh Yaanahałbaalii) was used to push and haul dirt out of the way to make the road. The workers also used big farm horses, dynamite to blast rocks, and Navajo workers to widen and improve the old wagon trail. It went by Mitchell Butte, with a branch off to Goulding's, then into Kayenta. The dynamite used to blast the rock felt oily and was not very powerful. The farm horses dragged something around. This is how the roads were made. In Kayenta, there was a gas pole for fuel. Later the road was graveled, especially where the sand would usually pile up.[10]

Opening the Gates—Dolph Andrus

The familiar spires and monuments of the tribal park have been well known for decades and now the park has a seventeen-mile unpaved loop of road that threads through some of the most dramatic scenery of the Four Corners area. Thousands and thousands of cars move over this gravel, dusty road, spitting out tourists with cameras every day. But who was the first tourist to drive at least partway in a car and then photograph this magical setting? Perhaps that honor belongs to Dolph Andrus, who in 1916–18 was a car salesman living in Bluff, where he promoted the use of the newfangled contraption that has now become so indispensable. To create attention, prove its usefulness, and open a new aspect of tourism in southeastern Utah, Dolph became the first to make vehicular descent of Comb Ridge, a major obstruction to overcome in connecting Monument Valley to traffic from northern Utah. He accomplished this in October 1916, traveling as far as Totem Pole Rock with three companions—friend W. H. Hopkins, chief of the U.S. Land Office H. Stanley Hinnricks, and photographer O. C. Hansen. Andrus was very clear about what he hoped to achieve.

My premises were: 1. The trip would prove the sturdiness of the Maxwell car and I would be swamped with orders. 2. The Maxwell Company would ask for photographs and my story to use for advertising purposes. 3. The photos of Monument Valley would arouse such interest that Utah, Arizona, Colorado, and the US government would rush to my aid and at least fix the road down Comb Ridge. (Well if each brought one truckload of soil it could be made passable until it rained) 4. With Comb Ridge navigable, we would have cars streaming through Monument Valley. Never mind the sand patches, the road was good in between and we could have saddle horses or a team pull them through. We know now that it took about 50 years for this to come true, but it did come. Take a trip over Highway 47 [163] and you will find yourself going down the same dugway. The rocks are covered with earth and the soil is treated with asphalt to make it stable. The rains will not wash it away. The sand patches are oiled too. If you want to see what the sand was like just drive off the highway.

In about eight days all of the members of the party had arrived in Bluff and informed me that they would like to go with me to Monument Valley. I removed the turtleback from the Maxwell to provide room for food and bedding. This also created a seat for Hansen and Hopkins. Mr. Hinnricks rode in the front seat with me until we reached the dugway on Comb Ridge. Here he left me and the car to walk down the dugway ahead of me. Hansen joined him and they made a fire at the foot of Comb Wash where we had planned to camp the first night. It was dark before we crossed Butler Wash as I could not leave until school was out on Friday night. Dr. Hopkins remained behind the car and followed me down. Every time the car made a loud thump going over a small ledge, the Chief would shout, "Dolph are you all right?" and Hopkins would shout back to him, "Nothing to worry about Chief. Take it easy!" I was never sure who was meant to "take it easy," but I took it easy and as slow as I could. Mr. Hinnricks was a very emotional man. When we arrived safely in camp, he put his arms around me and sobbed, "Boy am I glad you are safe! I was sure you would be killed." Mr. Hansen was concerned about getting back up and wanted to know if we had to come back this way. I told him that I had arranged for a team of horses to meet us Sunday evening and pull us back up. I informed him that I had made the trip once before this way and knew that it could be done. We spent a very pleasant evening and all slept well that night.

Early morn found us on our way up Comb Wash. Up to this point we were retracing horse steps with automobile tracks. I was wild with joy. What fun! We left Comb Wash and the horse trail to head for Lime Ridge and Mexican Hat. No trouble with Lime Creek this time for I had learned to avoid the stuff that looked like gravel and acted like quicksand. We passed Mexican Hat Rock without a comment about Pedro or his upside down sombrero nor how it got there. No stories about Moors as we rolled past Alhambra Rock. On we went! It was still early morning when we arrived at the oil drillers' camp, where we unloaded our gear and headed for the monuments. They looked so close, but were far away. We fought our way through sand patch after patch, but they became deeper,

Dolph Andrus and W. H. Hopkins, framed by Monument Valley rock formations, make their way across the desert floor, blazing their own roadway through the sagebrush. Andrus had a strong desire to connect northern Utah to the valley by going through Bluff, over Comb Ridge, and past Mexican Hat, a journey he made for the first time in 1916. (Courtesy Photo Archives, Utah State University)

longer, and closer together. The monuments were still distant. We were forced to turn our back on the monuments and Mr. Hinnricks said to me, "My boy you have a wonderful idea, but you must wait until they build roads!" We returned to the oil drillers' camp. The men who were hauling wood for the oil rig offered to take us by team and wagon to the monuments. They unloaded their wood and we climbed aboard. They followed our road back for some distance and then turned right on one leading to their camp. They proposed to continue northwest on this road, maintaining it was the shortest way to the monuments. I protested that they would never find anything worth photographing in the direction they were going then proposed that Hopkins and I go on foot and head southwest for the Mittens. Hansen could not go on foot with his big camera. Hopkins agreed and we took off. We were soon among the best of them. Hopkins trotted with glee from "shot to shot." I thought he would split his lens when we found an old Navajo hogan. I took a picture of him at the door.

I had hoped to make it to the Totem Pole, but we had lost so much time that it was getting too late for picture-taking when we arrived at the Mittens. He took the last "shot" of me and the Mittens. I am standing near the spot where the Navajo Tribal Park Building now stands. "We have a six mile or more hike to camp so we had better be on our way," I said. "Which way do you think camp is?" he asked. I pointed to the northeast. I had kept looking back as we went forward and had picked a monument that I could see against the skyline after it got dark; I was sure this would guide us safely back. "You are wrong," he protested. "I think camp is that way." He pointed due south then started on his way, expecting me to follow.

I had to shout at him, for he had already taken off in the direction of where he thought camp was. "Let me give you some advice before we part. By daylight you will find yourself lost. You should be able to see the Totem Pole. Head for it and stay there. We will come in the morning and bring you into camp. There is a spring near the Totem Pole so you will not suffer for water. If the Navajos scalp you, we will rename Totem Pole rock Hopkins Butte to keep company with the Mitchell and Merrick Buttes. So long and happy wanderings."

I had not gotten out of hearing distance when I heard his faint cry, "Wait for me. If we are going to be lost it is better for us to be lost together." I waited for him. He followed along behind, grumbling all the time about being lost. When we came in sight of the campfire he said, "Of course this is not our camp, but let us hope the Indians are friendly." I replied, "I do not think Hinnricks and Hansen would like that and I am sure the wood haulers would not relish being called Indians either."

When we got near enough to be heard I gave a shout; Hinnricks jumped up where he had been sitting, wailing over the fact that we were lost. He placed his hands to his mouth and shouted back, "Are you all right? Is anybody hurt?" I shouted back, "We are all okay." His only answer was "Thank God!" Before we came within easy earshot of the camp, Hopkins said quietly, "It would not be nice to tell them about our disagreement over the direction of camp, would it?" I agreed that it would not and the matter was left just between "us girls." As far as I know, I am the only surviving one of those who were there that night, so I feel that I am not breaking my promise to tell it now. Hinnricks was in tears and greeted us each with a big hug. "I was sure you had been eaten by wolves," he sobbed. Hansen reported that they had ridden all day and never fired a shot. No monument's worth taking a picture of and unless we got something the trip was a flop. Hopkins told him to wait and see. The next morning, we headed back for Bluff. We arrived at the foot of the Comb Ridge dugway without incident and waited for the Hyde boy and his team to drag us up the rocky incline.[11]

This photograph of Totem Pole Rock, the goal for Andrus's first journey into today's tribal park, is one of the first pictures taken of this site. No doubt it was an achievement that he and Hopkins could chuckle about years later. (Courtesy Photo Archives, Utah State University)

Education—Opening the Door to the Tiger or the Lady

Indian education across the United States has had a long and checkered history. Many books have been written about the boarding school experience, government policies, aftershocks of dissent, and how some people found it a wonderful blessing and others a disaster. This huge topic is briefly touched upon here, focusing on it as an agent of change. A few personal thoughts and experiences from Navajos living in Monument Valley suggest that the topic of education, whether or not attending school, enlisted powerful attitudes for and against the educational experience. Common themes found here and elsewhere include how families resisted losing their children as an able workforce around the home; the difficult interactions between those operating the school and the attendees; internal friction between students; and the imposed structure—from classes to clothing, and from intense discipline to dorm-style living. While it is popular today to point out all of the wrongs for those forced to go, many elders were also grateful for what they gained.

Samuel Holiday, a future Navajo code talker in the U.S. Marines during World War II, offered his thoughts.

By the time my mother had given permission, classes were already in session in Tuba City. She tried to tell the government officials that she needed me at home to help and that she did not want me to go. Leading His Horse Around (Bilį́į' Neilózí) and an interpreter had come to visit her, insisting I enroll and reassuring her that I would be alright. She tried hard to tell them not to take me but it was no use. I did not want to go and was very sad when I left. Another boy, William Weaver from Farmington, and I traveled in a car the seventy-five miles to the Tuba City Boarding School. During that trip I thought about my mother a lot, worrying about how she would be alone without my help. I felt strong compassion for her and imagined how she would have no one to herd the sheep now that I had left, even though she was very capable and knew how to take care of everything. My stepfather also had horses, a mule, and a cornfield to care for while he worked hard at other jobs. I knew that by leaving home for school I would learn things for my future life if I were to succeed in the white man's world. Knowing white ways could open the door for the future, although I was still not sure whether to trust them or not.

As Willie Weaver and I traveled to school for the first time, we talked in Navajo. Although the car made its way down the graded dirt road slowly, it seemed the trees whizzed by at amazing speed. We arrived that fall afternoon at a strange group of buildings—the boarding school with a lot of children. I was scared; as soon as we got out of the car someone informed on us that we were talking in Navajo. It did not take long to learn how wrong that was. The first thing I noticed was that many of the children were playing outside. All had been separated by sizes—the little children stayed in one place and had a different dorm than the middle-sized ones. I was put with the bigger, older children in a different part of the dorm and then met my dorm advisors. I could tell right away that the Navajo woman working in our dorm was strict, mean, and bossy. Each group had one adult assigned to take care of the students' clothes, laundry, mending, and to supervise the living quarters. There were also Navajo male dorm advisors in charge of the athletic program and daily morning exercises. Harry Sloan was the one assigned to my dorm. He looked at me in disgust as if he did not want me to be there. It seemed these advisors were trained to have nothing to do with Navajo traditions and language but instead were instructed to push it out of our lives. I looked like a traditional Navajo to Sloan so he announced that we must always speak English and never Navajo. I was very scared and apprehensive of these dormitory advisors. Now we were to learn the white man's way.

The next thing the school employees did was to have me get rid of my plain store-bought clothes in exchange for an issue of three sets from the school—one for class, another for church, and one for play, as well as some all-purpose socks and shoes. I thought they were alright. At least I had new clothes and besides, everybody else wore the same thing. On Sunday the boys put on a church uniform comprised of white pants that tied in the front with a white shirt. Coveralls that buttoned all the way to the underneath side served as everyday clothes to work and play in. I also received blankets and sheets then was soon assigned a bunk bed. That evening we lined up to eat. Some of the older boys who understood and spoke more English received the title of "captain" and made us line up, something we did everywhere we went. They kept us in line and were our leaders. After dinner we went to the dorms to sleep.

We arose early in the morning and formed up to do exercises, one of which was to march around the buildings. Then we marched to breakfast, ate, then lined up and marched to class. When I got there, my teacher, a white lady, put me in a classroom with all of the new students labeled Beginner Group B. I was the oldest and tallest one in the room. Those little children were very naughty and would kick me saying things in English that I did not understand. The teacher reminded me again that I should not talk Navajo but only English. There was also to be no more Navajo religion and traditional ceremonies. "Learning English will help you in your future," she said. "Navajo language will not help you; it has nothing so you must speak only English." This was very hard for me because I had always spoken Navajo and this new language was difficult to learn. I did not even know how to say chair. Then I thought I would try hard to learn and speak English; that was the only way.

The first week in the classroom and in the dorm was very difficult. All the adults were very strict; the dorm advisor woke us up early in the morning to exercise; the teachers had spelling tests with fifty words every week; the bigger boys in the dorm were rough, made fun of me, and picked on me constantly, real bullies, while the little boys in my class were just plain naughty. Even my height became a problem since I was middle-sized for my age, but when I went to class I was the only tall boy there. I was very stressed and scared and wondered how I was going to speak only English. I made up my mind at that point to be just as good as or better than the rest of the students, trying extra hard in everything.

In the afternoon we took out sleeping mats like sheepskins to rest on. When I lay down I was taller than everybody else and so the others teased me, calling me giant. Every once in a while, I would get kicked by the boys as they told me to move over. Once I kicked back and the boy started crying so I was punished by doing extra work. This often took the form of having to scrub the floors and walls or by having to stay in the dorm while everyone else played outside. Our class used to take walks and the white teacher and I were the same height. The boys teased me, saying that she was my wife. One time we went to an apple orchard after the harvest but the trees still had some fruit on them. "Hey boy! Reach up and get me an apple," the children teased since I was a tall beginner and they wanted to pick on me. I got mad and threw one of them down. He started crying and told both the teacher and dorm advisor so they punished me and said not to pick on the little boys. That was something I remember from one of our walks. It was a rough beginning.

One thing that did not seem to get any easier at first was always talking English. Once in a while some of the smart children would get away with speaking Navajo, but often they were caught and punished. The new arrivals in Beginner B received some leniency because they did not know any English words at all. Still the teachers did not approve of it. After we were in school a while, we were not allowed any Navajo words at all. Beginner B was mostly five-and-six-year-olds, while Beginner A was mostly eight-to-ten-year-olds. There the teachers forbid all Navajo: "Talk English," they yelled at us. Within three months after going through the Beginner B, then through the Beginner A group, I was in the second grade. This had the smarter boys and girls. Most of us were the same age, size and height, but there were also some younger boys.

Our teacher, Miss Handly, was very strict about our getting assignments done and turned in. She was mean and tirelessly enforced English-only, saying, "No Navajo, no Indian, no, no, no." Fortunately, by then I was able to speak more words, but now we had to learn subjects. I ended up staying after school a lot. We were given tests every week. When it came close to exam time, everyone was studying where there was light. Sometimes we stayed up at night to study in the washroom. I was sad and suffered greatly because I could not respond or ask questions about what I wanted to learn. My first year, I was very scared; the boys often told lies about me, saying that I was talking Navajo, so I received punishment many times although innocent. That is how I began my schooling.[12]

Families often depended heavily on their children to help with all of the work that had to be done. Consequently, a lot of parents did not want their children to attend boarding school to learn things that, at the time, did not seem relevant for the tasks at hand. Others saw it as an investment in the future, as the dominant culture became increasingly prevalent. Susie Yazzie attended for only two years because her father was forced to send her. She regretted not being able to go longer. Lucy Laughter, one of Susie's relatives, was sad because she had not been able to attend. "No, I do not read. During that time, we were not permitted to go to school because we had to herd sheep. They would even put us in rock crevices to hide us. If I had gone to school, I would have been somewhere else. I probably would not have made life. That was how it was at that time."[13] Sally Manygoats also wished that she had gone: "No, I do not even know my name. Not even a little bit. I did not go to school. I was told [to herd] sheep and that was why I did not go to school. I do not know anything about paper [reading and writing]. I do not know the Anglo language. I wonder, 'What if I had gone to school . . . could I have been in a Washington [D.C.] office?'"[14] These women felt that their desires and full potential had not been reached because they did not have the opportunity to try.

In spite of all of the shortcomings of boarding schools—and there were many—they did provide opportunity for those who applied the things they were taught. But that also could be an issue. How applicable were the things they learned upon returning home? Betty Canyon fell into that quandary after learning how to read. Even though she had minimal schooling, she wanted to hold on to what she had learned. This was not always easy.

We were less fortunate when we were young and going to school because we had to be taken on horseback. When I returned home in the summer, I did not have any books to read or paper to write on. I used to wish I had something to read. The only available material was the labels on the canned food items such as baking powder, salt, sugar, flour, and coffee—some of which also came in a bag back then. I was always happy to get back to school. My parents and everyone else at home were uneducated, so there was nobody to review the alphabet and numbers with us. We had to learn it on our own and at school. I stopped going to school in 1931. I could have gone longer if my parents hadn't told me to marry.[15]

Since marriage was a family decision, including whom and when, Betty followed her culture's tradition and stopped her formal education.

The CCCs—A Taste of American Labor

In addition to the formal environment of boarding school, there was also the Civilian Conservation Corps (CCC) program introduced to shore up the faltering U.S. economy and meet unemployment needs between 1933 and 1942 of the Great Depression. Throughout the Southwest, one of the more successful regions for Native Americans in the United States, the federal government recruited Indians into the CCC-ID (Indian Division), to the tune of 85,000 enrollees total with a final nationwide expenditure of $72 million.[16] The Navajo Reservation had one of the most active programs, consistently filling authorized slots for workers. Projects included soil conservation and water resource development, grazing and flood control efforts, road and trail construction, predator and pest eradication, and heritage site stabilization and interpretation. Navajos from Monument Valley and throughout the reservation flocked to join the program. John Holiday was one of those men, providing a representative example for what so many experienced. His casual introduction resulted in full-time employment that he later regarded as highly beneficial.

My family used to sell meat—a whole sheep carcass, leg of beef, or rump—at the trading post or CCC camps where the cooks often made purchases from the local people. One day my big sister told us that people needed meat at Road Coming Down. So we butchered three sheep, packed the carcasses on the horse, and took it to them. I arrived at the job site, brought the meat to the place where they cooked the meals, and sold it to them. My brother-in-law received the payment for the mutton but I did not get a nickel.

I stayed around this workplace for a while and was asked to take the horses to water at noon. The watering place was large and near a mesa and so a man named Charlie Salt and I took them there every day. He used to talk a lot and tell stories, so he would ride his horse ahead then stop in front just to keep talking. Because he talked all the time, he received the Navajo name of Talks a Lot. He told me, "I got married. I got married two months ago and became a son-in-law of Tall Educated One. She is only nine years old.[17] My parents herded the horses to my bride's place as payment, but she is still afraid of me so I haven't touched her yet.

The road heading out from Kayenta with the volcanic neck of El Capitan on the right and Owl Rock on the left was a familiar sight for John Wetherill, perched upon a rock. The deceptively smooth, open road was notorious for bogging cars down in windblown sand and slick spots of clay. As part of the "Billy Goat Highway"—a network of reservation roads—it saw steady improvement during the years of intense uranium mining. (Courtesy Harvey Leake, Wetherill Family Archives)

When I move towards her, she tries to run away, so I leave her alone. I'm still trying to get her used to me."

Another story he told me was: "One summer I planted a huge corn field at Red Rock Going Down (Mystery Valley) and worked in it all day hoeing weeds. This particular time, I was working in the middle of the field when my mother-in-law, who was not so fond of me, asked, 'What is that out there, in the middle of the cornfield? Is it a kitten burying his feces?' She never really appreciated me." I laughed and laughed and enjoyed working with Charlie for several days before getting paid in silver coins. I was so proud of myself that I took them out of my pocket every few minutes and lined them up to look at.

Later, I was herding livestock at the base of the La Sal Mountains when I heard that I had a letter at home. I returned to Monument Valley and began working for the CCCs. The program operated out of several large white offices in Kayenta. The BIA constructed these buildings just like the BIA boarding school with a cafeteria, where the workers lined up to eat. My clan grandfather, Man with Gray Face (Hastiin Binii'łibei), was our cook. He used to get up early in the morning, prepare breakfast, then come in and yell, "Come and eat!" Many Navajo men labored on these crews. The metal census tags used to count and identify our people by number when being paid for work or food distribution, was also used when employed by the CCCs. We were asked, "Do you have your metal?" (census tag). The pay was only $1.25 per hour. We worked to "kill the washes" in Chilchinbeto by filling in the water-eroded land and by putting up fence barriers across gullies. Other men built water wells, the remains of which can still be seen in some places. But most of these structures have fallen apart due to age. We also built many dams using wheelbarrows, big trucks, as well as arm and leg work. Some dams are still visible, but others have filled in with sand and debris.

For relaxation, we played baseball. There were other CCC groups in Tuba City, Slim Cottonwood, Shiprock, Teec Nos Pos, and by the Anasazi dwellings northeast of the San Francisco Peaks and Flagstaff. There were additional outfits in Blanding, Monticello, and Moab. In this last place, the houses were green, not white like other camps, and were located just across the bridge by the Colorado River. Each crew had a baseball team that played against different camps. We would pile into a long, green bus and travel to our games. Sometimes we won, sometimes lost, just like high school students playing sports. We had games in Window Rock, Moab, and against a Mormon team. I was always asked to be the pitcher because I tossed the ball fast and the opposing team could not hit it, would get mad, and throw their bats down. I offered to have others pitch, but they told me to do it so I had fun. On work days, our supervisor loaded us in trucks and transported us to the site, wherever a well was to be built. One day we were working on one at Sitting Willow Tree just below Rough Rock, AZ. Our foremen were Dressy Woman's Son (Asdzą́ą́ Hadit'éhí Biyáázh) and Little Tower House (Kinyaa'áanii Yázhí) from Chilchinbeto. We worked really hard hand-mixing the cement because there were no electric mixers. The cement, gravel, and water blended in a baking pan-like container, was mixed with shovels, then poured into the square frame boards and mesh wire prepared as forms. These kinds of projects were done throughout Navajo land.[18]

Technology, roads, boarding schools, and government programs like the CCC were just a few of the forces moving the Navajo people of Monument Valley in the direction of the dominant culture. There were many more—World War II, war industry work, tourism, new technological innovations—the list goes on. Much of the pressure for change was subtle, in other instances, quick and gut-wrenching. Some was self-imposed and in other instances enforced top-down by the federal government. In each instance, there was an action and reaction that either strengthened the bonds of traditional culture or opened the gate to Americanization. Always it was a matter of the direction and the rate of change.

CHAPTER TEN

Tall Sheep—Short Change or Good Gain

Early Promotion of the Valley

A s Monument Valley became more accessible, its photogenic wonders and financial opportunities began to appear before the world. Livestock, agriculture, and associated crafts and products formed the basis for the nonmonetary Navajo economy, but once the dominant society's wealth and wage system opened to the People, the promotion of earning a different livelihood became available. As more and more of the outside world intruded or was invited to become a part of the daily life of the Navajos, the greater the "rising expectations" for those who wanted to try new things. The last chapter pointed out that rapid and greater change unfolded with the introduction of the car, roads, schools, and government programs. The chapter following this one dis-cusses the development of the uranium industry, which, along with oil and gas production in other areas, vaulted the Navajo economy into the twentieth-century financial limelight more than anything else had in the past. Here, this interim chapter centers on Harry and Mike Goulding, who played an early part in shaping and attracting different elements of Anglo culture to this high desert environment, an influence that would play out for sixty years.

First, a caveat. As mentioned previously, there is an entire book based upon an oral history of Harry and Mike Goulding and their Monument Valley experience.[1] The intent here is not to duplicate what that says, but rather to emphasize the Navajo view when possible. No other chapter has centered on an Anglo, but to ignore the Gouldings' presence in Monument

214

Valley is an impossibility. They affected many different aspects of Navajo life, including livestock production and sales, arts and crafts, a trading post, visitor accommodations, roads, moviemaking, archaeology, uranium mining, the Navajo Nation Tribal Park, and a Seventh Day Adventist Hospital, and they created a major emphasis on tourism.

No single individual had a greater impact in the history of developing the valley than Harry Goulding. He got along well with the Navajo people, participated in community and traditional activities, and was generally a good steward of the land. Many Navajo people who worked with him agree. Yet, there is always another side of the equation. There were those who did not like, understand, or trust what he was doing, especially in the realms of economic development. He was an astute businessman. Many of the things he started have come to fruition and have turned a handsome dollar. However, there were also conflicts—over rangelands, business deals, elements of traditional culture, outside influences, land ownership, and mining efforts. Some of these issues will surface here. In mentioning them, there is no intent to either harm or praise the Gouldings, only to report different Navajo perspectives and the very human interaction that played out between two sometimes opposing forces.

First Impressions

Samuel Holiday was born next to Eagle Mesa at a site where his family could see the dust from the construction of the Goulding's Trading Post, starting in 1927. Samuel was three years old at the time, when workers began shaping sandstone blocks from the side of the adjacent mesa and wagons hauled in nonlocal supplies and materials. Two years prior to this, Harry and Leone "Mike" Goulding drove into the valley in an old Buick and a Graham Brothers truck to pitch their tent near a wash by Mitchell Butte. Life was hard that first year, as the couple lived off melted snow and spring water, moved their tents to various locations, and established relationships with new neighbors. To now have another trading post closer than the relatively new Oljato store (1921) was an important addition to the community of Navajos living in the area. Samuel recalls:

> At that time there were only a few white traders who ran the trading posts in Oljato and Kayenta. My mother told me that others were moving into the area which both scared and made me curious as to how they appeared. Mother told us that a white man and his wife had moved to Tsé Gizh (Gap in Rock), a narrow defile near present-day Gouldings' trading post

later renamed Dibé Nééz (Tall Sheep) after the man, Harry, who was tall and went around purchasing sheep from the People. They were living in a tent and seemed like a happy, kind couple. Even though my mother said they were very friendly, she still did not trust them because they might help the white government agents looking for Navajo children to be taken away to schools far from their homes. Later I learned that the Gouldings were only buying rugs and sheep but my mother still did not trust them as they visited hogans in the area. They might come and identify her children to be taken away.

One morning, Harry Goulding and his wife, Mike, were traveling about taking pictures of Navajo sheep in Monument Valley. Since they had gotten to know my mother and had quickly learned to speak Navajo, they paid us a visit. Both rode in on packed horses and began pointing at all the rock monuments, saying, "Beéso (money), beéso, beéso, beéso." Mother was puzzled and asked me, "Why is he pointing to the rock monuments and calling them money." Later I realized that he had made a lot of money by taking pictures of the rock monuments and selling them. At this time, he was planning for the future when he said "money." To me he became a millionaire by taking lots of home movies and photographs of the rock monuments and selling them.

I was told that this white couple was building a house out of cut stone near Gap in Rock. My brother-in-law, Billy Nez (Tall), who was husband to my oldest sister and whose name later changed to Nash because of the English pronunciation, had a couple of children and lived close to us. He and others helped with the construction while Ted Yellow used his wagon and a team of mules to haul stone. Even with all this help, it took three years to finish the project. Once the structure was completed, Mike ran the store and Harry took tourists into Monument Valley on horseback for four-or-five-day trips to see all the canyons and rock formations. Most of the mesas and buttes are named after what they look like—Bear and Rabbit, The Rooster, Stage Coach, Eagle Rock, King on the Throne, The Three Sisters, and many more. Later the tourists traveled in jeeps, requiring only a day to tour the valley. The Gouldings also brought movie makers to Monument Valley. Among the films created there, I remember *Stagecoach* and *She Wore a Yellow Ribbon* with John Wayne starring in them. Later my wife, my sister-in-law, and I had our picture taken with him when he was filming *The Searchers*.[2]

Samuel was too young to be aware of what actually faced the Gouldings in those early days, but Harry remembered well sixty years later.

Reminiscent of what John Wetherill encountered in Oljato twenty years previous, the Gouldings met one winter morning with a delegation of six or eight elders who asked when the couple was going to get off their land, which incidentally had not been officially given to the Navajos at this time. Harry remembers the confrontation.

Well I didn't feel too easy about it because you could feel the atmosphere strong. There was a .38 Smith and Wesson that I carried clean through the war, hanging on the front post of the tent. I stepped right up beside it; I wasn't leaving it too far. A Navajo can put out an atmosphere—oh, it's like a breeze if it's nice, or it's like a terrible whirlwind when they want to be. They have that ability whenever they want to use it. It was their land and they had the atmosphere that they were wanting us to leave. They didn't *ask* us to leave, they just wanted to know *when* we were going to leave. . . . I didn't talk the best Navajo right then. I didn't know what the word for "hair" was, so I pointed to my hair and went over and put my hand on the white tent, and said, "When my hair gets as white as that tent, maybe I'll go out." They laughed at that a little bit. So then it was all fine. We shook hands. I think they seen that the bluff wasn't going to work, and that joke kind of softened the whole thing out.[3]

No doubt Harry knew that when a trading post was established on a reservation in those days, the federal government had major control of what and how things were sold and strictly screened individuals who applied for a license to operate it. The trader only owned what was on the shelves, while the land belonged to the tribe. There was a way around this, however, which the Gouldings understood, as Fred Yazzie explains.

The government divided the land into small sections; a few private owners obtained allotments that had been set aside for specific uses like schools. My father, Adakai Yazzie (Little Gambler), saw all of these lands divided, when there were few Navajos living here. There were posts that marked the land, and a person could be fined $250 if one was pulled out. For us at that time, that amount seemed like $250 million would today. My parents told me, "Yiiya', stay away!" I listened to them and left the markers alone. When money was abundant, Tall Sheep came along and knew where the school sections were. He had some traps with him and pitched a tent near Mitchell Butte, which was part of a school section. After trapping animals for about a year, he moved to where the junction is now onto another school section. Then my father gave a sheep to him for some supplies. White men are smart. First, he trapped coyotes, skinned them, and sold the hides so that he could get money to set up a trading post. He got along well with the Navajos, made many friends, and traded fairly, obtaining a lot of livestock from them. In a short time, he moved again to where his post and lodge are now.

Still, he upset some Navajos over the use of the land and got into an argument with my father often. My father told him that he should move out and that white men did not belong here. During the argument, Harry took out his gun and they were about to kill each other. Soon my father became sick with pneumonia and almost died from it, and so that cooled down the fight between the two. After my father got better, he went to Harry, who agreed to pay my father $85 a month for the use of the land. This led to another argument and Harry getting his gun again. This time my father said, "I could have died and so now it does not matter how long we drag out our fight." He went and got his gun. "You can shoot me and I will shoot you and have no regrets." Harry did not want to die, so he made peace. He gave my father a small sack of flour and some coffee, then called a truce. Later, the argument broke out again, which resulted in a fist fight. One of my uncles served as a representative and came to talk to my father, telling him that he should not take the law into his own hands. "Go to the government and tell them about what Tall Sheep is doing."

My father went to a lawyer and the police in Shiprock. They told him to be at Goulding's in the evening. He went to the trader's place at the appointed time and did not wait very long before he saw an automobile come up the road carrying a lawyer and two police officers. The lawyer told Harry that he had to take his sheep off of the reservation. Maurice and Paul Knee, Mike's brothers, herded them across the San Juan River; the two were crying. They kept them there for a year. Harry hired another man to herd the sheep, but he killed two white men over there, which caused a lot of commotion among the Anglos. Harry's herd vanished and I do not really know what happened during that time because I was in school, but as this was taking place, we did not see him for a whole year.

Harry Goulding is a good example of how Anglos make money. Whites are intelligent and when they put their mind to something, it can be accomplished in no time. Navajos, on the other hand, observe the white man to see what he is doing and how he makes his money. Anglos make money just talking about their part or how to make a fortune. You can see photos of Navajo sheepherders across the country, but what did they get from it? Maybe a nickel. What did the Anglo get for taking the

Harry Goulding—Tall Sheep—with a customer, stands outside of his two-story trading post built by Navajo labor. The downstairs was devoted to the trading business, including a store and storage rooms, while upstairs was the family's living quarters. During the John Ford years, this site became the center of activities, hosting stars and supporting the nearby tent-city, staging area for much of the filming throughout the valley. (Courtesy Photo Archives, Utah State Historical Society)

picture? Much more. Now they look at the natural resources and so they are making money and getting rich from them. The Navajos did not get any money even when the Anglos discovered uranium, but the white man got rich. As my father used to say, "look at the land carefully—the buttes and monuments that are all around us as well as the open space in the middle. Look at El Capitan, then Train Rock. You would think there is nothing. You would think you have nothing to show for it as you gaze across the barren land. You would think I will just starve because I have nothing, but here in Monument Valley, there are lots of riches. If you make room for a white man, he will get rich." This is what I was told and so I did not leave here. People have asked me to move out, but I observe what is going on around me and think how to get rich. As I look about, it is true, one can get rich like Harry Goulding, but it killed him. He swindled and cheated people as did Maurice Knee. So you see, a white man always has a dishonest side. Observe your surroundings and ask questions. Navajos could have lots of money, if they carefully thought out what is before them. They could become wealthy. Many of the good spots on the land are already taken by the states. For instance, the junction is a school section and is heavily developed. The only way to learn about these kinds of things is by going to school and not giving up. I talked to one of my sons who is in college about what I have observed about Anglos and how they are swindling us.[4]

Positive Perspectives and Promotions

These harsh judgments are honest evaluations by individuals who have been hurt by past actions and transactions, no doubt. Yet there were many other Navajos who harbored no such feelings. Take, for instance, Gladys Bitsinnie, when discussing the role of both the Oljato and Goulding's trading posts. Here she is referring primarily to Harry.

> He really understood the people's language very well and helped them, like when he gave my father flour, shortening, and coffee while buying hides and rugs. The price was high when the women brought them in. We received a lot of food when we took a rug there. We got much more than expected. A person might arrive hungry and he would give you tomatoes and crackers for free. Both the traders did this. Now, nothing like that is done. Traders now will not even give you anything, even of little value. At that time, the traders had hearts. If a person is going to have a ceremony, the traders helped with food and extended credit. Tall Sheep used to help us a great deal. We were sad when he was no longer there. When an Anglo is helpful, they are like a grandmother.[5]

Ted Cly felt the same way. Excerpts from his interview with Samuel Moon illustrate the close connection that the Navajos felt toward the Gouldings.

> He was a trader who bought rugs, skins, and wool then took it to market and brought something back to give to our parents. He ordered all kinds of things for us like nosebags for the horses, wheat, barley, horseshoes or collars, wagons, wagon grease, axes, and shovels. He traded so that we all could have a shovel and an axe. Otherwise, we would not have them. . . .

When we left the reservation, we would write to him. We got paid and we always sent money to our mother or father. We sent it to the store and then he would take it down to my father's place. . . . He was close to us, like brothers and sisters. He traded with our family the way we traded with each other. . . . The other Navajos here in the Valley think the same of the Gouldings. They all came here to trade. He was their friend, just like brothers, so he sat down and talked to them. When people got old and sick, he would come around and have a ceremonial for them. He would go down in the Valley, just drive around when the snow was on the ground, and bring down kerosene or something. . . . Mrs. Goulding was the same as Mr. Goulding. She traded in the store and helped others. She found some girls and showed them how to sew clothes using a pedal sewing machine. They got all different sizes of material and she showed them how to make good clothes. . . . We used to bring meat to their freezer, butcher a goat or sheep and give them half of it. We also helped in the winter by chopping wood for their fire to keep them warm. When she went to town, she would return with boots to wear in the snow and heavy clothing. Oh, they used to take good care of us. We were all coming and going with each other, feeding each other, and helping each other.[6]

Another arena in which the Gouldings receive a positive grade is in promotional efforts to bring and support the movie industry in Monument Valley. Harry tells a lengthy story about how he went to Hollywood and wooed John Ford and others into coming to see what the land in the Four Corners region had to offer. The movie *Stagecoach* was Ford's first attempt in a filming relationship that lasted from 1938 to 1964. Personal bonds with the Gouldings and the Navajo people continued until both Ford and John Wayne had died. The initial undertaking was no mean feat. To bring all of the equipment and other logistical support to such an isolated setting showed commitment and a love for the spectacular scenery that turned many of Ford's hits into national box office successes. Other films followed to the point that eight years later, in 1946, Ford quipped, "I think you can say that the real star of my Westerns has always been the land. . . . My favorite location is Monument Valley; it has rivers, mountains, plains, desert. . . . I feel at peace there. I have been all over the world, but I consider this the most complete, beautiful, peaceful place on Earth."[7] The Gouldings were the ones who introduced Ford to all of this. In a previous chapter, Navajo feelings—both pro and con—are shared, but for the most part, they appreciated the employment, enjoyed the experience, and thanked Goulding for getting the process started.

The movies made an important contribution in another way not so apparent—healthcare. Starting in 1947, budding to fruition by 1950, the Gouldings opened dialogue and encouraged members from the Seventh Day Adventist Church to establish a clinic, later a hospital, to help the Navajos overcome rampant diseases such as tuberculosis, trachoma, and other pressing medical needs ranging from childbirth to end-of-life maladies. In Harry's words, "I'm having to bury too many of my friends! They just don't have anything."[8] He offered a parcel of land in the Gap, worked with the tribe to get initial funding, assisted in road construction, and hauled materials to build a clinic. Gwen and Marvin Walter, two medical missionaries from the church, brought in two trailers, one for a home and another for a temporary clinic, had three hogans built for patients and visitors, and immediately began work to build a permanent structure. A good part of the initial materials came from the movie sets—Tombstone near Eagle Mesa and the fort used in *Stagecoach*—with permission from the tribe, while Harry encouraged the missionaries to take his truck for additional supplies to Flagstaff. He also allowed them to quarry rock on his property for the two-room clinic and other structures, including a small schoolhouse. None of this and the subsequent expansion into a twenty-six-bed hospital and dental facility would have been possible without his support.

In general, the Navajo people very much appreciated having this healthcare facility available. The Anglo medicine dispensed there dealt with physical remedies, in keeping with western knowledge informing medical practices. Traditional healing uses herbs and ceremonies to cure an illness, seen as a symptom that the patient is out of harmony with the holy people because of an infraction of spiritual laws. Western medicine primarily treats the physical problem. Each side practices its healing powers based on a different set of beliefs, and each attains success in different ways. Most traditional Navajos do not have a problem with employing both sides of the medicinal spectrum, being pragmatic in that whatever can cure the affliction—be it physical or spiritual—is a good thing. At times, especially in the past, some medicine men warned their patients away from western practices, encouraging strictly traditional methods, while others encouraged people to try what the white man had to offer.

This approach could be a two-way street, but one worth examining to understand how the Goulding-promoted healthcare interfaced with the Navajo worldview and how two different perspectives could be shared. Gwen Walter, as an Anglo nurse, tells of a night she was summoned to Oljato where two girls were having extreme fits and seizures.

As I drove up to the hogan, I could sense a power as I heard the medicine men in there singing. Out of respect to the medicine men, I would always stay in my car or take my time coming in until they knew I was there then signal that I could take over. When I came up they were singing and the air was charged.

I waited until I heard a pause in the singing then went in. The mother and father were sitting on either side of the girl, holding her wrists because they said that this thing would seize her and just throw her everywhere; she'd roll and thrash around, and they were there to hold her. When I came in, after prayer, which was my custom, soon the atmosphere was quiet and the medicine men calm, the girl was calm, everything was calm. We talked it over and the mother and father indicated that they wanted me to take her to the hospital. There was nothing for me to do there; all of her vital signs were okay. So I said, "Alright"—this was ten o'clock at night—"I'll take her to the hospital," 103 miles over dirt roads. We got in the car, the three of them in the backseat of the jeep station wagon, which was very tight, so they could control her in case of one of the seizures. We started out from the hogan, and things remained quiet until I got down the road about a half mile, and a coyote went slowly across the road with his tail hanging down. The coyote was a bad omen. A normal coyote will go fast across the road and his tail will be out straight in back. It was a coyote man. This means to them, "No. Don't go any farther." They didn't speak English. I knew what they wanted, but just to test them I kept going, and finally the father got hold of me and said, "Stop!" in English; it scared his English up! So I said, "We'll go around on the other side where the coyote hasn't been." "Oh no! No!" This was a bad omen; we must not go to the hospital. So we went back to the hogan, and I talked to them again. I said, "You know I have babies to take care of, you know I have work too. I've been up all day; I must sleep tonight. If you decide you want her to go to the hospital, you get Patterson." He was a Presbyterian minister that lived not far from them, and he and I worked together nicely. I said "Tomorrow morning, if she isn't better, you ask Patterson."

As I drove away from there, all hell broke loose! The girl screeching and screaming, those medicine men rattle-shaking and singing; the atmosphere came back—fast. It's the kind of thing that makes hair stand on end. I'm telling you there was power there! . . . The next day, Patterson took her down to the hospital, and she had a mild convulsion while he was taking her, within five miles or so of their camp. Then when he got past a certain hogan, everything was quiet the rest of the way down. She was fine, normal when the doctors checked her—nothing wrong. They came back and got close to this same hogan again, she tensed up, the parents tensed right up, and I think she had another episode. . . . Patterson and I came to the same conclusion—witchcraft—and there was nothing we could do about it except to pray. In about ten days, the whole thing cleared up.[9]

Change was not always one-sided or in the expected direction that characterized many interactions on the reservation.

Community involvement by local traders was an important part of relationships. They were expected to contribute to local ceremonies, just as Harry (left) watches medicine man Hite Chee pour blue cornmeal mush into a heated hole lined with corn husks. The batter is baked into a cake for a young girl's puberty ceremony (kinaaldá). (Courtesy Photo Archives, Utah State Historical Society)

The Bones of Yé'ii Tsoh

While the Gouldings sought and brought positive change to the valley, the Navajo people also had issues with other things that proved to be both beneficial and harmful. A prime example to conclude this chapter and serve as a segue to the next is that of the uranium mining industry. Context is important. In the Morrison and Chinle geologic layers of the earth, water eroded elements of once-living matter such as that of a tree, bone, or other organic material and replaced it with mineral deposits. Uranium was one of those elements that easily dissolved, then solidified and remained in prehistoric streambeds or as one part of petrified wood. Two of the largest deposits of uranium were discovered on the Navajo Reservation—one at Grants, New Mexico, the other in Monument Valley. To the Navajo, petrified wood fragments were remnants of a mythological monster, Yé'ii Tsoh, who was killed at the beginning of this world's existence when evil creatures roamed the earth. Armed with four types of arrows—two made from different types of lightning, one from sunbeams, and another from a rainbow—the Twins, Monster Slayer and Born for Water, destroyed him. Trapped in his bones that moldered in the earth was the energy given off by those arrows, hence radioactive power. Uranium, often associated with vanadium, a nonradioactive element used to strengthen steel and fortify paint, became increasingly important during World War II and especially during the Cold War that followed. Monument Valley became a progressively prominent source for both of these elements.

John Wetherill, during World War I, prospected two claims for vanadium, but lost them to the Vanadium Corporation of America (VCA). Uranium, while present, was a nonissue at this time and would remain so until the Manhattan Project and the explosion of nuclear bombs over Hiroshima and Nagasaki. In 1944 the Office of Indian Affairs leased its first uranium claim in Monument Valley. The mine, located on the eastern tip of Oljato Mesa at a place called Tsé'haageed hahsání, yielded fifty-two tons of vanadium the first year. The tribe, anxious to receive its 10 percent royalty, willingly signed for a group of Utah miners to work this claim called Utah One. They transported the ore in a cable-and-bucket system from the mesa's edge down to a loading platform and onto trucks for shipment to Moab, where it was evaluated, then sent for processing.

Guy Cly worked at this site and became well known for his skill in working with the buckets. "I took care of the buckets that are going into and out of the mine. Once one was filled, I would guide the buckets out as an engine nearby provided the power to move it. I was in charge of the guiding and returning of the buckets. When the buckets that were full got out to where I was, I dumped it out. I got paid more for this work."[10]

Kayo Holiday remembers those very early years during World War II.

Anglo miners were looking for vanadium at that time to harden metal. They dug around in the rocks and were the only ones who knew what they were looking for. This was the start of all the mining that occurred for vanadium and uranium. At first, people just looked on the surface, but they eventually turned to drilling into the earth. Soon the search for uranium had people digging in mines. The price of it was high. Some of the Anglos owned sheep and kept them on the La Sal Mountains, but once the boom for uranium started, they decided to go after it, but we Navajos knew nothing about it. I started working for the VCA because it seemed like big money was there. This foreman picked two people, one of whom was Luke Yazzie, and brought them down to Cane Valley. This place in the old days was known as Chííhaagééd because this is one of the places where women obtained chííh—a red, very fine mineral that they put on their face to protect from sun and wind burn. At this same place, there was lots of uranium.

When Tall Sheep went there, the Geiger counter needle showed there was a high level of radiation affecting the meter because of the heavy deposits beneath. The Anglos became very busy and discovered more sites where this mineral could be mined. They soon began to drill all over the place, discovering more uranium. At first we did not know what it was for, but only that the Anglos were handling something very dangerous. It eats into flesh and is cancerous with a sore that never heals, bothering vital organs. White supervisors asked us if we wanted to work and told us that the money was good. At that time, I think it was about $1.50 an hour. The Anglos, however, were probably raking in big money. This is how it started out. They were actually greedy with the money and everything had to be done in a hurry, with mining going from dawn to dawn with no stopping. There was a load in the ground in Cane Valley that was circular, almost the size of this house, and looked like balls. It was greasy and yellow and a pick could not even pierce it, so it had to be hammered. There was another deposit that was powdery and felt like it just flowed in the air. This one was red and green. We dug it up, but it was dangerous and gave us terrible headaches with the pain going into our eyes. We worked like this for several years.[11]

Goulding took a growing interest in the possibility of having mines in his own backyard. By June 1950 he, with the help of Navajos, brought in samples, having located seven deposits of uranium.[12] Harry invited Denny Viles, field manager of VCA, who was still operating in the area, to visit the sites. The trader realized that he could not receive any royalties from these discoveries, but he was anxious to improve the Navajos' standard of living while increasing employment, which in turn benefited his own operation. He showed Viles the poverty that was part of reservation life and exacted a promise that wages paid to Indians would be comparable to those paid to white men.[13] One of these deposits would become Monument Two, one of the most productive mines on the reservation.

John Holiday explains how he and his friend, Luke Yazzie, became intimately familiar with the location of this uranium deposit.

When a boy, I was aware of the presence of uranium in the VCA area across the wash from our hogans near Black Rocks. As adolescents, four of us children had the responsibility of carrying water in buckets from the holes on top of some of these small pillar-like formations. We ascended the mesas in the springtime after it rained. While we were there, we played hide-and-go-seek. Luke Yazzie and I climbed into a large crevice that was narrow at the top then widened at the bottom. We climbed all the way down and found an overhanging ridge with a sudden drop and a high cliff on the other side. We looked around and found a layer of rough rock in the wall where someone had dug here and there. Some layers of the rock were reddish in color and some black. I also saw a pillar of uranium ore that had been dug into quite deeply by the Anasazi, I think. Luke and I wandered around for a while before the other two boys found us. We wondered what had happened here and said, "Hey! This would be good for clay to mix with seeds then eat." So we gathered some, took it home, and Luke brought some samples to Harry Goulding. He and Goulding went to the spot where we had found it and the trader probably struck it rich from there. For those of us who actually discovered it, we never got a penny. We also saw the strips of ore on the hills and mesa at Moonlight before it was mined. The uranium was very visible to the naked eye.[14]

Luke Yazzie is generally credited with discovering this tremendously rich vein of ore and making entrepreneurs aware of its location. He tells his own story of what happened.

I am Kinłichíi'nii and born for Tódích'íi'nii. My footprints come out of
there. I was herding sheep and there was a hole under a rock. When you
are a boy, you do crazy things. There were red rocks all over the place,
some were very small, others were green, and some black. I thought they
were very pretty. I picked up a green one and scraped it, then did the
same to a black and a red one. A yellow color appeared underneath each
of them. I put the colors on my hand. I thought about this as I walked
around. These rocks were smooth and so I thought I would make something from them—perhaps a toy horse or wagon or even an automobile.
You do this when you are a child. I went to that place many times because
it was near our home, but nobody else knew about it. Even my father
did not know about it. I went in the hole under the rock, where the red
rocks were large, and brought one out. I made some more automobiles
and horses and donkeys, but left them there. Every few days I went over
there. I kept thinking what will I make. It was like this for several years.

One day I went into Goulding's Trading Post. Laid out on top of the
counter, arranged in a neat row, were all types of rocks, the kind I used to
play with. I asked what they were for, and since Tall Sheep understood
the Navajo language very well, he answered that there was an Anglo
who really wanted them, then asked if I had seen any others like them
because people were looking all over for similar ones. He said the Anglo
really wanted them. He asked me where I had seen those kinds of rocks.
Anglos are looking for them all over this place and if a truckload could be
dug out and hauled away, I would get a lot of money. I was in awe.

Tall Sheep told me that I would be paid by this Anglo but that he
was now away on business and that I should return in seven days. I put
some samples, just small rocks, next to the pile of other rocks. The dial
on the meter went very high, "round and round." It exceeded the power
of all the other ones that had been brought in, so I thought I would tell
the Anglo who wanted them. I agreed to return a week later and when
I did, the man was there. He told me not to say anything about this. He
was probably tricking me, because these Anglos are very sneaky people.
They just want to trick people, and now we are like that. I agreed not to
say anything about it.

Soon he returned when the sun was about midmorning, and he and
Tall Sheep told me to put my horse in the corral. I put my horse in the
fenced area and was directed to get into an automobile. There were no
roads to the site at that time and so I told them that the car would not
make it. This made no difference, they said, and as long as I knew where
the site was, that was what was important. The man said, "I will do the

Navajos visited trading posts for a variety of services. This uncharacteristically large crowd was attending a Christmas Day celebration, but at other times, when things quieted down, receiving mail, writing letters, recruiting for on-and-off-reservation work, dispensing medical advice, and a host of other activities kept the people returning to these important community centers. (Courtesy Special Collections, J. Willard Marriott Library, University of Utah)

driving and we will get there." We followed a wash that went in between the rocks, then went up and down hills until we reached the place where the grass grows. All this time I directed him around sandy spots where we would get bogged down. I really knew all of the places around here. We drove through the grassy area and up to where the mine would eventually be, stopped, and went the rest of the way on foot. The men began discussing the situation, Tall Sheep saying that the deposits were on his land. Later, it seemed that this was one of the reasons that I never received any pay for showing them the rocks. The two discussed things further, we took a picture of us standing at the site, and the man told us that he would write back to let us know what was going to happen. We agreed that we wanted to hear what he and his company thought. He wrote my name down as the person who had found the deposit and showed him. Now that it was recorded, it could not be changed. This is what the man in the picture said.

Tall Sheep, however, was putting himself between me and the discovery and there were many people who said the place was his. Anglos are very sneaky people and perhaps he even received a little bit of money for this. I don't know. If it did happen that way, one day he would stumble over his sneaky deeds. Still, it was my name written down and I am in the picture taken over there. This Anglo who tricked me is now gone. He used to sit for the store and talk to people the way we are talking now because he really knew the Navajo language. It is said there are a lot of words over this and so he said let him be because we were the first to find the rocks. I was told that I would be paid for this by the trader, but as time went on, it never happened. He said since I was the first to find it, that as long as I walk about, I would receive payment. There was only this exchange of words. The trader told me that the mineral hunter would pay me a lot of money if two or three truckloads of uranium were taken away. If I get to see this man again, I will ask him. At the time, however, he told me to wait until the rocks had been taken out of the ground.

After that I would have lots of money, perhaps even get paid into old age. Maybe I would receive a large lump sum or a little at a time. This is how he talked, but all the time he was just tricking me.

Look at what the Goulding's Trading Post, Lodge, and other businesses are like today. There are many buildings over there, with lots of rooms to sleep in. The owners brought in water the same way, using their understanding of the law and land, so the site has really grown. Tall Sheep worked it that way just as he did with the uranium, and now he is gone. It is said there are words against what has happened over there. Now, before anything similar takes place, there is a lot of talk and signing of papers to make sure there is a clear understanding on both sides of an agreement. Everything is discussed before anything is done. There is still talk about the trick that has happened and I have been asked if I have been paid. When I replied no, people said there would be talk about it and perhaps those men involved would go to jail, but that we needed proof. Still, nothing has happened.

At the time that men were taking the yellow mineral out of Monument Two, there were well over a hundred people employed there. They lived all over the place and chopped down many trees for firewood. They finished it off around here. Many Anglos also worked there, with lots of trucks hauling rocks and dirt away. The man who started this business must have really had money. Those involved took this wealth to their money home [bank] and probably bought vehicles with it along with many other earthly goods. But no one has bothered me with this matter as of yet. Tall Sheep said that the boy who had given him the first rock was now dead. For about three years, there were miners who would come and go and work sporadically, then the site really began to operate full time. I went to work over there and was paid for my effort like any other miner. I also became involved in mining closer to the Goulding's post. One of my main jobs was to separate rocks that had uranium from those that did not. One day, as I was picking through the rocks, an automobile drove up. An Anglo approached me and asked who was in charge. I pointed out our boss, but a little later, he returned with some other men to see me. They told me that they had come to talk to me and that the mine would be starting up full time. The equipment was there and preparations were underway. They asked if I would go with them and I agreed that I would meet them there the next day. When I arrived, I started working immediately. I think it was because I was so aware of the area and what was going on. When they asked me if I wanted to work there, I said yes and ended up employed at this site for twenty-seven years.[15]

Before closing the doors on the opening of the uranium industry, Cecil Parrish discusses how some Navajo entrepreneurs were able to work successfully with white counterparts and receive benefits. He said,

Anglos came by several times, asking me if I knew of any places that had certain kinds of rocks. They would tell me what they looked like and ask that I search for them. I followed what I was told and started searching for those kinds of rocks, finding them on a mesa nearby. The more I looked, the more I found, not just on one mesa but two others as well. When I reported their locations, the man told me that I should get my own papers and permission from the tribe to do mining, so that I could then have part ownership in the mine. This man and his partners said they would provide the equipment so that we could work together. I agreed to this since he had to work with a Navajo living on the reservation in order to obtain permission and I needed the equipment, which I could not afford. I went to Window Rock and received the initial paperwork. Later I worked with the Navajo government when it came time to weigh and measure the uranium taken out of our mines.

The Anglo that I worked with lived in Farmington and there were others who assisted him. It was through them that this was able to happen. We located a likely spot and began to drill, so that once we knew there was uranium present, we dynamited and mined it out. The Anglos brought the equipment in while Navajos provided almost all of the labor.

Once they got permission to mine, they went right to work immediately. Many of them have since suffered from the effects of the yellow sand. There were many who worked for us at all three mines. Once one location was depleted of uranium, we went to the next and then the next until finished. We did everything quickly but not always carefully. We dug it fast, there was no teaching about how to operate in a mine, while dust and smoke blew everywhere. In some places, there were spaces between the rocks and slippery substances within them. If these were not taken care of, there could be cave-ins and tumbling boulders. When they were handled effectively in a well-managed mine, there were no problems. We were often warned about this and told to remove all of the loose rocks first, before trying to dig the uranium. All of this would be fixed before we let the men in to drill. I used to be one of the drillers, although I never went to school for this kind of work. I just followed what the Anglos were doing. Part of the hurrying about, which seemed constant, was due to the government needing uranium for ammunition to fight our enemies. There seemed to be a desperate need and so we mined as fast as possible. This was how we did it.[16]

The opening up of Monument Valley—from tourism and trading posts, to moviemaking and healthcare, to uranium mining and infrastructure—is a story of accelerating development that moved the Navajo in the direction of loss of traditional practices and into the nuclear age of the twentieth century. Indeed, the uranium industry catapulted these quiet desert dwellers into a world threatened by nuclear holocaust. The next chapter provides insight into how their culture influenced their reaction to the demands placed on them by uranium mining. In conclusion, much of this chapter has clustered around the activities of Harry and Mike Goulding and their efforts to improve the lot of the Navajo as well as furthering economic development. While there were a wide variety of Anglo people who brought about change on the reservation, from healthcare workers to miners, no other exerted a greater influence in the valley than the Gouldings. For better or worse, the reader will have to decide how to best characterize that influence, one that did not stop even after Harry's death (1897–1991) and Mike's (1905–1992) a year later. Many of the things they started are still in full bloom, emanating from the land they settled and the causes they promoted.

CHAPTER ELEVEN

Mining the Monuments

Digging the Bones of Yé'ii Tsoh

There are a number of ways to understand the uranium mining experience (1944–69) in the Monument Valley District, comprising land found in Arizona and a small portion of southeastern Utah.[1] One could look at its success and note that it produced 3,900 processed tons of this mineral, more than any other mining district in the state of Arizona. Within the Oljato Chapter boundaries alone, there were ninety-five mines developed during this period. Other ways of understanding the experience are to evaluate the economic impact on the Navajo or the mining consequences on the environment. Here, the main emphasis is on how Navajo culture dealt with this twentieth-century influence that was suddenly thrust upon a people who had been relatively isolated until World War II. It should be emphasized that this approach generally looks at the far end of a traditional spectrum with those people who followed ceremonial practices and had been part of the old livestock economy. There were others who had been raised in boarding schools or in an off-reservation environment where Anglo education removed many of the old teachings and replaced them with standard Anglo learning of the mid-twentieth century. A secondary concern is the price paid for not understanding the dangers involved and how many of the activities of daily life compounded the problems.

Violating One's Mother, Protecting Oneself

From the beginning, Navajo people have had a relationship with the earth, considered in traditional thought to be their mother. She is a provider whose bounty is found in the mountains and deserts and whose veins, the rivers and lakes and springs, bring forth life. Embedded in the songs, prayers, and teachings are the cultural roots that foster this distinct worldview. As a mother, it provides what its children need, while respect is returned by those appreciative of what has been given. To traditionalists, the whole idea of mining flies in the face of the type of relationship that should be fostered by those who are grateful. Shone Holiday, who spent two decades as a Navajo miner, shares his thoughts about this relationship.

> Prayers to the holy beings—Haashch'ééyálti'í and Haashch'éé'ooghaan—and offerings to the sacred mountains and earth are provided by miners because they will be digging up her body. The medicine man names all the important mountains in his songs and prayers when singing the "earth songs," keeping these activities sacred at all times. The prayers are continued in a miner's home, even after he leaves for work, just as it is done for one who is departing for military service. The prayers can be said in any way an individual prefers and according to his belief or religion, whether Christian, Native American Church, or Navajo way. One cannot do without prayers, so we pray for everything, wherever we go and whoever we are.
>
> Mining, as we did for uranium, was not of our own doing, but was how the white man instructed us. They wanted to take from the earth the minerals they needed, but it was mined out by the Navajos who had the prayers for protection. I personally would not do something like that, but since I did it according to the white man, then it was not my doing. If one has to destroy the earth, there needs to be a "prayer of forgiveness" to the holy beings, or else that person may be hurt. We have many prayers for all occasions. Many of my coworkers, some white and some Navajo, died from health complications. I have some problems, too, but I've gone to a Hopi medicine man who took out small stones from my body. They were an oblong shape, like the ones drillers get with their drills; I would have been gone by now if I had not had his help or said my sacred "forgiving prayers." I have also been treated at the hospital and was told that my health problems were caused by the mines.[2]

Sam Black agrees.

All the good things on earth can also harm someone if they go beyond the limits of what they are supposed to do with it. Water and air become dangerous, plants poisonous, as does the land itself. Uranium is like a big snake in the earth that breathes poisonous air and can kill a person. The white man did not know that he was violating Navajo traditional ways that we are taught.[3]

The power of protection from physical harm, such as the effects of radiation or collapsing mine walls and ceilings, resides in the ceremonies and prayers offered before, during, and after the work experience. Kayo Holiday explains.

The stories about Mother Earth teach that there needs to be proper respect and that to poke holes in her surface is dangerous. When an Anglo asked if I wanted work and I said yes, he did not tell me about the danger involved and that it would start to kill me in the future. I just did it without defense. The ones who had a ceremony performed on them believed that the earth is our mother and we are hurting her when digging inside and affecting her veins and other parts. This is what they were thinking and so had a specific protection ceremony performed for them, but I did not. Some other people had the Hózhǫ́ǫ́jí or Blessingway performed, but I do not know how the ones specific to mining are done. There is a prayer for Mother Earth that has the four directions' songs that come back together. These ceremonies deal mainly with illness; when one has pain inside, it is diagnosed, so that a person knows what is killing him. Some medicine men really perform on the patient and heal them, while the Hózhǫ́ǫ́jí establishes harmony in the mind.[4]

Luke Yazzie took a different approach.

Corn pollen is placed on the main trunk of a young juniper tree that is still growing. This tree represents the well-being and future of the one who leaves the offering. This was done only with a juniper, because that is how the holy beings established the practice in the palm of time. If one talks and prays through this, no matter how much of the yellow uranium gets on them, it will not cause harm. This is how I think about it, and although some people have died from this [radiation exposure], it is because they did not live in the manner they were supposed to. They may have ridiculed the place they were working, which should not be done, because one does not make fun of their mother and the land. We live on it, our livestock drink and eat from it, and then we eat the livestock. This is why we offer corn pollen to the land.[5]

No stronger testimony of the effectiveness of prayer and ritual is offered than by John Holiday, who spent years mining and was a powerful medicine man in Monument Valley for most of his life. While some Anglos may doubt the type of power summoned to protect a person working in this environment, John had total belief and conviction.

Once, while I was working at the mines, I stayed in a tent close to the job site where I had been working for only a short time. I had a dream one night that someone, maybe a holy being, told me to make an offering of corn pollen and prayers to the cliffs and mesas nearby. "It will be dangerous if you don't," something told me. I thought that I could not make the offerings because my sacred corn pollen was in my medicine bag at home near Train Rock. I awakened in the early morning when the dream was still fresh in my mind. There was no water in the camp and the weather was windy with light rain showers. I grabbed a bucket and headed down the hill to where the big water barrel was. The wind and rain had erased our footprints on the trail, but as I walked along, I spied my sacred corn pollen pouch sitting in front of me. I did not believe it at first because I knew it was at home in my medicine bag, but I examined it very carefully, and sure enough, it was mine. This was strange, but I picked up my pouch, put it in my pocket, and walked back to my tent with the bucket of water.

My dream kept bothering me. I made breakfast then went to work, arriving at the sheer cliff wall close to the mine shaft just before the other workers. I stood at its base and placed my offering of corn pollen and prayed towards the mine, saying a prayer to the uranium and the earth for my safety on the job and other things. At this time, my responsibility was to blast the ore, help my father-in-law scoop it up with big coal shovels, take it out of the mine in a wheelbarrow, then down the hill.

I had just blasted a very thin layer of ore that my boss told me to remove from the low ceiling. I quickly shoveled the ore and thought I would help my father-in-law haul it out, since I was in a hurry to complete the work. Just when I left my spot, a large piece of rock came crashing down right where I had been seconds before. The slab was so huge that it nearly went all the way up to the ceiling and missed my backside by inches. I managed to climb out of the mine, with barely enough room to crawl around the fallen slab. I was saved by my dream and the holy beings because of my prayers and offerings that morning. Somehow, my pollen pouch had followed me there and enabled me to perform the sacred prayer. If I had not done so, I would not be here today. Something like this has happened to me three times during my work as a miner and are examples of why I believe that there is a God.

I often prayed before going underground because I knew which prayers, songs, and offerings to make to the earth, mountains, or mesas. It was a sacred routine that I followed throughout my entire mining career. Many other miners had it done for them. It is said that the holy being, Black God (Haashch'ééshzhiní), was in charge of Black Mesa, where the present coal mine is located. Black Mesa has a prayer and song of its own and some of the employees working there still use these sacred rituals. One of my sons works there and I have often performed songs and prayers on his behalf.

Another time when I was mining, my partner from Chilchinbeto and I were putting in bolts and mesh wire on the ceiling and walls of a wide-roof shaft. Together, we put up a very wide sheet of mesh wire on the ceiling as directed by our boss that morning. We bolted some heavy-duty boards against it every few inches all the way across. By lunch time, we were finished in that area, so we moved all of our equipment around the corner and went outside for lunch. After eating, we returned to the mine and our work site, but there was none. The work area was replaced with a long, large slab, where the whole ceiling had fallen to the ground. My co-worker was stunned and frightened, quitting his job immediately. I never saw him again. He should have had a ceremony or sing, but he did not. This incident did not bother me at all, so I just went back down alone, moved my equipment, and drilled farther down the tunnel. The close relationship one has with the holy ones pays off throughout life. They take care of you, keep you from harm and danger, and give you strength and courage.[6]

Many of these incidents are spectacular and hinge between the physical and spiritual worlds. Most of the time, mining in Monument Valley was just hard gritty work, day in and day out, tedious and dangerous, occasionally punctuated by the miraculous. To put much of this in perspective, Bud Haycock described a typical mining day and how he felt about it.

During that time, everything just went too quickly, which seemed like one of the main goals. There were few roads around here and so we worked with the Anglos to build them along the mesa. We dynamited the rocks, putting roads where needed in some of the most unusual places. I used to work close to home. I would get up in the morning with work starting at 8:00 a.m. sharp. When I got to the mine, I'd put my food and water at the entrance of the mine, then dress in my hardhat and steel-toed shoes, adjust my headlamp, light it, then go down into the mine. When I first reached the work place in the morning, there would be lots of water before the compressor started to pump it out. When it was just right, I went directly to where the deposits were, then used a metal detector that gave a reading as to where the most ore was located. That is where I drilled until noon, placing the dynamite. While we ate lunch outside, the boss might set off the charges or he might choose to wait until evening, which was better because it allowed the smoke from the blast to clear out. At first, we used to work in the smoke, just as it was clearing. Later, we became aware that it was harmful and so switched to blasting in the evening. Next, men hauled out the shattered deposit while the driller was busy making new holes and setting charges for the next round until the work for the day was finished.

We were not taught about the dos and don'ts in mining, but just came to work. If we had been instructed better, we probably would have worked in another way, but the main emphasis was to get the deposit out as soon as possible. I felt like it was for our people that we did this—for the young men and women and our land. I think when we worked in these places, it was for a good cause, even though it may have harmed us. We will just let that be. I have worked in many places and am happy about what I did because it has advanced my life. I am not in hunger and I have all my needs taken care of as I walk toward the end of my days. I am being paid for what I did and have helped many of my people.[7]

Shone Holiday paints a similar picture of his work, adding detail as to what miners encountered.

I got a job at the VCA mine near Mexican Hat, where I worked for six months before moving to the mines on Oljato Mesa, where there were several of them. There was also one by Promise Rock, and another near Narrow Canyon called Starlight, where I worked for a white man we named White Mustache (Dághaałigaii). We were employed at these sites, about six of them, for several years, which entailed a mixture of horizontal and vertical mining. It was while I was working at Starlight that the mine collapsed. We had just barely cleared out the area and were getting ready to leave when one acre of the roof fell in. It buried my cousin, Paul Begay, under it all, but we were able to dig him out. We left the mucking machine that removed water with all of the hoses attached plus all of our tools; they are still down there.

As with so many aspects of Navajo culture, mining is based on relationships—not just with other workers or employers, but also with Mother Earth itself. These vanadium miners protected themselves from harm by saying prayers, sprinkling corn pollen, and maintaining harmony with the land around them. (Courtesy Special Collections, J. Willard Marriott Library, University of Utah)

Our working relationship with our white foremen was good. Some Navajos spoke English while some white men spoke Navajo and got along fine. I can't remember the exact amount of our wages, but it was enough, varying between $100 and $200 for the drillers every two weeks. The owners of the mine furnished rubber clothes—coveralls, overcoats, gloves, and hard hats—which we changed into when we went to work. Some of us took them home and hung them with our personal things, unaware of the contamination.

Usually the drilling area was as wide as a doorway or a little wider. The "jack leg" allowed one to drill higher up the wall. This was done section by section, taking about three hours or so, then we went outside to eat lunch. Following this break, we took in a box of blasting powder and filled the drilled holes with a wooden stick, not metal. After they were in place, we connected the wires to each one and made sure they would ignite correctly. By then, it was usually close to quitting time and everyone left the mine except for the two men who lit the fuses. In a few minutes, one could hear the blasts underground, filling the mine with dense fumes that had a foul smell. The miners usually kept a fan blowing air out at night, otherwise the shaft would fill up with heavy gases. We were not allowed to enter when this happened because it was difficult to breathe. The air smelled like butane, sometimes making us weak. Both Navajos and whites went through this together. It was usually warm in the mines even during the winter when it was freezing cold outside. Underground springs in the mines were warm, producing steam.

One thing that helped prevent cave-ins was to have enough support columns. An accident occurred, one time, when our white supervisor told us to shoot out several of these columns. He said they contained a lot of ore and he wanted to have them dug out. We did not want to do it, but had to obey him. Sure enough, the roof collapsed. This happened twice. Once I got into a heated argument with one of our supervisors about doing this, but he got his way because he was angry and chased us all down into the shaft. We were barely finishing when the roof collapsed, burying all our machines and a man. It is safer to have more support columns, but if that's all that is left and they hold plenty of ore, then it is time to shoot them out, but it is dangerous. They should have been left alone for safety's sake.[8]

Cecil Parrish, who worked with Shone, noted that there was no place to take baths or showers, and that their clothes felt greasy even after washing them by hand. Likewise, traditional sweat baths did nothing to remove the oily feeling from a person's skin. Uranium seemed to permeate everything. As for the white bosses, some of them were nice.

We would joke together and they would tell us we were doing a good job, but once he left, the foreman got after us if we were not working properly. Some of these foremen wanted us to work faster, even though the physical body could not do it, pushing us to "hurry and dig that out. Hurry and fill it. You only took out five ore carts when it could have been ten." We were in constant motion with our work. When I first began in the uranium mines, there was one called Stumped Ears behind Promise Rock. There were no hydraulic tools, so we had to hold up the jackhammer while we drilled. There also was no water to blow out or settle the dust, so the mine was full of it. Sand filled our throats, noses, and ears; it was a mess! This was in the beginning.[9]

A Clear and Present Danger

By now it should be obvious that working in the mines, from either a long range or short range perspective, was dangerous. Today it is so much clearer what these dangers were, from exposure to radiation to the physical collapse of a mine's ceiling. By the 1950s, a substantial understanding of the health issues was known so that, in one sense, there was no excuse on the government's part in not making the public more aware. Dissemination of that information was the problem for all of the miners—white and Navajo. There was no OSHA (Occupational Safety and Health Administration, started 1970), communication was comparatively slow and limited, and in the case of the Navajo, translation was necessary. Much of this could have been solved, but many of the miners lived a hand-to-mouth existence, the pay was good, and a lot of the harmful effects would not become apparent until later. While there could have been intentional deception on the part of the mine owners, there were those who did not know, others who did not understand, and those who did not care. What follows is a series of accounts, pointing out the many ways uranium mining affected the Navajo.

Starting with problems most visible, we will continue the stories of collapsing mines. Seth Clitso begins: "I was working at a mine on Boot Mesa when the ceiling collapsed on some people. It was near Boot Mesa. I was working with explosives at that time. Several people died in the mine because of it falling down, which almost happened to me, too. I was somehow spared from the mud as it started to slide down in big chunks without warning."[10] Luke Yazzie remembered several instances where mines collapsed and people were killed. "Those that I knew were Lee Chief, Paul Begay, and a Mr. Jones, the latter two being buried and killed in a cave-in. There were many other major and minor accidents, like cutting off a finger or dropping something on one's foot, etc. Mr. Begay was crushed under a huge slab of rock that fell from the roof of the mine. It took them several days to dig out his body. This accident took place at the Moonlight Mine where there were about 125 men working in three different shifts."[11] Kayo Holiday dynamited the road that went up onto Oljato Mesa where he worked in the mine on top, and also at Mine Number Two, as well as a mine in Oljato. "It was there that a Navajo man had the mine cave in on him. The rocks were about to fall down when I stopped working there; a little later they crashed down on him."[12]

Marjorie Haycock, Bud's wife, remembers one of these incidents (most likely the death of Paul Begay), recalling,

A younger cousin-brother of mine was killed in a mine cave-in many
years ago. He was hauling out the waste with a wheelbarrow when it happened. I often wondered if the company and the white men he worked
for cared about his death. From the day it happened, no one ever said
anything about the cause of his death. Not his mother (my aunt) or any
other relative. I remember how his body lay out on the ground after he
was removed from the rubble. The white men from the company quickly
made a wooden box and laid him inside, nailing it shut. Then a bulldozer dug a hole and they buried him next to the job site where he had
been working. Someone had asked that the body be taken to the Tuba
City Indian Hospital, but for reasons unknown, they buried him on the
spot. To this day, it still hurts and bothers me to think how ruthless the
company was in dealing with his death. Shortly after this incident, my
mother, father, and my cousin's widow went to Window Rock to check
into the matter, but were unsuccessful in getting any help or compensation on behalf of my cousin's death.[13]

*Mining underground could be extremely dangerous. This was especially true in the
small, underfunded "dog hole" mines operated by individuals or small companies when
compared to the larger VCA holdings. Still, there were always accidents, not to mention
issues with radioactivity. (Courtesy Special Collections, J. Willard Marriott Library,
University of Utah)*

Inherent in every job was danger. Luke Yazzie, who worked with dynamite, tells what it was like setting off the charges, then watching walls and ceilings collapse:

> I just drilled and drilled at the end of a tunnel. When there was about an hour to go before lunch, I put the lines between the charges in the drilled area, after all the men were signaled to get out with the blast of a horn. It was then that I and five other men started lighting the lines to the dynamite, which was usually around one hundred drillings. We had an igniter that lit the end of the highly flammable split lines. We ran as we did this, with the dynamite going off behind us, blowing sand out of the tunnel and collapsing walls and ceilings. It fell down when we were out of there.[14]

The exposure to radioactive dust was constant. Billy Yellow was well-named when working in the mines.

> I almost had two cave-ins on me. My job was to drag out the quarried rocks in a cart. When I was through with a day's work, I looked like I was covered in yellow powdered flour. I bagged the uranium by hand and then went outside to eat my meal—rib-meat for lunch—with my yellow hands that looked like they were covered with corn pollen. I think I am still living because of the herb I used. I ate only a little bit, but I think it made harmful things stay away from my body. When taking it, one vomits, which causes great suffering; I do not think I can handle the potion now, so sickness will just do whatever it wants to me.[15]

Miners got a "dusting" in other ways. This is what Sam Black remembers.

> When we got paid, we brought our checks to Jim Hunt at the trading post to cash them. We all hopped on one of the big trucks that went into town and were dropped off at the post. On the way we all got dirty and dusty from traveling on the dirt road and from the yellow and white sand they hauled, but we didn't care. Whatever the color of sand the truck was hauling was the color we became by the time we hopped off. Sometimes the sand was hauled to the river and dumped in it.[16]

Sandpaintings, used to heal the sick, provided a limited radiation exposure through the sand and ground rock used, according to Bud Haycock.

They used to say that it [uranium] was the same clay or sand that was used in making sandpaintings or painting the sick with sacred symbols during a ceremony. Some called it "clay," and some called it "yellow rock." I do not know if it caused any serious sickness or injury. We did not know then that it was extremely dangerous. We used to drink the cool water that drained down deep into the mine, about 112 feet underground, and ate our lunch down there, too. When one was in a hurry to get the job done, he usually held and ate his sandwich with one hand while drilling with the other. Once we got off work, we went directly back to our homes and families dressed in our contaminated work clothes. We knew nothing! Our wives did our laundry by hand, and our children played with our hats and headlamps. I have taken my whole family with me to every mining job site that I ever worked in.[17]

Water in the desert, whether in or out of a mine, was still precious to the Navajo. Sam Black's grandfather had an uneasy feeling about his grandson working in the mines, and so Sam had limited exposure, but while he was there, he saw many Navajo men living by their worksite. Their families were drinking and bathing in the water pumped out of some of these mines as well as allowing livestock to drink the water. Nearby springs also met this need. Many of these people, according to Sam, have contracted different kinds of sickness, in his mind, stemming from radiation exposure. Mine water was also hauled by families to their homes, but he never used any of it. Kayo Holiday did. "When you enter a mine, you sometimes got a headache from the dynamite powder that mixes with a mist of water that causes the odor to be very strong. In the mine, where water seeps out of the ground, puddles formed. The water was cold and refreshing and so we drank it."[18] Bud Haycock also experienced using this underground water.

After work, we went home from the mines without changing. One time I went to work when a man was drilling where water was oozing out of the ground from a hole that was so very deep that the men had to rope each other in and out of it. I worked there with him as he drilled into a rock where the water was running out. The miners put a pipe into where it had been drilled and the water flowed easily. We drank that water but now realize it was very dangerous to do so. The workers also took their food into the mines and ate in there. If we had been told that this was dangerous, we would not have done it. Even the boards used in the mines were given to us when the job ended, so we used them in our homes. I still have some as part of my shade house.[19]

Inadvertently eating uranium on a sandwich or roasted ribs was one thing, but intentionally using it as a sweetener and food extender was another. Traditional Navajo cooking called for certain types of clay to be incorporated into some recipes. Ada Black explains.

There were a couple of mines not far from here that had yellow rocks that we used for food. One year there was a lot of rain in the summer and snow in the winter that gave rise to abundant vegetation. A plant with red berries called haashch'éédą́ą́' (wolfberry) also has a root used in cooking. At first, I did not know it could be eaten, but my husband's (Harvey's) mother and sisters and uncle's wife consumed a lot of it. They boiled it with the uranium, now said to be dangerous, but we were not aware of it at the time and ate it as food. The rock was said to be a special mud (hashtł'ish) that was ground with a mano and metate, while the water used to boil it was also consumed. I was herding sheep at the time, and they were living out in the valley. As I brought in the flock, I rode by their place on my horse. There were often different types of food set out, including meat and haashch'éédą́ą́'. I spooned some up, tasted its sweetness, then ate lots of it. Many times after that, I continued to eat this special mud that tasted like milk.

This food extender was like the white mud found in the mines, used as a sweetener. Lots of people worked there, and many died from it. Harvey's uncle and his wife passed away, as did his mother. They probably did not take any preventative measures, but I offered earth prayers to the rocks where the mine is. In this way it does not bother you. We both have reached old age even though we really ate a lot of it. Before the mines in Monument Valley opened up, we used to gather the white clay from a mine called Dleeshbii'tó (Clay's Water) close to Comb Ridge. It provided very white clay that came from a vein of rock that had a seep with the water trickling down. The people dug out the clay and took it with them. The uranium and the clay were used in the same way even though one was very white and the uranium was very yellow.

There was also water pumped from the mines, lying around in pools that the sheep drank in the Oljato area. The pipe carried the water to the surface as people worked below. Although animals went there to drink, we did not use that water, but people did eat the sheep. Our water came from a windmill that had a drum attached to it. Since that time, we have learned about the dangers associated with radioactivity from uranium. There are other people throughout Monument Valley that were either hurt by accidents or by exposure to radioactivity. Some had sores

Miners taking a noontime break still faced health issues. Drinking radioactive water from the mines, eating food without washing, and inhaling the gases from blasting powder or the dust from working had future consequences on the miners' health. (Courtesy Special Collections, J. Willard Marriott Library, University of Utah)

on their legs that took months to heal. After I treated them with herbs, they became better. Harvey, now, does not go anywhere. He cannot even ride a horse but just stays home. We heard that there is an application for help for those who worked in the mines and are bothered by sickness coming from the uranium. People came to visit us about this, and I told them part of his story.[20]

Physical and Spiritual Healing

For some traditional Navajos, from start to finish, the process of mining and healing from its effects were rooted in the realm of spirituality. Sickness is not just a physical indicator that something is wrong in a body, but it is also viewed as proof that an individual is not in harmony on his or her spiritual path in life. That person has offended the holy people or broken a law instituted by them since the beginning of time. In its simplest, generalized form, Anglos have no problem accepting the results when a physical rule or law is broken. For instance, if a person does not have supplemental oxygen or a controlled environment at a high altitude, their body will react to the deficit and could even die. In the Navajo world, the same is true when a spiritual law is broken, with the severity of the consequence depending on the infraction and the holy being offended. Equally logical, just different. So it is not surprising to find that songs and prayers, as well as ceremonies and rituals, for traditional practitioners can be just as effective or ineffective as those remedies provided by skilled physicians.

Protection and healing expressed themselves in a number of different forms. Bud Haycock said, "Before the workers entered the mine, they would have a prayer to prevent anything harmful from happening. We would go in after the first prayer, but we also prayed for and to our equipment. In this way, things went well. A person also pleaded on one's behalf that nothing would go wrong and that there would be a spiritual shield of protection."[21] On the other hand, Guy Cly discusses what happened to those who did not address the holy people and follow their practice. When asked about mining accidents and their causes, he reported that they occurred at specific mines.

> Only the ones over here I have heard of this happening. It was because the individuals had no sacredness in their manner. They joked about everything. The rocks have the power to harm, but probably felt kindly toward those who were using them to feed themselves and their family. Others did not take it seriously and so suffered. Where I worked, the people offered prayers to these rocks and had sacredness in the mines, so no one there was harmed in that way. The only incident I recall was with a man called Hastiin Dooahotehi, who had a tractor he was operating flip over with him. He used to joke about the job that he had, and it harmed him.[22]

Fred Yazzie gives a more complete explanation of his understanding of how spirituality affected mining operations.

> In the story about Mother Earth, it is said that she can be dangerous, and to create or to be in a hole in her can bring on problems. Those believing these teachings and having ceremonies performed for them said that the earth was our mother and that when we are digging inside, we are hurting her. What she was living on, her veins, we were digging up, and so ceremonies for protection had to be performed for the miners. I did not have the one done on me because all I wanted was work. I was told that

Billy Yellow, a medicine man, was very familiar with the prayers and rituals needed to protect miners from harm and to avoid offending Mother Earth. As a miner, he understood the importance of maintaining hózhǫ́. (Courtesy Monument Valley High School)

those rocks were valuable and that I was to dig for them and that was all. Some people had a ceremony performed for them, like the Hózhǫ́ǫ́jí, the effects of which were very real. My wife (Susie) and I each had this done at different times, me for my mining and her to protect herself and the children while at home. This way she could lead them to a happy future. The ceremony placed a shield around my family and created harmony in their lives. I do not know how specific mining songs were performed other than there is a prayer for Mother Earth and in it there are four direction songs that come back together.[23]

Billy Yellow describes his understanding of the protective prayers.

This is done with the miner's entire family before he actually started working. The medicine man would take from his bundle a mixture of ground turquoise, jet, and other sands along with corn pollen, then scatter them on the ground, offering a blessing as part of an act of returning something to the earth since something was going to be taken from it. Then the miner would repeat this action, saying a prayer for himself for protection. Next, each family member did the same, with the mother helping infants to also do it. This prayer ceremony could be done any-where, not necessarily at the mine. Another way to obtain protection from harm in mining was to drink an herbal medicine once a year, then take a sweat bath. Doing these two things together left the men lying in the sand all day without strength. In the evening, they would drink a solution of broth to regain their strength. This cleansing is best done in the spring when the weather is not too hot or too cold.[24]

In spite of the spiritual and physical precautions that may have been taken, sickness and exhaustion visited the miners and caused long-term debilitation. John Holiday gave a complete report of his activities, from start to finish. Each miner has their own story, but John's could certainly be accepted as somewhat representative. The sheer volume of work he accomplished as an active worker is indicative of the type of effects the stress, strain, and injury had on an individual. Miraculously, unlike many miners, his exposure to radiation did not kill him the way it did many of his contemporaries. No doubt he attributed long life to his being a med-icine man and practicing the teachings of the holy people. Following his initial experience at Stumped Ears, he began work in a series of mines that developed his use of more sophisticated technology. Still, the work was physically challenging.

The second mine I worked in was Rough Rock Point. I was one of the first workers to open this mine and the job was just as bad as the first one. We had no hydraulic jacks and had to tie the drill bit to the tip of the jack hammer. The process was slow because of the inconvenient equipment and sometimes we had to use hand shovels to complete the job. I next worked at the Moonlight mine as a driller then in several mines on the mesas above Oljato where I was promoted to foreman. Later, I moved to the mouth of Narrow Canyon for additional work. Today, I sit here as if I had never done such labor.

When I was transferred to the old VCA mines because the work was slowing down, I rode my horse from Train Rock to the site and spent one week, sometimes two, then came home. My white employers would not let me go. At times I worked for 14 days straight, then took a week off and performed several ceremonies before returning to the mine. Harry Goulding must have told my employers I was a medicine man and pre-arranged my busy schedule so I could perform the ceremonies and work in the mines at other times. Goulding was somewhat of a supervisor and

I am sure he invested a lot of money from his Monument Valley trading post into mining.

The white bosses who supervised the operation entered the mines only once in a while. They feared them and came in only long enough to give instructions as to what they wanted done. This was usually at the beginning of the shift so that the miners could follow through with the job. I drilled most of the time and learned how to blast, even though I never went to school. Observation, specific instructions, and then working were how I was trained. I was appointed lead man several times and mastered drilling and blasting vertically and horizontally. I really worked hard during my mining years.

In this job, I waited for the men who did the blasting to come in and blow off the surface. One day I decided to dig a ditch along the base of the wall inside the mine tunnel. There were streams of water everywhere, so I thought I would make just a small canal to funnel the water into one stream. Just as I was about to connect the two streams, I heard a loud crack above, and in a matter of seconds, part of the ceiling came crashing down. The rush of air from the falling rock pushed me clear of the slab, wrenched my shovel out of my hands, and threw it several feet ahead of me. I looked up and saw a huge, oblong piece of rock lying where I had been digging. The stone was so large and long that it covered all the ditches I had dug. This was a miraculous escape. I believe my sacred prayers and songs truly protected me and I was meant to live this long. I was very lucky.

Later, I was hired in Mexican Hat at the uranium processing mill to work the graveyard shift. The ore was ground to sand, sifted, and refined then mixed with water and run through some pipes overhead. Underneath were huge pots of black tar heated by flames which dried the ore all night long. Once dried, workers loaded the ore into wheelbarrows and dumped it in a pile. The sifted, powdered form was dried separately and then shoveled into the dump trucks by hand. The ore was as fine as flour and covered us from head to toe in powder, but we never knew how dangerous it was to our health. Then I worked near Denver, in a place called Rico, Colorado, in another uranium mine. I spent about two years there before moving back to Train Rock where I was hired at a new mine not too far from Moonlight. I worked there for about three more years as a driller.

One evening, a group of white men came to my home. They had been inspecting the drilled areas and told me to prepare a huge space. I began drilling with my assistant and we hurried along as fast as we could, putting explosives inside the holes and preparing them for blasting. When the inspectors came around, they saw that I had finished and was waiting while the men in other areas were still drilling. They found that I had drilled 280 holes during my graveyard shift. The roof was fuzzy with fuse wires. The men could not believe that I had made so many holes; they counted all of them and sure enough there were that many. "How many years have you worked like this?" they asked. I told them how many and they recorded it in their records. "This man can sure work! He does a job equal to that of four men. He's a real hard worker!" they said. But they also told me I was working much too hard and warned me that I was overdoing it. So they transferred me to another job for five days and gave me a raise and had me haul ore. They said I must be working equal to 100 hours each week. I remained in the haul-out area for some time, then was transferred to the "lift-out" area where I took care of the machines. I worked there for about a month.

Soon my supervisor assigned me to care for the entrance of the mine shaft where the workers brought up ore in small rail cars. Some of the men who worked at the entrance did not break the large rocks into smaller pieces which created problems, so my boss had me make sure the rocks were the right size. I worked there for two months. One cloudy, misty fall day, a rail car came to the surface with a big slab sitting on top. I unloaded it and let the rock roll back down the shaft then took the sledge hammer and walked down to where it lay. I hit it with the hammer four times then felt a flash of electric shock go through my arm and body. My limbs fell to my sides and I collapsed to the ground. I became paralyzed and could only move my head a little before blacking out. A horn blew each time a rail car brought a load to the surface, and since I could not unload it, the whistle kept blowing and blowing. Two workers came running up the mine shaft, asked what happened to me then quickly called for help. They tried to lift me, but could not, so summoned an ambulance and I was taken to the Monument Valley Hospital. The doctors finally revived my body after two days and then I spent several more days in bed. After that, I had to slow down in mining and could not work like I used to; it was the doctor's orders. My job had failed me, and now I could not work like that again.

My final mining injury occurred at a new mine that had just barely opened. The shaft had not yet become very deep and we were preparing to blast. I drilled the sides of the high walls then filled the holes with explosives and waited. I sat down on a pile of sand and rocks near three other men sitting on another pile. The wall across from me was very smooth, but suddenly exploded, sending flying rocks at us. One of these rocks hit the wall behind me and came down on my back, knocking me out. I spent four days in a coma while the doctors in Gallup performed surgery on my spine. They told me that one of my disks was destroyed which made it worse. I should have stayed home that day then I would not have had this injury and health problems.

I left mining for the last time after that back injury, which totally misplaced all my vertebras and disks. I feared I could not return to a normal life because it had affected my health so badly. My speech became distorted, I could not swallow properly, and the mist from the ore was dangerous. It nearly got me. I had to hire medicine men several times to get my health back to normal. Traditional medicine is very strong and healed me. It is good to have medicine men with their powerful songs and prayers and sacred herbs for healing. I feel very fortunate to be alive and to be well again. That is what I used and that is why I am here today.[25]

While John recounts many of the visible, physical challenges he and many other miners faced, radiation exposure became a primary concern toward the end of the uranium boom and for decades thereafter. Indeed, all Navajo miners today mention how many of their fellow workers and relatives associated with the industry are now dead. Very few good quantitative studies have been done on the thousands of men—Anglo and Navajo—who worked in the mines. An impression of the toll uranium took on health, however, was given in the 1982 hearings held by the Senate's Committee on Labor and Human Resources to determine radiation exposure compensation. During this meeting, Harry Tome from the Navajo Tribal Council and member of its Environmental Protection Commission painted a representative picture from a survey of sixteen miners. At the time of this hearing, the men were relatively young—an average age of 54.4 years old—with an annual income of $5,184. Fourteen of the sixteen men had averaged fifteen years in the mines, sometime between the 1940s and 1950s, and thirteen of them suffered from "serious medical problems." Only four of them had medical insurance, and many of them were too young to receive Social Security benefits, Medicare, and Medicaid.[26]

Perry Charley, who worked for the tribe's Division of Health Improvement, offered a similar report, testifying from personal knowledge of twenty deaths directly associated with uranium mining. Fourteen of these men had died from lung cancer, five from respiratory failure, and one from "another type of cancer." He also stated that his agency had "documented that 50% of the miners examined, who are living within the Shiprock Agency, have clinical and radiological evidence of chronic lung disease."[27]

These Senate hearings bore fruit very slowly. In 1990 the U.S. Supreme Court determined that it could not hear the case since the uranium industry during the 1940s to the 1970s was immune from suit because of its governmental status. However, Congress passed legislation entitled the Radiation Exposure Compensation Act, stating a possible award of up to $100,000 to deserving miners, widows, or children if the parents were deceased. President George Bush signed the law and Congress eventually appropriated funds for the compensation.[28]

The wheels of progress continued to grind forward. Although there have been some positive moves, such as completing the burial of the tailings at the Mexican Hat mill in 1994, individual Navajos have still had problems.[29] Briefly, each year millions of dollars are allocated to help miners and their families. The filing process has proven lengthy. The U.S. Department of Justice has the responsibility to determine if an individual qualifies for compensation. Couples who had traditional weddings and lacked a marriage certificate find difficulty in proving their marital status and subsequent eligibility. Lawyer's fees gobble up 10 percent or more of what could have gone to the victims, while documentation of mining careers is sometimes hard to obtain. Many Navajo miners have trouble understanding and have little faith in this bureaucratic system.

What follows are the voices of some of these miners, explaining the effects that the experience had on them. Kayo Holiday shared his situation.

It was not until about three or four years ago that I started to suffer. I lost much of my eyesight so the doctors sent me to Gallup. There they worked on it so that I could continue to see a little. My eyes were checked and worked on again. I then went to Phoenix, where I spent seven days, but my health worsened and I went into a slightly comatose state. I stayed there for seven days. When I got better, I returned home only to catch pneumonia again. I went to the Monument Valley Hospital, where I almost died and spent eleven days, much of which I was semiconscious again. I pulled through with the help of ceremonies such as the Enemyway. The doctor in Kayenta asked me if I had once worked at the VCA mine. I told him that I had for about two years and explained that there was no vent and nothing but smoke in the mine. Although the air was smoky, my supervisors still placed me in there and asked me to drill, which almost killed me. Just as I had completed drilling, my heart began hurting. I threw my tools away and started crawling in the dark to the surface. I finally reached it when the explosion in the mine went off. I lay there in the darkness until some miners came out to me and asked what had happened. I said my heart was hurting and that I was by myself. They took me to the hospital, where I was told that I could no longer work. Uranium was the problem, my doctor advised.[30]

Jesse Black reports:

In my body, it hurts, even in my head. The doctors tell me there is nothing wrong, except for high blood pressure, but I tell them there is. They cannot see it. I am not well, but they say I am okay. Maybe there is nothing wrong with me, only my heart, but throughout my body I ache and sometimes feel hot all over, itch everywhere, have trouble hearing and seeing, my head aches, and I have a lot of cramps.[31]

Kayo Holiday noted:

Many men died from this [exposure to radiation]. It bothered their vital organs, so some died quickly. The same thing happened to Anglos. To this day, we are suffering from it. Sickness bothers my throat, my whole body does not feel right, and there were sores all over me. Now I just have scabs. The people in the Shiprock Hospital often do not believe us and wonder if we are telling the truth. I have to show them proof that I have worked in the mines, but they are still suspicious that we are not being honest. There was no doubt when they asked us to work in the mines and get uranium to fight in the war.[32]

Shone Holiday had a different attitude, convinced that he was in the service of his country, which was something to be proud of.

The Navajos did not do this alone. It was the government's idea to mine the ore to make the ammunition for the war. It wasn't just for money, but for our protection against foreign enemies. They praised our fine work. I don't think the mining was worthless because we did our share to help keep our freedom in the United States. Our older men were contributors, too, by working in transporting ammunition on the railroads. As far as having ill feelings toward the mining personnel, it has all but vanished. What they did leave behind is a big controversy today. Since we know that it is hazardous to human life, we feel it was not good. The dust from

Shone Holiday, unlike many Navajo miners looking back at their experience, had a more positive view, feeling that he was helping others and doing what he could to protect his country. Many Navajos, like Shone, have a deep patriotic spirit. (Courtesy Monument Valley High School)

the tailings still blows around in the wind and air. Our foods are contaminated, and it affects our digestive system, leading to fatal diseases. I personally know several of our people who now have such ailments. During the mining era, we saw nothing but money in the business, not what it was doing to our health.[33]

Perhaps no single experience in the twentieth century has catapulted the Navajo into the modern Anglo world in quite the same way as the uranium boom. While things like cars and education moved forward at a somewhat individualized and measured pace, the uranium industry swept in full blown with sophisticated technology, large sums of money to finance operations, an insatiable demand for labor, and a patriotic theme that appealed to the Navajo people. Its benefits and drawbacks need to be weighed through the thinking of the time as well as the twenty-twenty hindsight of today that points out its many ills.

Efforts have been made to correct some of the ills. In 2001, U.S. senators from Utah and New Mexico sponsored legislation to correct the poorly funded and politically manipulated Radiation Exposure Compensation Act to fully fund approved healthcare claims of uranium miners, estimated at \$71 million for that year.[34] Additional payment for each fiscal year followed. There were also experiments in which new stands of greasewood and four-wing saltbush, with their root systems growing forty feet in length, were used to clean nitrates and ammonium byproducts left over from uranium mining operations in the water table below. The experiments proved to be less costly than previous remedies while also restoring the land.[35] A greater sense of stewardship is now being expressed toward the land, as these steps, plus the closing of old mines and uranium site mitigation, unfold over the years in different areas of the valley.

A final note about past wrongs is that much of what was happening on the reservation was also taking place with white miners off the reservation. This is not to excuse the problems but just to recognize that it was not simply a Navajo-white issue. We end with whom we started, Luke Yazzie, discoverer of the largest uranium deposit in Monument Valley. Having lived through the entire experience, he noted:

> I did not think about this. It just happened, according to what the men used to tell each other. I live according to their words. They taught that the earth is our mother, as they tapped their feet on the ground. This was what they said. There is also the sun and water that is here with us. This is why there is nothing wrong. It is through these and our traditional teachings that we learn what is true to live by. If you do not understand this and do not follow these things, then there is tragedy. This is what I think, but I do not say it to many people. You are the only ones I am telling this to.[36]

CHAPTER TWELVE

Tradition, Tourism, and Trade-offs

The Price of Being Iconic

ourism, photography, and Monument Valley are inextricably entwined. Rocks, sand, sage, and sunshine compose a landscape with contrasting combinations of light and darkness, intense and muted images, that speak to the soul. Today, more than ever, people flock to see the valley's natural beauty, much of which has not changed since photography first captured its magic well over a century ago. Still, the truism that "people kill what they admire by loving it to death," is also becoming apparent, and what seemed so timeless is now showing the effects of large-scale ecotourism and development that capitalizes on capital. To some Navajo residents, there is more opportunity to improve one's life and financial standing; for others, it is a slow death of an old way deeply rooted in the land, a lifestyle that needs to be preserved. In previous chapters, we have caught a glimpse of O. C. Hansen accompanying Dolph Andrus during their maiden voyage traversing the desert to the outskirts of Monument Valley, snapping pictures all the way. John Ford and his romance with the land through the movie industry provided impetus for many to follow in his footsteps, taking photographs and trying to capture the land's essence. Many nationally and internationally famous photographers have taken their fair share of pictures, too. But it is the day-to-day tourists that, in terms of sheer volume, have acquired the most. This chapter focuses its lens on these people, what has been done to facilitate their experience, the impact that it has had on the residents, and the People's reaction to the change it has fostered.

Tourism and the Tribal Park

The first photographer in Monument Valley may never be known, but Fred Yazzie, who lived near some of the valley's most picturesque scenery, describes the first time he saw someone taking pictures.

> My family was living on the south side of Eagle Mesa in the midst of the juniper trees when some Anglos came to visit us. This was long before moviemaking took place. When these people came, they brought cameras, something we did not know about. My father was butchering a sheep when one of the men went over to watch, took an object, aimed it at him, and remained there for several moments. Later, there was a paper that came out that had a picture of my father butchering. These pictures were black and white and the Anglo told him that that was his image on the paper, but it was not too clear. This was the first time we got to know about the camera. My father put the photo in a safe place. This was perhaps around 1919.
>
> Time went by, and then there was talk of Anglos looking for Anasazi ruins, and the number of visitors increased. Picture-taking evolved. Another group of white men visited us, sometime in the early 1920s, but they were carrying a different kind of object that produced images with strings going into them. Maybe they took movies because it made a sound like chii chii chii, and it was rotating. They did not show us the finished product. Time passed and then Harry Goulding came. Anglos visited from great distances, starting the regular filming of movies.[1]

Seth Clitso, like Fred, ties picture-taking and the influx of white men in those early years to their interest in the Anasazi.

> The first picture-taking probably started with tourists coming through here. They came with small cameras and took pictures of the land back with them. That is how other Anglos found out about this place. They came together and had money to do this. Movies followed through the film industry and were circulated far and wide, making many more aware of this place. That was the palm [beginning] of things, with small cameras coming first.
>
> These people said amongst each other that the land was good. Anglos usually want to live in beautiful places where there is a rock standing, or a mountain and stream flowing by. They take photographs of these places,

stealing the land through pictures of scenery. This started with some-thing small at first like a few pictures they would talk about. Anasazi ruins provide a good example of what happened. At first these travelers would journey about, often led by Navajo guides, some going to Tsegi Canyon, others around Navajo Mountain, taking pictures of these places. Now many white men come to take photos to bring home with them. It seems like this is what they mostly come here for, even traveling from other lands to do this.

When you think about it, maybe the Anglos are taking images of our land away; this could be why there is no rain, while other places have plenty of it with no droughts. This is what the elders among us say. Why is our life set up at an angle? Not until winter do we get any moisture, then we get too much snow, which does not really help when it gets frozen solid. It used to rain from July on, but we have had several summers recently where we have not had much rain. It always seems like we are at an angle since it used to rain constantly. Maybe it is because the Anglo has no respect for the land we have. This is what the feeling is now. The elders used to sing several rain songs that started with the east, then went all the way around. This was how the rain was requested when the elderly men came together. No one is doing this now. It is hard to find a person who knows the rain songs. Nowadays, when drought arrives in the summertime and mud and cold creates hardship in the winter, this is how it is looked at.[2]

As more and more people visited this little-known but heavily pho-tographed land, there grew an increasing need for tour guides. Everyone from professional archaeologists and anthropologists to a housewife from Hoboken, New Jersey, requested assistance in getting off the beaten track and into seldom-seen sites and scenery. Navajos led and guided major ex-peditions down to day trips throughout Monument Valley and as far west as Navajo Mountain. Guy Cly tells of his older brother, Lee Sani, being among one of the first.

In the past, my older brother Lee Sani took the ones who wanted to go among the rocks and revealed them to these tourists. He did this for money and led these people in there. That is how the Anglos learned about Monument Valley so that now they take pictures of these places, which are then sent all over. When my elder brother guided them, I went with him. Some of these white men did not travel fast, especially the older ones. We would even pull them up to the place where they could

Dolph Andrus, an avid promoter of the "Monumental Highway," was one of the first to advocate for tourism. Little could he have imagined not only the sophisticated cars being driven today, but also how his effort to get people to Monument Valley was only a trickle compared to what was to come. (Courtesy Photo Archives, Utah State University)

see far away. They were looking for the Anasazi in the cliffs that were still buried or sitting upright. The Anglos also dug up some of the pots and footwear made of braided yucca woven into sandals. My brother was the one who led them in the Monument Valley area. Now, they just stream over the land and I don't know how to slow it down, as they crawl all over behind our back.[3]

The Navajo Tribal Park—Curse or Blessing?

The growing demand for access and facilities to enhance visitation grew. When I conducted my interviews in the early 1990s, tourism was well-advanced from the sandy roads and relative isolation of the 1930s. It and uranium mining were the prime movers that got highways paved and minimal services into the valley in the 1950s. By May 1960, the Navajo Nation solidified its investment in the tourist industry by dedicating the Navajo Tribal Park with its iconic rock formations, dramatic vistas, and historic culture. Development of the 94,000-acre park cost an initial $275,000, which included a visitor center, campground, and network of roads that snaked between and around some of the most photographed monoliths and mesas in the world. The growing number of visitors attests to the park's popularity: in 1960 there were approximately 22,000 fee-paying tourists; in 1983, 100,000; in 1993, 292,721; in 1999, 380,575; and 2019, an estimated 600,000.[4]

This kind of growth with supporting infrastructure has fostered two opposing camps—those for and those against development. Both sides have their promoters beyond the valley. Indeed, one of the major complaints of those living within is that there is too much control from without. The lines between these opposing sides were drawn long before 1997, before much of what was being discussed came to fruition. At that time, a former secretary of the interior, Stewart L. Udall, living in Santa Fe, argued for development. He said:

> I am convinced there is an unparalleled opportunity to double tourism in our region in the next decade. This can be accomplished by reaching out to the international tourism market and by making our Indian neighbors full partners in upcoming tourism. My argument rests on these realities. First, tourism is the biggest, fastest-growing industry in this country. Second, the area I am delineating as America's Scenic Circle contains a singular display of natural and cultural resources. And third, tourism benefits that will flow to all communities in the surrounding area can be attained if a new dimension is added to existing efforts to enlarge access and understanding of our unique assets.[5]

Albert Hale, president of the Navajo Nation at that time, proffered an opposing view. His question: "At what price?" The idea of world-class tourism on the Navajo Reservation seemed a bad fit. High prices, exotic cuisine, unrealistic demands, non-alcohol regulations, and other issues made the idea unappealing. After citing the Harvey Houses coupled with the Santa Fe Railroad and other unsustainable marketing efforts in different parts of the Southwest, Hale closed by pointing out that the efforts to bring wealthy American tastes into a non-Native environment did not create a natural flow of events and products that were self-sustaining.

> Instead, for a century we have had tourism that says, "Take only pictures, leave nothing but footprints." That is precisely what the last era of grand hotels left us—nothing but footprints. It is time for a new approach. Instead of imported ideas, public relations slogans, world-class hotels, and beluga caviar snacks, it's time for a Navajo approach. A shift in thinking is required. To start, perhaps we need to think of building

without nails. Once that approach is understood, then we can start
thinking about suitable tourism for the Navajo Nation.[6]

While both sides have their proponents, big business and international
tourism tipped the scales. The question is how the elders interviewed in
the late 1980s and early 1990s felt about these things as they watched
increasing infrastructure and growing hordes of tourists, many of whom
were international visitors, walk upon their land.

Starting with what was known by the elders as the ranger station, but
is now called the Navajo Tribal Park, there were a number of older women
who did not want it from the beginning. Jenny Francis said that initially,
those who lived in that area opposed it but to no avail.

> My husband put up a fence so that the Anglos would not get into that
> land, but they paid no attention to it. Harry Goulding was in favor of
> opening Monument Valley to movie companies, and there were some
> huge disagreements with the Navajos, and the company would leave.
> After some sort of settlement, it would return and make the movie. Some
> of the sacred places were ruined and are not used anymore because of all
> of the people visiting them. In the early morning there used to be a great
> strength in the sunrise. As it rose, the strong rays would grow dimmer
> until the strength was gone. From the sun, one could see the redness of
> the rocks and the green trees and the rich vegetation. Corn grew just over
> the hill from where the ranger station is. Now, there is nothing like that.[7]

Gladys Bitsinnie agrees.

> We were not told everything, and we have no power to do anything about
> it. We have leaders, but they are not given information, so the Anglos just
> do as they wish. There is no such thing as the people having a say in this
> matter. It seems like the white man just came for a visit to eat out of our
> home. To this day we are of no value to them. We don't like it. There were
> elderly men there once who were like guardians, protectors of that place
> [Navajo Tribal Park]. Now that they are gone, only their children are left,
> and most of them have moved out. The people who own that land do not
> bother with it now.[8]

Bessie Katso expressed fear that the road down through the monuments might be paved, even though the Navajo people opposed it.
Underlying part of the resentment was that with the improvement, the

Anglos would take away the land. Plus, their presence was "ugly" as those with "bushy hair crowd into the stores," bring "bad tobacco through here," and desecrate sacred places. "A long time ago, we were told there were certain things that should not be done in these holy sites and not to harm Mother Earth. Now we cannot chop trees for firewood. There never used to be words against this, and there was not a lot of sickness going around. I think that is the reason we have problems now."[9] Nellie Grandson adds to Bessie's thoughts:

> We should have not abused Mother Earth, but the Anglos are doing it. They have also gone to the heavenly bodies like the moon. We are abusing the element of harmony in every direction—up, down, and in the sacred places. That is why sickness comes to us without hesitation. In this day and age, things have changed and are not like they should be. The earth attacks us without hesitation. Some of us say no to this outrage of destruction, but it is becoming clear that the earth is of no value to many. We are at a stage where we say our prayers but feel like there is little response to our pleas. White men are designing things so quickly that we will come to a point where there will be no way of avoiding what they have done.[10]

Navajo men had similar responses about the park and existing conditions, given the sacredness of the rock formations. Guy Cly, an elder who lived within it, felt that much of the sacredness of its trees and rock formations had been forgotten and that the circumstances had caused stress between families. Things had become topsy-turvy. For example, at one time there had been a tall spruce at the base of one of the large rock formations near his home. The tree was chopped down.

> It almost went up over the top of the rock wall and was very thick. This tree received offerings of sacred stones (ntł'iz) for rain, which made it rain all of the time. When the people asked for it, there was a sound that went throughout the valley, as the thunder rolled and the rain came. Sometimes the rain arrived before the people who prayed for it had even gotten home. Often it started with a small drizzle, but upon returning home, the rain came down harder, puddles formed, and haze arose as the water splashed and then ran over the land as the downpour continued. This is what the tree brought. Now it is gone and the people fight, telling each other to go away, that this is not their land. That is why I am up here

One of the concerns of the elders and traditionalists is that they have lost the land to tourists and the tribal park so that now ceremonies cannot be held as in the past. The place where these structures were set up as part of an Enemyway ceremony lies in the heart of the park's valley, now inundated with sightseers. (Courtesy Photo Archives, Utah State Historical Society)

and overlook the land from above the valley. My grandchildren tell me to stay here. They tell me I am their only root that is of strength.

I know of numerous places where corn pollen and the sacred stones and prayers were offered for water and as a shield for protection. When the coughing sickness came, there was a thin rock that stands over there called Tsé Ałtsoozí Íí'áhí. People used this because it was made of electricity in every part of it and could shield against sickness. It was like a banner that worked against any illness. Then there is a mesa where prayers are offered; it represents a fire and accepts prayers to fight against sickness. When a prayer was offered there, things returned to normal, but now it is not used. Offerings have not been taken there for a long time and so the holy people are probably wondering where the Navajos have gone. Maybe they are thinking that the elders have died of old age.[11]

In terms of the park as an administrative unit, Shone Holiday was not happy.

I don't think it has been going like it was agreed upon. Today, it seems as if residents in the local area are being shoved away. When the project was first introduced, they told us it was for the people on our land, but now they say this area belongs to the state or the tribe. We were promised a lot of things—tourists visiting, our selling arts and crafts in the park to make some profit—instead, we are chased off the premises of the tribal park and its vicinity. The white businessmen are reaping all of the profits, not us, as planned. In spite of this, some of our people still peddle their crafts along the roadsides, pinching off a few dollars every now and then.[12]

On the other hand, Cecil Parrish felt that there had been good benefits that helped the residents.

I think it is okay because there are many Anglos visiting and putting money back into Window Rock, some of which probably comes back to here. The tourists are paying money to look at the scenery, but a long time ago the people used to offer the sacred stones in the valley at the standing rocks and several places where water comes out of the earth. These are sacred places, but now there are many Anglos going down there, traveling back and forth, and so these sites are not used.

In the past when our older men had not mixed with the Anglos, they prayed and asked for things through prayers. They said they would walk on the corn pollen path. Now there are paved roads all over the place. They said they would travel on great horses and here are the automobiles and airplanes. They said they would travel in safety and that is here. We are traveling in that way now. It is said they used to pray in the valley and climb on top of a large rock to pray and leave an offering or in places where the rocks talk (echoes). Those men have passed on now. This is how I think about the park and how our forefathers prayed there. I think they were answered. I am happy about this and glad that they had prayed about these things. These places where the rocks are sitting and offerings made are still sacred.[13]

John Holiday, as a practicing medicine man, shared his informed opinion of how he viewed the park with its attendant changes.

Today our land is overcrowded with tourists and the movie outfits secretly do their filming in our area. They are guarded by the police, who keep the complainers, even those who live a few feet away, from them. None of us get paid for use of our land, which is not good. In earlier times, our elders were always in charge of such events, but today it is not that way. The movie outfit informs our local people that they have already paid the tribe in Window Rock, but we do not hear anything from our Chapter officials about how the money was used. In fact, no one tells us about an upcoming movie. We no longer have the rights to our land and are being trampled by everyone. Our forefathers were quite stern, never letting any white men move in as they wished. They must have had closer connections with the government, but today we are not as close. We are in a difficult period and continue in that direction.

I also do not like what the Navajo Tribal Park is doing. Our chapter officials and tribal representatives initiated the plans for this park. They negotiated these plans "under the table," taking sides opposite our people. The residents were shut out of the discussions and had no say. These secret negotiations have totally blocked our chapter officials' future plans on many things. The land now belongs to the government and the Tribe. A lot of money is made in the park, but residents feel they do not get any and that nothing can be done. Some people say the government does not do anything for us, but I say it does because I see the government helping a lot of people. I see young pregnant mothers receive assistance with food to keep them healthy and the money continues when their babies are born. There are funds that provide food stamps, as well as help with firewood, coal, and housing. The government assists with many things. I feel that we cannot say anything against the government because the money made at the visitors' center goes back to the government which helps us. That is my understanding of our government money.

Still, the sacred places have been trampled and no one speaks up for them. Even if someone did protest, the opponents always say they are abiding by the laws. For some reason, our best-educated people agree with them and do not speak against them. I am sure there are other alternatives, but they do not look into them. There is nothing; it is hopeless. If only I could speak and understand English. Although I have to use an interpreter to communicate, I sometimes ponder a problem until I get it right, especially if it does not make sense. I'm steadfast and observant. I might not go places or participate in planning activities, but I know what goes on. Even though I am uneducated and do not understand the English language, it is still obvious to me.[14]

Time moved on—more tourists, more development, more money. In 2006, Marie S. Holiday, a resident of Monument Valley, saw the handwriting on the rock wall. The tribal park administrators and a company named ARTSCO never approached the Oljato Chapter for permission to withdraw land from the park to build a motel. Rather, they worked directly with the Navajo Nation. Next, ARTSCO requested a liquor license for its clientele—something the chapter opposed through resolution. And finally, without local input, construction of a motel called The View started, opening for business in December 2008. The ninety-five-room complex with its high-end restaurant, swank gift shop, and other amenities fulfilled exactly what Udall had suggested eleven years before, capitalizing on what has been called by some the Eighth Wonder of the World—Monument Valley scenery.

Marie echoed two hundred community members' sentiments in a letter to the editor of the *San Juan Record*. After expressing concerns about what the residents living within the park could and could not do, the lack of interest the operators of the park exhibited in Navajos' welfare, and the disconnect between local and tribal government, Marie went to the heart of the matter.

> We seem to have lost a sense of the sacredness of this natural land. Our government in Window Rock has failed to protect our cultural and spiritual values. Our Nation's legislators are looking like Washington, only legislating for the well-to-do and giving a deaf ear to our local Navajo tour operators in Monument Valley and displacing them. We feel victimized by the terrible political assaults in Window Rock through the self-serving efforts of the administrators of the Parks, the legislators, and the Nation Administration Office through legal manipulations. . . . Oljato Chapter people had originally given authorization to withdraw the land for the Monument Valley Tribal Park and the Chapter deemed its inherent right to govern the people and land within the Oljato Chapter boundaries, including Monument Valley Tribal Park. If ARTSCO builds a hotel near Monument Valley Visitor Center, the development will completely ruin the beauty, natural scenery, and awesome views.[15]

But that is what happened.

If one believes history repeats itself, then there were indicators, alerting the people about what was around the corner. Without going through the complexity of what occurred previously, suffice it to say that Harry and Mike Goulding, in 1962, relinquished ownership of their trading post and related holdings to Knox College (Illinois), who later sold the property to the LaFont family, today's current owners, in 1981. These facilities, including the Seventh Day Adventist Hospital, were located on a school

Tourists in the Oljato Trading Post are treated to a candy bar and cold soda, but they are probably unaware of the unique history and role it played for the Navajo people. Saddles, washtubs, bolts of cloth, and sacks of flour have given way to a figure of Gumby, imitation bird house, and Pepsi. (Courtesy Special Collections, J. Willard Marriott Library, University of Utah)

section that belonged to the State of Utah and not the Navajo Nation. Consequently, sale and use of that land was under different regulations and open for development, unlike any other piece of real estate in the valley. Still, it is an island surrounded by Navajo land; the LaFonts learned what that meant. In 1995, the tribe cut off the water flowing to all of the Goulding facilities. Reason: the pipeline carrying the water from a well crossed Navajo land; part of the LaFonts' airplane hangar stretched onto a piece of tribal land, as did part of their sewer lagoon. After trucking water for a month, the RGJ Corporation and LaFonts declared bankruptcy and had to agree to pay hefty fines before the tribe turned the spigot on and business resumed.[16] RGJ purchased more trust land in 1999 to handle expansion, and although there were many complaints from within the Navajo community, there was no recourse for the complainants.[17] Since that time, expansion at Goulding's includes additional rooms and cabins, bringing the number of accommodations for tourists to around 160 spaces, a market, gas-and-convenience store, and expanded airstrip. Other entities followed suit by building a large clinic, fire/first responder facility, a high school, an elementary school (Tsébii'nidzisgai), Church of Jesus Christ of Latter-day Saints chapel, a vendor village/welcome center, and a KOA campground. There is even a traffic rotary at the "crossroads" with the nearest traffic light over twenty miles away. Not all Navajos are particularly happy with these changes.

Education and Employment: "To be or not to be, that is the question."

Returning to the elders and traditionalists of the 1990s, what were their thoughts about change? Knowing how to do things has always been an important quality in Navajo culture. While observation and family instruction were an important part of traditional education, Anglo culture promoted formal schooling and is now the one emphasized on the reservation. While each form shares similarities, they are fundamentally two different approaches that achieve two different results. The elders recognized that their children and grandchildren were being raised in a very different environment compared to the one they knew, and that it was shaping the younger generations in different ways. This has become a two-edged sword. With the high value placed on learning and earning a living, traditional teachings can sometimes cloud the path to embracing what lies in the future. For instance, Sloan Haycock had strong feelings about education but bemoaned some of the accompanying discordant notes that went with it.

> I believe education is extremely important. Any uneducated person will tell you how much they wish they had gone to school because it opens many good opportunities for an individual, and helps one to find a well-paying job to make a decent living. A good education will assist a person to go far in life and be competitive. He or she will have the ability to make it in this world. I have seen many women working in business offices or teaching, and that is good. One has to know how to read in

order to learn and understand how things work. I can't read my Bible because I don't know how. To be illiterate is to struggle. Unfortunately, some of our young people are taking their schooling for granted. They would rather waste their time and get into trouble with drugs and other harmful things. Many of these youth have gone crazy and do not respect others, much less themselves and their clans. They do not want to listen to their parents and teachers. I think this is happening because of all the social activities that go on in the schools, like dances, movies, and so forth. In some cases, they have become hostile.[18]

Stella Cly sees similar problems.

Our children seem to be more respectful, but the youngest generation is not and likes to argue and raise trouble. They get mad because they don't want anybody else moving into the valley, while the older generation is not like that and is kinder. People used to live in harmony when they lived in the tribal park valley. This land was made for everyone. We cannot say it is ours. For those who were born and lived here the longest, they are the ones with seniority. The land was always here; it has not changed, but the people have. I do not know why everyone is fighting over it because that is wrong. It already belongs to the unborn, who have their right to live on this land, too. Some people in the valley claim the famous rock formations saying, "This mesa is mine," but that is not so. These mesas were there long before their time and our land sculpted itself—not us humans—so we should not argue over it. When I visited the valley, that was all I heard among our people. I was fortunate to have lived there, all alone, before this commotion. It would be nice if the people would quiet down.[19]

Ada Black was another longtime resident who has lived with change. Her devotion to traditional ways was unwavering, having served in her community as a medicine woman, assisted with male-dominated ceremonial practices, and suffered through the livestock reduction years. Her views are important and her position balanced.

I think to myself that I am improving my life. Many of the things my children and grandchildren have learned in school, I do not use, but that is how they get their jobs. Since they get paid for it, they like the way it is. None of my children are working at the ranger station, but I do have a grandchild employed there. I hope they will continue to work at that place for a long time; the only thing that hinders them is that thing that they put to their mouth [alcohol]. Once they start to drink beer or wine, it ruins their work at the job. If they do not get involved with it, they will lead a very productive life. I do not want someone to haul in liquor to sell to the people because it ruins everything.

Tourism in Monument Valley has been growing and growing. Some of the development that comes with this is good, and some is bad. What if in the future a tractor is brought to start clearing the area and buildings are put up? I think that would not be good, but at the same time we need a store and places for tourists to stay and eat. In return, our children who did a fine job will cook food, make beds, and work as tour guides to earn good pay. It would be of great joy to see such a sight. There may be those who feel the urge to become managers of these stores or motels. These are the roads I think of for them. Kayenta is like that with homes being built and the town growing out. But this can also bring in things that are not appropriate, like alcohol and crime. Still, white people coming to see Monument Valley is good. We do not want them to move here and do the terrible things that come when people live in large groups. Perhaps our children and grandchildren will return to their senses and remember their home, automobile, and livestock. They will figure out where they stand in life and return to the earlier values they had when growing up. That is what I did. They will evaluate what they did when they reach old age and think differently about how they live their lives.

One thing that has always been an issue in Monument Valley is water. Our livestock has existed with hardship in getting enough of it. We have had to haul it in for our sheep and other animals, and I do not even own an automobile, an important tool for our livelihood. The water that flows underground is sent to the Monument Valley Hospital and Goulding's grocery store. The motel uses it for cooking, bathing, and other things; I wish that someone would help me get water. I have asked for assistance from our chapter officials, but they are not strong in their office. Our council delegate does not talk to others to solve the problem, and he does not think. Many issues face us here, but that is just the way it is. It would be good for our children and grandchildren to have some money put aside for them for the future. There should also be regulations against people who want to build really fine houses in the area. A lot of clearing, grading, and construction disturbs the ground. The earth provides all of the herbs needed to heal ailments. Those plants should have a place so that they can continue to help. In the future, people and all living creatures depend upon them to provide every type of healing upon this earth. I have made many herbal remedies for many people, and now they are in good health.

I do not want the traditional teachings messed up, as today's life confuses a lot of it, and it is not getting any better. Our children's children are learning only in the Anglo language, the girls are wearing pants, and the young people do crazy things to their hair. Navajo hair is said to be the dark clouds filled with water that is falling to the ground and is very sacred and powerful. When one's hair is cut, it is cutting the dark clouds off that person. Little wonder it does not rain.

Our present day has turned things away from these teachings and is horrible. If only the wine and beer could be stopped for a year, perhaps the people would come back to their senses. There would be no stealing, spouse abuse, or fighting among the people, and violence would slow down. This would be a thankful thing to do. Our children's scars will heal, and those who live in uncertain ways would change and live differently. The number of thefts and automobile accidents will lower by stopping the flow of things that make people crazy. They will come back to their senses.

I never went to school to learn how to read and never made a mark on a paper. I stayed home and learned of what was to be done there, like herding sheep and working around the home. These are the only things that I grew up on. What I have learned in my lifetime is what I have made my home of. I was able to bring things home through weaving rugs, basketmaking, fashioning moccasins, planting crops, and taking care of livestock. Whatever I made, I exchanged for money and purchased from the white man. Even though I did not go to school, I have seen everything and feel rich in experience. It is like that.[20]

In comparing the past to the present, Betty Canyon also felt that a tremendous amount had been lost and that Navajo culture, as she knew it, was in great jeopardy.

We no longer have or live by our elderlies' teachings; they are gone. Our people live as if they were small children tending a household while their parents are away. As far as our environmental conditions, we have more devastating windstorms and less rain, and when it does rain, there is more lightning and thunder, which is scary and dangerous. Our vegetation and water supply for livestock has become depleted, the land exhausted and barren, and ceremonies diminished. I believe this is due to our people no longer practicing or believing in the sacredness of our traditional faith.

Three or four generations of women sit outside the Oljato Trading Post in 1946. This skilled workforce, trained in tasks for daily life in a desert environment, has provided a strong backbone for preserving traditions in a matrilineal society. What would a similar gathering of today's generations look like? (Courtesy Special Collections, J. Willard Marriott Library, University of Utah)

All we hear nowadays is, "Ch'į́įdii bí" (It's the devils). The sacred corn pollen, arrowheads, and "hadahoniye'" (sacred mirage stone) belong to the devil, therefore, I do not want any part of it. I only want Christian religion. That is what some of our people are saying. I remember, when I went to school in Fort Wingate, we had many people and preachers come to speak to us. They preached, saying, "You don't steal, use foul language, or tell lies, etc., because the end will come in five years." I never understood what they meant by that. It has been many years since then, and nothing has happened. They must have meant the end of their own lives, for they are no longer with us. When I hear people say, "It belongs to the devil," I think to myself, "Of course, he is the owner of this world. The devil has been here since creation, along with everything else." I believe it depends on our prayers, and that is all we can do—pray.[21]

As Ada pointed out, alcohol is a great concern. Although the reservation has historically been "dry," there have still been far too many drunk-driving accidents, broken homes wrecked by booze, and lives captured by the bottle. However, the exploding tourist industry that constantly tries to attract more and more people has to compete with other venues that sell liquor in its many forms—an after-tour beer, a drink with supper, a social drink in a friendly gathering, or an evening wind-down. The dominant culture has integrated alcohol into a variety of settings and promotes drinking for celebratory occasions, whereas Navajo culture eschews the vice, yet many partake. Nellie Grandson testifies that "our children" are seduced by drink and "go crazy" with beer and wine. They fail to listen to the voice of reason.

> Beer has no relatives. We plead to the people not to drink, but the Anglos keep selling it to our children because of money, and there is no power to remove it from our land because they have papers claiming they can sell these items. When our children consume it and something happens, we are blamed by the police officers who say, "This is what your child did," how much the bail is, how many days in jail, and that our children cannot be visited. Yet it is the white man who is selling it, but it is our children who step off the road. This is what I say.[22]

As with the views of the women, the men are split as to the benefits and drawbacks of what is happening to Monument Valley. While both are concerned about future generations, the women expressed more concern for that while the men discuss opportunity and avoiding past mistakes. Bud Haycock, after all of his years in uranium mining, maintained a positive attitude. The tribal park was a benefit to the community.

> I think it's okay. I'm not sure what the future holds, but we'll see. My daughters work there, and they are gaining some valuable work experiences from it. Who knows, perhaps some of our children might learn how to run the same type of business on their own. Other people are already offering guided tours and making pretty good money. The peddlers who sell by the roadside make a living that way, which for many of our local residents has become their main source of income. When we had the mining industry, that was our main income, but that is long gone. I have a very strong feeling that tourism will continue to benefit our people for many more years to come.[23]

John Holiday, as a medicine man, looked more at the loss of cultural teachings and how uninformed Navajos are about different sites within the park and traditional practices in general.

> The younger generation does not realize the sacredness of these stories. When I start telling them, they begin telling their own stories and mock mine. There are Navajo people who live around here who do not know the traditional teachings about these rocks and mesas. The old people like Bitter Water, He Who Starts to Jog, and Mister Lefty, who lived here, knew but they are now gone. Today's generation does not know about the old stories, so just hears them but does not know what to do with them. They only see the place, live there, and do not preserve the beauty of it.[24]

Many of the residents of the valley are aware of the issues surrounding the tribal park as well as the different status of trust lands still controlled by the state of Utah or those sold to various entities. Fred Yazzie speaks to both issues.

> There are many Anglos who want Monument Valley. There are school sections all over this place, and they are putting boundaries around them and filing papers to get them. I am told that I am not in charge of this, but really, they are not in charge either. I grew up around here, so I know the land and the land knows me. My children are also here, but I do not see these officials living in this area. They first put boundaries around here in the form of school sections. Next came allotment, but my father said no to that and encouraged leaving the land as one whole plot. Small pieces of land are not good because it belongs to all of us in the community. Regardless, they put boundaries on school sections. These buttes around here are my fences and inside is where I live. I look at them every morning, the rocks never changing, just as the sun coming up is the same. Sunrise is beautiful and I am happy about it, making my frame of mind strong. With this I am strong, my plans are strong. This is how I think when I am sitting here. Some people want my land and are dying to get their hands on it. People in Window Rock and Anglos are like that, lining up with their cameras from the junction all the way into the valley, and also on the way to Mexican Hat. Every day they are swarming around here, making their money. I do not count and so people walk all over me.

Anglos made millions on the things they took out of this land and we have nothing. We are not aware of what is happening to us and so do not talk about changing the circumstances. I am sitting on this land, but there are some who are trying to push their way onto it. It is my land as I leave my tracks on it until the day I die. The place called Window Rock is where they approve without consulting us. It was said we will have a strong government that would work with us and help plan and make money here in Monument Valley. That is how they were able to build the tribal park. They should think of us when they make these kinds of decisions, especially when working with white men, but they always side with the Anglos. This is what is on our minds. The land was in good condition at the beginning, but now it has boundaries, and mixed nationalities trudge all over it and dig away the scenery in our sacred places. Even in open flat places, we sprinkled corn pollen as well as where the rocks meet the earth and under a young blue spruce. Now we are just stumbling all over without much thought and have gotten to the point where we no longer use our songs and prayers. We do not even think about values, while the Anglos are compiling their riches to see who can get the most. They think, "I will be in the lead on an elite path."

As young people mature today, they go through a series of steps. First, their way is to do what they are supposed to do, in a religious sense. Soon they are not practicing the beliefs properly and start having different goals. Their religion slips away from them to the point that they no longer know the songs, but rather have stepped out of it into new sets of ideas. Whatever was good, they have rejected and forgotten. They only know the edges of the songs, have mixed up the prayers, and have forgotten the teachings. There are some who keep and understand the traditions, but there are many more that have forgotten.[25]

Today

The elders have spoken and are now gone, taken by old age. Their monumental description of the knowledge and understanding they held sits here for future generations, who are now producing their own elders. Before concluding, however, there have been events over the past twenty-five years that continue to put Monument Valley "on the map," giving recognition to its people. Now that you have had an opportunity to view life through traditional Navajo eyes, look at four events and think of how John Holiday, Ada Black, or others might view these more recent activities. How would they explain the recognition of arts and crafts, the 2002 Olympics, the Red

For decades jeep safaris, horseback rides, tourist trucks, and private vehicles have opened Monument Valley to hundreds of thousands of tourists each year. National and international organizations book large groups to visit this part of Navajo land. Some residents see it as an opportunity, others as an inconvenience akin to a plague. Whatever the view, the land is capable of speaking many different languages. (Courtesy Carolyn Davis, obtained from Billy Crawley)

Bull competition, and the COVID pandemic? These events were all part of Monument Valley's late-twentieth- and early-twenty-first-century history and iconic reputation. None of them will be dealt with in detail, but enough to see how well the reader has absorbed teachings from the past.

The Navajo people are well known for their weaving and silversmith abilities, following traditions that are still healthy but decreasing in number of participants. There is no immediate danger of these craft skills disappearing, but in the era of the elders discussed in this book, "every" Navajo woman at least knew how to weave, and the majority were prolific in creating blankets and rugs. Today, many of the younger generation have not acquired this skill. Even more endangered is the knowledge of basketmaking (note: in the true sense of the word, it is not weaving, although most people still use that term). Monument Valley still has a half dozen families that are involved in the craft, and none was more exceptional than Mary Holiday Black. Starting in the 1970s, Mary ventured away from the traditional Navajo wedding basket pattern to create baskets with innovative designs and images. By 1995, she had become famous for her creations and setting an example for other basket makers, who had increased in number, with an estimated thirty-five women pursuing the craft. That year, Mary received a National Heritage Fellowship Award and $10,000 at a White House ceremony, making her the first Utahn and first Navajo to receive this recognition.

The accomplishment was not without its struggles. When Mary began creating pictorial baskets, she used symbols that were considered sacred, based in stories from traditional teachings and ceremonies. Her father, who was a medicine man, performed protective rituals to prevent harm for depicting images that should not be used or seen in everyday life. Just as the Anasazi had taken the sacred and made it profane, some felt that Mary was following suit. Weavers, inspired by her success as some of her baskets sold for $6,000, also took protective measures. While many viewed these women as preserving heritage and giving growth to a dying art, others saw their work as another desecration of traditional values and selling their culture for money.[26] Which is it?

In March 2001, Monument Valley received the national and international honor of hosting part of the torch run that preceded the 2002 Winter Olympics held in Salt Lake City. Kelsey A. Begaye, president of the Navajo Nation, selected this place because, "For as long as I can remember, Monument Valley has served as a doorway to the western world. . . . The Navajo people here are able to maintain a traditional way of life."[27] The Navajo Olympic Committee, named "Discover Navajo: 2002," had representatives accept the torch at the Goulding's airstrip. They then moved it to Totem Pole Rock, where seven Navajo runners ran it back to the park's visitor center for a short acknowledgment ceremony before flying the torch to Bryce Canyon and Zion National Park and eventually Salt Lake City. Monument Valley, a well-established icon for the Navajo Nation, met all of the marketing criteria to promote tourism that highlighted its history and culture. February 4, the day of the run, an intense blue sky with brilliant sun warmed the chilly air and the estimated 10,000 spectators as they watched the runners make their way to the visitors' center and the lighting of an Olympic cauldron.[28] Mission accomplished.

Monument Valley received more attention at the Navajo pavilion built in Salt Lake City by the tribe to highlight its history and culture, again with an eye for tourism. Its theme—"Discover Navajo: People of the Fourth World"—played out through a variety of well-known symbols including a hogan, sweat lodge, and shade; exhibitions of weaving, silversmithing, basketmaking, and sandpainting; dramatic visual presentations and storytelling about the Four Worlds along with other traditional beliefs; and the history of the Navajo code talkers, some of whom were present. All of this was arrayed within an 11,000-square-foot pavilion. Pictures of Monument Valley were prevalent; the basket weaver—Peggy Rock Black, influenced by Mary Holiday Black—was from Douglas Mesa; and participants teaching cultural values shared their knowledge. Approximately 30,000 visitors viewed the exhibits, two-thirds of whom paid an entry fee, but it proved insufficient to offset the $3.5 million expended by the Navajo Olympic Committee, resulting in a final loss of $786,000.[29] There were a number of factors that created the loss, which will not be discussed here, but many Navajos viewed it as a successful promotional effort that encouraged more tourism—and no area on the reservation was better represented than Monument Valley. How would the elders of yesteryear view this?

If the goal was to bring more tourists to the land, then five years later, they may have encouraged the next spectacular occurrence. In 2007, Monument Valley hosted one event of the twelve-event Red Bull Air Race Series held in various countries throughout the world. This extreme flying competition was between fourteen professional flyers who raced between obstacles—some man-made from fabric while others were natural such as the spires, buttes, and mesas of Monument Valley. Time and finesse translated into points that accumulated during the series of races. To conduct the competition, 280 tons of equipment transported on forty-five trucks brought the airshow from Rio de Janeiro, once it was in the United States, to Monument Valley. Just to set up this equipment required ten days; the event itself, held on May 12, was billed as being in one of the most dangerous locations for this type of activity. Fortunately, no one was injured. One of the pilots, Mangold, was part American Indian and claimed to "feel the spiritual support of thousands of Native Americans. . . . They want to see a 'red man' get in there somehow. They're happy that I'm here, and all of the locals are pulling for me."[30] He came in third.

Monument Valley has also been the scene of balloon festivals, such as the fourth one held in 2013. Twenty hot air balloons registered for the three-day event. Pilots received their flight briefing at John Ford's Point, launched around the Three Sisters, Rain God Mesa, and the Mittens, then sailed above the land at an altitude of 1,200 feet. Other activities took place on the ground such as a concert with a reggae band and Apache Crown (Ghan) dancers. But perhaps the most unique event was the screening of *Star Wars, Episode IV: A New Hope* held in the Monument Valley High School. The entire film had been dubbed in Navajo, and prior to its showing, the tribe's vice president, Rex Lee Jim, talked about Navajo language preservation.[31] *Star Wars*, Navajo language, powerful rock formations, hot air balloons, holy people—what would the elders say?

The final large-scale event, which is still unfolding at the time of writing, is the COVID-19 pandemic. Like the influenza epidemic of 1918, this disease attacks the respiratory system and is transmitted in a number of ways—airborne and tactile being the primary means. By March 13, 2020, the Navajo Nation had declared a state of emergency, closing down tourism, most outside visitation, and public forums. There was good reason for this as seen through a statistical evaluation concerning southeastern Utah. Half of the 15,000 residents of San Juan County are Native American, primarily Navajo. Of the roughly 700 cases of COVID-19 in the county, 550 were American Indian, with 90 percent of the hospitalizations and 90 percent of the deaths belonging to the same ethnic group. Reasons for this included lack of medical supplies, less access to water and washing facilities, multigenerational homes, close-knit communities with more contact, and a higher percent of elders and those with underlying health issues.[32]

Tourism was now one of the largest employers in the valley, and so the closing of the tribal park affected hotels and dining facilities, tour guides, and related industries, while the closing of school and switching to classes held through telecommunications affected teachers and students alike. The independence of the past, where people grew their own food, raised their own livestock, and owned their own tools, was gone. Most people depended on trucks delivering the necessities and money to purchase them. Large infusions of federal money distributed by the government or the tribe saved the day for most. Not until the tribal park opened at 50 percent capacity in mid-July 2021, following well over a year of closures, were people able to resume some of their normal activities. Even then, in the park the trails and museum were closed, and visitors who wanted to see the rock formations had to go in a licensed tour vehicle, could not take their own car, and had to wear masks the entire time.[33] At the same time, the tribe ardently pushed for total vaccination. The schools and every business also had to follow a safety plan. What would the elders say about both the cause and the cure?

Life is ever changing as today's youth become tomorrow's elders. The rocks, sage, and sand will always be there, but what is done with them is decided by the People. The elders of the past used Monument Valley's resources, lived a life based on traditional teachings, and preserved the land for future generations. What those generations now do with those things determines the quality of life and what is available for their children, down to the seventh generation. May they walk in beauty.

NOTES

Introduction

1. See Deni J. Seymour, *From the Land of Ever Winter to the American Southwest: Athapaskan Migrations, Mobility, and Ethnogenesis* (Salt Lake City: University of Utah Press, 2012).

2. Google "Reader."

3. John Holiday and Robert S. McPherson, *A Navajo Legacy: The Teachings of John Holiday* (Norman: University of Oklahoma Press, 2005); Robert S. McPherson, *Navajo Women of Monument Valley: Preservers of the Past* (distributed by Boulder: University Press of Colorado, 2021).

4. Frances Gillmor and Louisa Wade Wetherill, *The Traders to the Navajos: The Story of the Wetherills of Kayenta* (Albuquerque: University of New Mexico Press, 1934, 1979); Samuel Moon, *Tall Sheep: Harry Goulding Monument Valley Trader* (Norman: University of Oklahoma Press, 1992).

5. Robert S. McPherson and Perry J. Robinson, *Traditional Navajo Teachings: A Trilogy*, vol. 1, *Sacred Narratives and Ceremonies*; vol. 2, *The Natural World*; vol. 3, *The Earth Surface People* (distributed by Boulder: University Press of Colorado, 2020).

6. Robert S. McPherson, *Dinéjí Na'nitin: Navajo Traditional Teachings and History* (Boulder: University Press of Colorado, 2012).

Chapter 1

1. Luke and June Yazzie, interview with author, April 8, 1993.

2. Betty Canyon, interview with author, September 10, 1991.

3. Fred Yazzie, interview with author, August 6, 1991.

4. Tallis Holiday, interview with author, November 3, 1987.

5. Shone Holiday, interview with author, September 9, 1991.

6. There are many excellent versions of the creation story and beginnings of Navajo culture, including the emergence and the events

surrounding Changing Woman, Monster Slayer, and Born for Water. Here I have included, in alphabetical order, some of the most readily available examples. See Stanley A. Fishler, *In the Beginning: A Navaho Creation Myth*, Anthropological Paper no. 13 (Salt Lake City: University of Utah, 1953); Pliny Earle Goddard, "Navajo Texts," in *Anthropological Papers of the American Museum of Natural History*, vol. 34, part 1 (New York: American Museum of Natural History, 1933), 127–79; Berard Haile, *The Upward Moving and Emergence Way: The Gishin Biye' Version* (Lincoln: University of Nebraska Press, 1981); Jerrold E. Levy, *In the Beginning: The Navajo Genesis* (Berkeley: University of California Press, 1998); Washington Matthews, *Navaho Legends* (Salt Lake City: University of Utah Press, 1897, 1994); Franc Johnson Newcomb, *Navaho Folk Tales* (Albuquerque: University of New Mexico Press, 1967, 1990); Aileen O'Bryan, *Navaho Indian Myths* (New York: Dover Publications, 1956, 1993); Mary C. Wheelwright, *Navajo Creation Myth: The Story of the Emergence by Hasteen Klah* (Santa Fe: Museum of Navajo Ceremonial Art, 1942); Leland C. Wyman, *Blessingway: With Three Versions of the Myth Recorded and Translated from the Navajo by Father Berard Haile, O.F.M.* (Tucson: University of Arizona Press, 1970); and Paul G. Zolbrod, *Diné bahane': The Navajo Creation Story* (Albuquerque: University of New Mexico Press, 1984).

7. Susie Yazzie, interviews with author, August 6, 1991, and November 10, 2000.

8. Gladys Bitsinnie, interview with author, March 26, 1993.

9. John Holiday and Robert S. McPherson, *A Navajo Legacy: The Life and Teachings of John Holiday* (Norman: University of Oklahoma Press, 2005).

10. Stephen C. Jett, *Navajo Placenames and Trails in the Canyon de Chelly System, Arizona* (Frankfurt: Peter Lang, 2001).

11. Holiday and McPherson, *A Navajo Legacy*.

12. Samuel Moon, *Tall Sheep: Harry Goulding, Monument Valley Trader* (Norman: University of Oklahoma Press, 1992), 7, 19, and 40.

13. Holiday and McPherson, *A Navajo Legacy*.

14. June Black Yazzie, interview with author, April 8, 1993.

15. In this and subsequent endnotes, unless otherwise indicated, additional information about the rock formations in and around Monument Valley is taken from ethnographic information collected by Stephen Jett, a noted scholar of Navajo geography. Stephen graciously provided this unpublished information based on interviews with local elders and a search of the literature. These are hereafter cited as "Jett notes."

El Capitan is an extraordinarily dramatic, pointed tuff-breccia volcanic neck rising from the floor of southern Monument Valley. [Robert W.] Young stated that it is the center of the world, and the pedestal for a Sky Supporter, who holds up the sky like an umbrella. However, according to Monument Valley Blessingway singer Billy Yellow, this function actually belongs to Chaistla Butte, another neck not far to the south. El Capitan was formerly used to communicate with the Sun, First Woman, and White Shell/Changing Woman in her home in the ocean and possibly with other holy beings above.

Paul Blatchford stated that an elderly singer had told him that El Capitan and Tuba Butte are the breasts of the great recumbent Female Mountain figure. Another statement is that it is female and paired with the male Shiprock.

El Capitan has close associations with the Western Water Clans created by Changing Woman. Some of their number arrived at Oljato, via here, and settled there for a while. During their stay, they sometimes camped around the pinnacle for hunting purposes. Hides from the game secured were scraped on the rocks, and tanned then made into clothing by the women; the wind blew the hair all over the peak until it was almost covered, giving the landmark its name.

16. Ada Black, interview with author, October 11, 1991. Her reference to having sheep in the area relates to the Navajo concept of keeping domestic livestock and wild animals separate. The two should not be mixed, even in the preparation of food. When sheep come in contact with deer hair, they become unruly and wild, requiring ceremonial cure.

17. Randall Henderson, "With Harry Goulding in Mystery Valley," *Desert Magazine*, vol. 20 (August 1957): 4–8.

18. Guy Cly, interview with author, August 7, 1991.

19. Marilyn Holiday, teleconference with author, September 17, 2020.

20. Luke and June Yazzie, interview with author, April 8, 1993.

21. "Mixed waters are used for similar purposes as pollen. Originally these waters were gathered at Navaho Mountain, San Francisco Mountains, San Juan Range, Pelado Peak, Mount Taylor, Taos, river forks in the south, and from waters in the west and north; from salt lakes below Zuni, or rather from the springs at the female and male mountains at the salt lakes. To this was added clay from the bottom of water, pollen, water pollen, and flag pollen." From Franciscan Fathers, *An Ethnological Dictionary of the Navajo Language* (Saint Michaels, AZ: Saint Michaels Press, 1910, 1968), 400.

22. Holiday and McPherson, *A Navajo Legacy*.

23. Tallis Holiday, interview.

24. Jett notes.

25. Kayo Holiday, interview with author, October 11, 1991.

26. Jett notes.

27. "Rain God and Thunderbird Mesas are the homes of thunderstorms and lightning, and have War God associations. People should not go on top of these mesas. Billy Yellow attributed the crash of a B52 bomber near there to the plane having flown too low over these mesas and their power having prevented it from ascending rapidly enough." Jett notes.

28. John gave the following information as he stood at the southeast corner of Rain God Mesa looking directly east at Totem Pole Rock. The rock formations he refers to start on his right and go to his front (Totem Pole Rock). As travelers then follow the road to Artist's Point they will see an abandoned, weathered male hogan surrounded by a fence, to which John referred previously. Once at Artist's Point, one can see White Tipped Mountain, a sandstone formation on the desert floor to the north.

29. Water Sprinkler is the clown at the Fire Dance. His actions are contrary to those of the other dancers, appearing to undo through opposition what the others are doing.

30. Holiday and McPherson, *A Navajo Legacy*.

31. Tallis Holiday, interview.

32. Holiday and McPherson, *A Navajo Legacy*.

Chapter 2

1. Robert S. McPherson, *Viewing the Ancestors: Perceptions of the Anaasází, Mokwic̆, and Hisatsinom* (Norman: University of Oklahoma Press, 2014).

2. Fred Yazzie, interviews with author, November 1, 1985; November 5, 1987; and August 5, 1991.

3. Ada Black, interview with author, October 11, 1991.

4. McPherson, *Viewing the Ancestors*, 65.

5. Billy Yellow, interview with author, November 6, 1987.

6. Guy Cly, interview with author, August 7, 1991.

7. John Holiday, interview with author, December 10, 2004.

8. Don Mose, interview with author, June 11, 2012.

Chapter 3

1. See L. R. Bailey, *The Long Walk: A History of the Navajo Wars, 1846–68* (Pasadena, CA: Westernlore Publications, 1978); Peter Iverson, *Diné: A History of the Navajos* (Albuquerque: University of New Mexico Press, 2002); Broderick H. Johnson, ed., *Navajo Stories of the Long Walk Period* (Tsaile, AZ: Navajo Community College Press, 1973); Lawrence C. Kelly, *Navajo Roundup: Selected Correspondence of Kit Carson's Expedition Against the Navajo, 1863–1865* (Boulder, CO: The Pruett Publishing Company, 1970); Gerald Thompson, *The Army and the Navajo: The Bosque Redondo Reservation Experiment, 1863–1868* (Tucson: University of Arizona Press, 1982).

2. Louisa Wade Wetherill and Harvey Leake, *Wolfkiller: Wisdom from a Nineteenth Century Navajo Shepherd* (Salt Lake City: Gibbs Smith Publisher, 2007), used with permission of author.

3. Fred Yazzie, interview with author, November 5, 1987.

4. Susie Yazzie, interview with author, November 10, 2000.

5. Charles Kelly, "Chief Hoskaninni," *Utah Historical Quarterly* 21, no. 3 (Summer 1953): 219–26.

6. James H. Knipmeyer, *Pish-La-Ki: The Lost Merrick and Mitchell Silver Mine* (Self-published: 2020).

7. Frances Gillmor and Louisa Wade Wetherill, *Traders to the Navajos: The Story of the Wetherills of Kayenta* (Albuquerque: University of New Mexico Press, 1934, 1979), 95–96.

8. "Murder by the Indians at the Field of New Discovery," *Dolores News*, March 13, 1880, 1.

9. Ralph Grey, interview with Dean Sundberg and Fern Charley, June 1974, O.H. 1621, in *The Navajo Stock Reduction Interviews of Fern Charley and Dean Sundberg*, Southeastern Utah Oral History Project (Fullerton: California State University, 1974), 6–8.

Chapter 4

1. Susie Yazzie, interview with author, November 10, 2000.

2. Sloan Haycock, interview with author, October 10, 1991.

3. Gladys Bitsinnie, interview with author, March 26, 1993.

4. Nellie Grandson, interview with author, December 16, 1993.

5. Robert S. McPherson, ed., *The Journey of Navajo Oshley: An Autobiography and Life History* (Logan: Utah State University, 2000), 30–35.

6. According to John Holiday, "This refers to the small black particles or debris floating on top of the San Juan River. This is used in the rain ceremony. Many medicine men will ask for a share of this debris and use a small-sized strainer to have enough to go around."

7. In Navajo thought, even once a tree is cut and becomes a log, the "growing end" should still be placed either down toward the ground or, if building a hogan and placing it horizontally, in a clockwise direction. John is referring to seeing this pattern reversed.

8. John Holiday and Robert S. McPherson, *A Navajo Legacy: The Life and Teachings of John Holiday* (Norman: University of Oklahoma Press, 2005), 92–97.

9. See Robert S. McPherson and Perry J. Robinson, *Traditional Navajo Teachings: A Trilogy*, vol. 1, *Sacred Narratives and Ceremonies*; vol. 2, *The Natural World*; vol. 3, *The Earth Surface People* (Boulder: University Press of Colorado, 2020).

10. Tully Bigman, interview with author, April 15, 1993.

11. George Tom, interview with author, August 7, 1991.

12. Jesse Black, interview with author, March 25, 1991.

Chapter 5

1. See Robert S. McPherson and Perry J. Robinson, *Traditional Navajo Teachings: A Trilogy*, vol. 2, *The Natural World* (distributed by Boulder: University Press of Colorado, 2020).

2. Robert S. McPherson, *The Journey of Navajo Oshley: An Autobiography and Life History* (Logan: Utah State University Press, 2000), 88–89.

3. For further information on divination, see Robert S. McPherson, *Dinéjí Na'nitin: Navajo Traditional Teachings and History* (Boulder: University Press of Colorado, 2012), 13–43.

4. Gladys Reichard, *Navaho Religion: A Study of Symbolism* (Princeton, NJ: Princeton University Press, 1950), 99.

5. Reichard, *Navaho Religion*, 99–100; Charlotte J. Frisbie and David P. McAllester, ed., *Navajo Blessingway Singer: The Autobiography of Frank Mitchell, 1881–1967* (Tucson: University of Arizona Press, 1978), 163; William Morgan, "Navaho Treatment of Sickness: Diagnosticians," *American Anthropologist* 33 (Summer 1931), 390–92.

6. McPherson, *The Journey of Navajo Oshley*, 49–50.

7. Susie Yazzie, interview with author, November 10, 2000.

8. Leland C. Wyman and Clyde Kluckhohn, "Navaho Classification of their Song Ceremonials," *Memoirs of the American Anthropological*

Association, no. 50 (Menasha, WI: American Anthropological Association, 1938, 1976).

9. Sacred names are bestowed upon the young and serve as a spiritual identification that is used only in a ceremonial context. It is an individual's sacred and secret identity recognized by the holy beings.

10. Lightning and lightning-struck objects hold powers from the holy beings. As such they can bring sickness and injury, or healing when used in the hands of a medicine man who understands how to control the power. Knowledge is the key to safe use. Just as the Twins used lightning to rid the earth of monsters and evil, so too can it represent protection and healing as well as danger and death.

11. John Holiday, interview with author, November 9, 2001.

12. Perry J. Robinson, interview with author, October 25, 2017.

13. Joseph E. Persico, "The Great Swine Flu Epidemic of 1918," *American Heritage* 27 (June 1976): 28.

14. Alfred W. Crosby, *America's Forgotten Pandemic: The Influenza of 1918* (New York: Cambridge University Press, 1989), 228.

15. Benjamin R. Brady and Howard M. Bahr, "The Influenza Epidemic of 1918–1920 among the Navajos: Marginality, Mortality, and the Implications of Some Neglected Eyewitness Accounts," in *American Indian Quarterly* 38, no. 4 (Fall 2014): 484; Persico, "The Great Swine Flu Epidemic," 84.

16. Gladys A. Reichard, *Navaho Religion: A Study of Symbolism* (Princeton, NJ: Princeton University Press, 1963), 19; Ada Black, interview with Bertha Parrish, June 18, 1987.

17. The color red signifies a number of beliefs in traditional Navajo thought. Reichard points out that when it is reversed from its normal role in sandpaintings, it can represent evil associated with lightning or storms. On the other hand, "white apparently differentiates the naturally sacred from the profane—black or red, for instance—which through exorcism and ritual, must be transformed to acquire favorable power." *Navaho Religion*, 182, 187. Thus, the red dawns and sunsets warned of the approach of evil, as opposed to having the white and yellow light associated with the normal beginning and end of day and the directions of east and west respectively.

18. Ada Black, interview with Bertha Parrish, June 18, 1987; Rose Begay, interview with Bertha Parrish, June 17, 1987; Tallis Holiday, interview with author, November 3, 1987; Fred Yazzie, interview with author, November 5, 1987.

19. Tallis Holiday, interview.

20. Fred Yazzie, interviews with author, November 1, 1985; November 5, 1987.

Chapter 6

1. Some of the more important works about trading posts as an institution are suggested here. For an overview see Klara Kelley and Harris Francis, *Navajoland Trading Post Encyclopedia* (Window Rock, AZ: Navajo Nation Heritage and Historic Preservation Department, 2018), and Frank McNitt, *The Indian Traders* (Norman: University of Oklahoma Press, 1962); Willow Roberts Powers, *Navajo Trading: The End of an Era* (Albuquerque: University of New Mexico Press, 2001); and Teresa J. Wilkins, *Patterns of Exchange: Navajo Weavers and Traders* (Norman: University of Oklahoma Press, 2008). There are many individual stories about traders and their experiences. A good place to start (alphabetical order) is: William Y. Adams, *Shonto: The Study of the Role of the Trader in a Modern Navaho Community*, Smithsonian Institution Bureau of American Ethnology, Bulletin 188 (Washington, D.C.: Government Printing Office, 1963); Hilda Faunce (Wetherill) *Desert Wife* (Lincoln: University of Nebraska Press, 1928, 1981); Frances Gillmor and Louisa Wetherill, *Traders to the Navajos: The Story of the Wetherills of Kayenta* (Albuquerque: University of New Mexico Press, 1934, 1979); Samuel Moon, *Tall Sheep: Harry Goulding, Monument Valley Trader* (Norman: University of Oklahoma Press, 1992); Franc Johnson Newcomb, *Navajo Neighbors* (Norman: University of Oklahoma Press, 1966); Gladwell Richardson, *Navajo Trader* (Tucson: University of Arizona Press, 1986); Willow Roberts, *Stokes Carson: Twentieth Century Trading on the Navajo Reservation* (Albuquerque: University of New Mexico Press, 1992); Susan E. Woods and Robert S. McPherson, *Along Navajo Trails: Recollections of a Trader, 1898–1948* (Logan: Utah State University Press, 2005); McPherson, *Both Sides of the Bullpen: Navajo Trade and Posts* (Norman: University of Oklahoma Press, 2017); McPherson, *Traders, Agents, and Weavers: Developing the Northern Navajo Region* (Norman: University of Oklahoma Press, 2020).

2. Gillmor and Wetherill, *Traders to the Navajos*, 71–97 (selections with slight revision).

3. Nedra Tódích'íi'nii, interview with Fern Charley and Dean Sundberg, July 13, 1972, in *The Navajo Stock Reduction Interviews of Fern Charley and Dean Sundberg* (Fullerton: Southeastern Utah Oral History Project of California State University, 1974), 13–14.

4. Sloan Haycock, interview with author, October 10, 1991.

5. Ada Black, interview with author, December 15, 1991.

6. Fred Yazzie, interview with author, November 1, 1985.

7. Moon, *Tall Sheep*, 24–33 (excerpts).

8. Anna Heffernan, interview with Margie Connolly and Fred Harden, February 11, 1994, in possession of Halene West, Cortez, Colorado, 9.

9. Moon, *Tall Sheep*, 24–33.

10. Elizabeth Compton Hegemann, *Navaho Trading Days* (Albuquerque: University of New Mexico Press, 1963), 229.

11. Roberts, *Stokes Carson*, 99–111.

12. Mildred Heflin, interview with Dean Sundberg, O.H. 1168, Southeastern Utah Oral History Project (Fullerton: California State University, 1972).

13. Tully Bigman, interview with author, April 15, 1993.

14. Roberts, *Stokes Carson*, 151–52.

15. Virginia Smith, interview with Elizabeth Scheib, July 20, 1971.

16. Virginia Smith, interview with Elizabeth Scheib.

17. Ada Black, interview with author.

18. Virginia Carson Smith lost her life as a passenger in a vehicle that plunged down a mountainside just outside of Ouray, Colorado, in 1985. With her were three sisters, all of whom were in the trading business— Mildred (survived), Josephine Drolet (died), and Marie Leighton (badly injured but survived). Two months later, Ed Smith died of a "broken heart."

19. Les Wilson, email communication with author, May 3, 2020.

20. Virginia Smith, interview with Sherril Burge, August 1, 1979, MSS A4090-2 (Salt Lake City: Utah State Historical Society Oral History Project).

21. Evelyn Yazzie Jensen, interview with Karen Underhill, February 10, 1998, Special Collections, Cline Library, Northern Arizona University, Flagstaff, AZ.

22. Evelyn Yazzie Jensen, interview with Karen Underhill.

Chapter 7

1. For a better understanding of the events that occurred during live-stock reduction see Kenneth R. Philp, *John Collier's Crusade for Indian Reform, 1920–54* (Tucson: University of Arizona Press, 1977); Richard White, *The Roots of Dependency* (Lincoln: University of Nebraska Press, 1983); and L. Schuyler Fonaroff, "Conservation and Stock Reduction on the Navajo Tribal Range," *The Geographical Review* 53, no. 2 (April 1963): 200–223. Books and articles that provide the Navajo perspective include

Dean Sundberg and Fern Charley, *The Navajo Stock Reduction Interviews of Fern Charley and Dean Sundberg*, Southeastern Utah Project compiled by the Utah State Historical Society and California State University–Fullerton, 1974; Ruth Roessel and Broderick H. Johnson, editors, *Navajo Livestock Reduction: A National Disgrace* (Tsaile/Chinle, AZ: Navajo Community College Press, 1974); and Robert S. McPherson, "History Repeats Itself: Navajo Livestock Reduction in Southeastern Utah, 1933–1946" in *American Indian Quarterly*, vol. 22, nos. 1 & 2 (Spring 1998).

2. Donald L. Parman, *The Navajos and the New Deal* (New Haven: Yale University Press, 1976); Lawrence C. Kelly, *The Navajo Indians and Federal Indian Policy* (Tucson: University of Arizona Press, 1968).

3. Annual Report, 1934, Bureau of Indian Affairs, Navajo Archives, Edge of the Cedars Museum, Blanding, Utah [hereafter cited as Navajo Archives], p. 4.

4. Annual Report, 1930, Bureau of Indian Affairs, Navajo Archives, n.p.

5. Annual Report, 1934, Bureau of Indian Affairs, Navajo Archives, n.p.

6. Annual Report, 1934, Bureau of Indian Affairs, Navajo Archives, n.p.

7. For an excellent explanation of the ecological and economic impact of livestock reduction, see White's *Roots of Dependency*, 212–323.

8. Hite Chee, interview with Dean Sundberg and Fern Charley, July 20, 1974, in *The Navajo Stock Reduction Interviews*, Southeastern Utah Project compiled by the Utah State Historical Society and California State University–Fullerton, 1974.

9. Nedra Tódích'íi'nii, interview with Charley and Sundberg, O.H. 1223, *The Navajo Livestock Reduction Interviews*, 1–25.

10. Guy Cly, interview with author, August 7, 1991.

11. Hite Chee, interview.

12. Hite Chee, interview.

13. Hite Chee, interview.

14. Fred Yazzie, interview with author, November 1, 1985.

15. Kayo Holiday, interview with author, October 11, 1991.

16. Guy Cly, interview with author.

17. Cecil Parrish, interview with author, October 10, 1991.

18. Ada Black, interview with author, December 15, 1991.

19. LaMar Bedoni, interview with Fern Charley, June 30, 1972, O.H. 1166, *Navajo Stock Reduction Interviews*.

20. Edward D. Smith, interview with Dean Sundberg, June 27, 1972, O.H. 1155, Range Riding and *Navajo Stock Reduction Interviews.*

21. Mildred Heflin, interview with Dean Sundberg, O.H. 1168, Southeastern Utah Oral History Project (Fullerton: California State University, 1972).

22. Willow Roberts, *Stokes Carson: Twentieth-Century Trading on the Navajo Reservation* (Albuquerque: University of New Mexico Press, 1987), 104–5, 108–9.

23. Mildred Heflin, interview with Dean Sundberg.

24. White, *Roots of Dependency*, 312.

Chapter 8

1. Robert S. McPherson, *Navajo Land, Navajo Culture: The Utah Experience in the Twentieth Century* (Norman: University of Oklahoma Press, 2001), 142–57.

2. Samuel Moon, *Tall Sheep: Harry Goulding, Monument Valley Trader* (Norman: University of Oklahoma Press, 1992).

3. Fred Yazzie, interview with author, August 6, 1991.

4. Seth Clitso, interview with author, January 20, 1991.

5. Bud Haycock, interview with author, October 10, 1991.

6. John Holiday, interview with author, September 9, 1991.

7. Cecil Parrish, interview with author, October 10, 1991.

8. Bud Haycock, interview with author.

9. Billy Yellow, interview with author, March 26, 1993.

10. Bud Haycock, interview with author.

11. Cecil Parrish, interview with author.

12. Moon, *Tall Sheep*, 156.

13. Ada Black, interview with author, October 11, 1991.

14. Betty Canyon, interview with author, September 10, 1991.

Chapter 9

1. See Robert S. McPherson, *Dinéjí Na'nitin: Navajo Traditional Teachings and History* (Boulder: University Press of Colorado, 2012).

2. John Holiday and Robert S. McPherson, *A Navajo Legacy: The Life and Teachings of John Holiday* (Norman: University of Oklahoma Press, 2005), 39.

3. Most likely, Navajos assigned these names to the car because of the chi-chi-chi sound of the engine. Some scholars suggest that another

possible origin of the name could be the Navajo verb *nishjiid*, which means "it sits or squats"; others believe the word comes from *dilchiid*, which means "to point at something quickly." For more about Navajo first reactions to the automobile and airplane, see Robert S. McPherson, "The Chidi and Flying Metal Come to the Navajos," *Navajo Land, Navajo Culture: The Utah Experience in the Twentieth Century* (Norman: University of Oklahoma Press, 2001), 84–101.

4. Holiday and McPherson, *A Navajo Legacy*, 228–31.

5. George Tom, interview with author, August 7, 1991.

6. Cecil Parrish, interview with author, October 10, 1991.

7. Fred Yazzie, interview with author, August 6, 1991.

8. Curtis Zahn, "The Automobile Is Here to Stay," *Arizona Highways* 22, no. 6 (June 1946): 22–23.

9. Jesse Black, interview with author, March 25, 1991.

10. Fred Yazzie, interview with author.

11. See Dolph Andrus, "What It Takes to Sell a Car: Dolph Andrus and the Bluff Experience, 1916–1917," *Blue Mountain Shadows* 56 (Fall 2017): 32–41.

12. Samuel Holiday and Robert S. McPherson, *Under the Eagle: Samuel Holiday, Navajo Code Talker* (Norman: University of Oklahoma Press, 2013), 53–57.

13. Lucy Laughter, interview with author, April 8, 1992.

14. Sally Manygoats, interview with author, April 8, 1992.

15. Betty Canyon, interview with author, September 10, 1991.

16. Wayne K. Hinton and Elizabeth A. Green, *With Picks, Shovels, and Hope: The CCC and Its Legacy on the Colorado Plateau* (Missoula, MT: Mountain Press Publishing Company, 2008), 251.

17. The age of this girl was not the norm for wives in Navajo culture, and John's specific mention of it conveys his raised eyebrow. In the traditional way, a girl is not of marriageable age until after she has had a kinaaldá following her first menses, usually around the age of twelve or thirteen. Ages fourteen to sixteen were considered preferable for marriage in the old days.

18. Holiday and McPherson, *A Navajo Legacy*, 123–25.

Chapter 10

1. See Samuel Moon, *Tall Sheep: Harry Goulding, Monument Valley Trader* (Norman: University of Oklahoma Press, 1992).

2. Samuel Moon, *Tall Sheep*, 29–30.

3. Samuel Moon, *Tall Sheep*, 29–30.

4. Fred Yazzie, interview with author, August 6, 1991.

5. Gladys Bitsinnie, interview with author, March 26, 1993.

6. Moon, *Tall Sheep*, 55–57.

7. Michael N. Budd, "A Critical Analysis of Western Films Directed by John Ford from *Stagecoach to Cheyenne Autumn*" (PhD diss., University of Iowa, 1975), 436.

8. Moon, *Tall Sheep*, 204.

9. Moon, *Tall Sheep*, 210–11.

10. Guy Cly, interview with author, August 7, 1991.

11. Kayo Holiday, interview with author, October 11, 1991.

12. Harry Goulding, "The Navajos Hunt Big Game. . . . Uranium," *Popular Mechanics* (June 1950): 89–92.

13. Moon, *Tall Sheep*, 175–81.

14. John Holiday and Robert S. McPherson, *A Navajo Legacy: The Life and Teachings of John Holiday* (Norman: University of Oklahoma Press, 2005), 163–64.

15. Luke and June (wife) Yazzie, interview with author, April 8, 1993.

16. Cecil Parrish, interview with author, October 10, 1991.

Chapter 11

1. For a more complete understanding of Navajo involvement in uranium mining, see Doug Brugge, Timothy Benally, and Esther Yazzie-Lewis, *The Navajo People and Uranium Mining* (Albuquerque: University of New Mexico Press, 2006); and Robert S. McPherson, "Digging the Bones of Yé'iitsoh," in *Navajo Land, Navajo Culture* (Norman: University of Oklahoma Press, 2001), 158–78.

2. Shone Holiday, interview with author, September 9, 1991.

3. Sam Black, interview with author, December 18, 1993.

4. Kayo Holiday, interview with author, October 11, 1991.

5. Luke Yazzie, interview with author, April 8, 1993.

6. John Holiday and Robert S. McPherson, *A Navajo Legacy: The Life and Teachings of John Holiday* (Norman: University of Oklahoma Press, 2005), 166–68.

7. Bud Haycock, interview with author, October 10, 1991.

8. Shone Holiday, interview with author.

9. Cecil Parrish, interview with author, October 10, 1991.

10. Seth Clitso, interview with author, January 20, 1991.

11. Luke Yazzie, interview with author.

12. Kayo Holiday, interview with author.

13. Marjorie Haycock, interview with author, October 10, 1991.

14. Luke Yazzie, interview with author.

15. Billy Yellow, interview with author, March 26, 1993.

16. Sam Black, interview with author.

17. Bud Haycock, interview with author.

18. Kayo Holiday, interview with author.

19. Bud Haycock, interview with author.

20. Ada Black, interview with author, October 11, 1991.

21. Bud Haycock, interview with author.

22. Guy Cly, interview with author, August 7, 1991.

23. Fred Yazzie, interview with author, August 6, 1991.

24. Billy Yellow, interview with author, May 15, 1991.

25. Holiday and McPherson, *A Navajo Legacy*, 169–70.

26. U.S., Congress, Senate, "Statement of Councilman Harry Tome . . . ," Hearing Before Committee on Labor and Human Resources, S. Doc. 1483, 97th Cong., 2d Sess., April 8, 1982, pp. 138–40.

27. U.S., Congress, Senate, "Statement of Perry H. Charley," Hearing Before Committee on Labor and Human Resources, S. Doc. 1483, 97th Cong., 2d Sess., April 8, 1982, pp. 142–43.

28. "Zah Vows to Battle for Due Payment," *Navajo Times*, August 22, 1991, p. 1.

29. "Radon Barrier Complete at Mexican Hat," *San Juan Record*, August 10, 1994, p. 1.

30. Kayo Holiday, interview with author.

31. Jesse Black, interview with author, March 25, 1991.

32. Kayo Holiday, interview with author.

33. Shone Holiday, interview with author.

34. "Funding Sought for Radiation Exposure Compensation Victims," *San Juan Record*, March 7, 2001, p. 1.

35. "Enhancing Natural Attenuation at Monument Valley, Arizona Site," Program Update, Office of Legacy Management, U.S. Department of Energy, January–March 2006.

36. Luke Yazzie, interview with author.

Chapter 12

1. Fred Yazzie, interview with author, August 6, 1991.

2. Seth Clitso, interview with author, January 20, 1991.

3. Guy Cly, interview with author, August 7, 1991.

4. The 94,000-acre Navajo Tribal Park in Monument Valley was dedicated in May 1960. Included in the initial cost of $275,000 was the construction of a visitor center, campgrounds, and a network of roads that wind between and around some of the most heavily photographed monoliths and mesas in the world. In 1999 alone, there were 380,575 people who visited the park according to statistics on file in the Economic Development Office, Monticello, Utah.

5. Stewart L. Udall, "More Tourists, Please," *Cross Currents*, July 18, 1997, p. 11–15.

6. Udall, "More Tourists," 12–13.

7. Jenny Francis, interview with author, March 23, 1993.

8. Gladys Bitsinnie, interview with author, March 26, 1993.

9. Bessie Katso, interview with author, March 26, 1993.

10. Nellie Grandson, interview with author, December 16, 1993.

11. Guy Cly, interview with author, August 7, 1991.

12. Shone Holiday, interview with author, September 9, 1991.

13. Cecil Parrish, interview with author, October 10, 1991.

14. John Holiday and Robert S. McPherson, *A Navajo Legacy: The Life and Teachings of John Holiday* (Norman: University of Oklahoma Press, 2005), 225.

15. "Concerned about Alcohol Permit Request," *San Juan Record*, April 26, 2006, p. 4.

16. "Navajo Tribe Turns Off Water to Gouldings Trading Post," August 9, 1995, and "Gouldings Declares Chapter 11 Bankruptcy to Get Water," August 30, 1995, *San Juan Record*; "Nor Any Drop to Drink," *Canyon Echo*, September 1995, p. 1.

17. "Monument Valley Residents Call 1999 Land Sale to RGJ a 'Betrayal,'" *Blue Mountain Panorama*, November 6, 2002, p. 1.

18. Sloan Haycock, interview with author, October 10, 1991.

19. Stella Cly, interview with author, August 7, 1991.

20. Ada Black, interview with author, December 15, 1991.

21. Betty Canyon, interview with author, September 10, 1991.

22. Nellie Grandson, interview with author, December 16, 1993.

23. Bud Haycock, interview with author, October 10, 1991.

24. Holiday and McPherson, *A Navajo Legacy*, p. 222.

25. Fred Yazzie, interview with author.

26. Lance S. Gudmunsen, "Navajo Basket Maker Wins Highest Folk-Art Honor," *Salt Lake Tribune*, September 24, 1995, p. E-2; "Navajo Basket Weaver Featured in *People* Magazine," *The Indian Trader*, February 1996, p. 5.

27. "Olympic Torch Relay to Travel through Stunning Monument Valley," *San Juan Record*, January 30, 2002, p. 1.

28. "Monument Valley Chosen as Olympic Torch Relay Stop," *San Juan Record*, March 14, 2001, p. 1; Neil Joslin, "Olympic Torch Goes through Monument Valley," *Blue Mountain Panorama*, February 6, 2002, p. 1.

29. Layne Miller, "A Look at What the Navajos Brought to Salt Lake City," *The Indian Trader*, March 2002, p. 15; "Navajo Olympic Exhibit Was a Financial Bust—Tribe Says It Lost More than $786,000 in Attempt to Promote Indian Arts and Crafts," *The Indian Trader*, August 2002, p. 3.

30. "The Red Bull Air Race Series Lands in Monument Valley," *Airport Journals*, June 1, 2007, airportjournals.com/the-red-bull-air-race-series-lands-in-monument-valley-2/ .

31. Krista Allen, "Orbs and Pinnacles, Balloons Enhance Monument Valley's Beauty," *Navajo Times*, December 19, 2013, p. A-9.

32. David Boyle, "Vast Majority of Local COVID-19 Deaths Have Been Native American," *San Juan Record*, September 23, 2020, p. 1.

33. "Navajo Nation Parks, Businesses, Schools Reopen with Restrictions," *San Juan Record*, July 14, 2021, p. A-3.

INDEX